Modernism

A Cultural History

Tim Armstrong

polity

First published in 2005 by Polity Press

Polity Press
65 Bridge Street
Cambridge CB2 1UR, UK

Polity Press
350 Main Street
Malden, MA 02148, USA

ISBN: 0-7456-2982-2
ISBN: 0-7456-2983-0 (pb)

A catalogue record for this book is available from the British Library.

Typeset in 10.5 on 12 pt Bembo
by SNP Best-set Typesetter Ltd, Hong Kong
Printed and bound in Great Britain by TJ International Ltd, Padstow, Cornwall

For further information on Polity, visit our website: www.polity.co.uk

For Nicholas

Contents

Preface

A cultural history of modernism? What else could one imagine: a natural history of modernism? In the wake of Giambattista Vico's declaration, as early as 1725, that *scire est facere, verum est factum* – which is to say that we can only really know what we construct as humans – modernity has tended to be defined by the closure of the cultural sphere; by a culturalization of everything in human affairs, in which all knowledge is mediated by symbolic forms; and in which all knowledge is historically specific. This has initiated a recurrent and progressive collapse of the distinction between culture and nature, between social, economic or even biological causes and cultural 'symptoms'. To consider modernism is thus necessarily to engage with culture defined in terms of an interconnected field of activity in which hierarchy and even causality is problematic; in which agreed boundaries are replaced by permeability and relatedness – in which economic thought is readily seen as influenced by ideas about the body; or literature might seem akin to science; or politics might become aesthetics. It is also to deal with the notion of modernity as a series of epistemic shifts in systematic regimes of knowledge, communication and perception, as proposed by writers such as Michel Foucault, Friedrich Kittler and Jonathan Crary.

To write on culture in this sense is to follow in the tradition established by the German sociologists of the late nineteenth century, Dilthey, Simmel and others, for whom human experience can only be understood in terms of its self-representation; for whom it might make sense to have, as Dorothy Richardson once suggested, a Ministry of Metaphors. Cultural history in the wake of Dilthey can involve a huge range of topics: anthropology (Dilthey's central discipline); the history of ideas; of philosophy, linguistics, sociology, political and legal thought; the histories of science, technology and medicine; even a broader phenomenology in which one might speak of a history of the senses or of feeling – as well, of course, as examining the arts and literature which register all these.

In this work I have tried to suggest some of the different ways of accounting for literary modernism in cultural terms: considering the experience of time and modernity in chapter 1; market culture in chapter 3; and in later chapters subjects including the discourse of reform across areas ranging from sexology to politics; the study of sensation and consciousness;

science, pseudo-science and technology; and cultural encounter. In a short study of a huge phenomenon, the avenues driven through the field are inevitably broad and selective, and detail has often had to be sacrificed in favour of suggestive example. Certainly it would have been possible to write a book with the same title with rather little overlap with this one – though the topics considered here have been chosen as representative of recent work on the field in which modernism has been re-connected with historical contexts from which it was disconnected by the formalist criticism of the post-war years. Likewise I have, throughout, attempted to place canonical modernism and its mythology into dialogue with the broader field of modernist writers in English suggested by recent studies.

Recent surveys of modernism by Levenson, Nicholls and others have continued to be preoccupied with modernism's own fascination with literary genealogy and the mapping of the field in terms of stance, aesthetics and genre. In its focus on culture, this short study attempts to strike a different note. This is not to say that earlier criticism is discounted, however; indeed, I deploy a version of genealogical criticism in chapter 2, examining such topics as modernist succession and women and modernism. And while I have nowhere offered a unified account of modernist aesthetics, I have tried to explore the linkages between the aesthetic and wider culture. Thus the reader will find suggestions about, say, the fragmentation of modernist texts: in terms of temporal dislocation (chapter 1); in terms of Walter Benjamin's account of epic as collage (chapter 2); in terms of the fluctuations of attention (chapter 5); in terms of the charged field (chapter 6); and finally in terms of the politics of nation (chapters 4 and 7). Equally, various cultural topics appear in different guises: the notion of an economics of plenty in relation to temporality (chapter 1); a fascination with waste (chapter 4); and in relation to the cinematic body (chapter 5).

A work such as this incurs debts not susceptible to systematic acknowledgement. I would like to offer cheerful apologies to those whose work is synthesized here; and thanks to my recent graduate students, who have taught me as much as I have taught them: Sam Halliday, Rodney Rosenquist, Mike Wainwright, Christabel Kirkpatrick, Elena Serraiotto and Jon Bell. My own teaching in recent years has been made easier by the huge range of texts collected in *Modernism: An Anthology of Sources and Documents*, edited by Vassiliki Kolocotroni, Jane Goldman and Olga Taxidou (1998); I often cite materials from its pages, and would like to express gratitude to its editors. I would also like to thank Royal Holloway and the AHRB Research Leave Scheme for terms of leave which allowed me to write this book.

1 Modernity, Modernism and Time

It is quite obvious that we do not all of us inhabit the same time.

Ezra Pound, 'Date Line'

Any account of literary modernism must begin with the category of modernity. In this opening chapter, I will explore the relationship between the literary and cultural movements we call modernism and social and cultural modernity. If one still fairly prevalent view of modernism is that it is a 'reaction against' modernity, 'a kind of soul trapped in the gross body of modern industrial society' as James Knapp puts it (1988: 22), then my argument throughout this book is that such a view must be displaced in favour of one in which the two are bound together in a relation which is often homologous rather than antagonistic. Because temporality is so important to modernity, I will discuss the modern understanding of time, and at the end of the chapter, the temporal rupture represented by the Great War.

Human experience changed in the early years of the twentieth century. In *Rip Van Winkle* (1820), Washington Irving imagined a character who sleeps through the American Revolution and wakes in the turbulent world of democratic politics. But he fits in well enough because little has really changed in his Catskill village. It is hard to imagine a Englishman sleeping twenty or thirty years from 1900 and adapting so readily: he would have missed the war; the Liberal reforms culminating in the National Insurance Act of 1911; the rise of the Labour Party; the enfranchisement of women; the Russian Revolution; the re-arrangement of Europe and the establishment of the League of Nations. And more: Einstein's demolition of the Newtonian world-view; the aeroplane, cinema, television; the *Titanic*. At the beginning of the twentieth century, the shock of change is intensified. Indeed, for a variety of reasons modernity is increasingly viewed in terms of crisis. If the Victorians saw themselves as 'modernists' in the progressive sense, in the new century progress could seem a cruel myth: how can 20,000 dead in a morning at the Somme or the genocide of a million Armenians be fitted into a progressive world-view? Was moral, cultural, even biological degeneration intrinsic to modernity? A variety of pessimists, from eugenicists to philosophers of history like Oswald Spengler or critics of mass culture like F. R. Leavis, were willing to say so.

SOCIAL AND POLITICAL MODERNITY

To talk of the crisis of modernity is to suggest that a long history was coming to an end, and we can begin with a sketch of that history. What is meant by 'modernity' varies greatly, and depends on the historical narrative one is constructing. But broadly speaking two things are usually at issue. First, a historical shift which begins as early as the seventeenth century, producing new forms of capitalist organization, social relations, government and technology, accompanied by the development of a scientific, secular world-view (Braddick 2000). Second, the rise in the Enlightenment of a discourse which actively promotes the modern against the inherited: the discourse of rationalization, progress and autonomy; the abolition of superstition and the mastery of nature.

Modernity in the 'long' sense is produced by a set of changes initiated by the Renaissance: the end of feudalism and the rise of capitalism, with its stress on the market and possessive individualism; the beginnings of humanism, with its roots in the rediscovery of lost forms of classical knowledge; encounters with other cultures in the Americas and elsewhere and the development of anthropological thinking; the development of the scientific world-view, and the extension of technology and instrumental reason. The expansion and integration of capital is central to this process: the intensification of overseas trade and investment; developments in banking, credit and such mechanisms as insurance and the incorporated company; and the changes produced by the agricultural and industrial revolutions of the early 1800s. The later nineteenth century sees the rise of monopoly capitalism and the vertical integration pioneered by businessmen like Cyrus McCormick, the American manufacturer of mechanical reapers and binders who in the period 1847–84 developed mass production techniques, standardization, advertising, and credit on an international scale. In the period of what is often called the 'second industrial revolution', roughly 1870–1920, new technological developments – electrification, integrated transport and communications systems and the rationalization of production – produce a shift to mass production, accompanied by standardization and specialization which subordinates the individual to large-scale systems. The bureaucracy developed by the modern nation-state represents a parallel development, generating cultures of surveillance and professional (legal, medical, educational, occupational) expertise intrinsic to social modernity. These techniques can be dialectically related to the fragmentation and dispersal intrinsic to modern urban society: it is the decline of fixed communities and stable class relations, along with geographical mobility and mass culture, which necessitate a new, statistical sense of the human population as the object of analysis and control.

The late nineteenth century also sees the development of new forms of mass consumption: department stores; catalogue sales; illustrated magazines which seamlessly integrate consumer advice, pictures and advertising. By 1900 *abundance*, that is an economy driven by desire rather than need, was something which needed theorizing in the work of the American sociologist Thorstein Veblen, economist Simon N. Patten and others; and the problem of over-consumption (including overeating) emerged (Birkin 1988; Leach 1994; Schwartz 1986). Economists like J. M. Keynes stressed the creation of forms of social credit to fuel a consumption-based economy. The engineering of consumer desire became the role of advertising and public relations experts and psychologists like Walter Dill Scott, Daniel Starch and Edward Bernays (Freud's nephew), who mobilized theories of subconscious motivation in the interests of industry and government. An economics in which waste, excess and mass consumption are central terms has important consequences for the arts.

The shifts in social relations which accompanies the economic changes sketched above are marked. In the UK, 1870 marks the inception of a new social order: the Education Act setting up school boards; the Married Women's Property Act which allowed women to retain earnings; and entry to the Civil Service by competitive exam; the following year Trade Unions were legalized and Oxford and Cambridge opened to non-Anglicans. The seeds of a more meritocratic society, and of a culture which would eventually be labelled 'middlebrow', lie in these reforms. The subsequent forty years see the rise of a new, aspirational lower-middle-class culture in Britain and America, shading into a salaried professional–managerial class. As gender roles loosened, women increasingly penetrated the workspace, especially in the new office jobs. At the same time the barriers between the professions and other forms of work were codified; professionalism became a way of concretizing masculine middle-class identity – a shift which is to some extent anticipated by the self-defined profession of author (Warner 1998), but which nevertheless challenged modernist authors into declaring their impeccable professionalism in contrast to their predecessors. Forms of identity are also closely related to the market economy: the notion of the self as describable in terms of a malleable 'personality' rather than (engraved) character which historians have seen in American culture in the late nineteenth century; and an identity founded on appearance and tokens of cultural distinction like 'branded' produce. The self becomes subject to technique and marketing, and takes on what Jackson Lears calls a 'weightlessness' born of social mobility (1981: 35–7).

Given all this, it is a truism that modernity involves a sharpened sense of the speed of change, famously described by Marx and Engels in *The Manifesto of the Communist Party* (1848):

Constant revolutionizing of production, uninterrupted disturbance of all social conditions, everlasting uncertainty and agitation distinguish the bourgeois epoch from all earlier ones. All fixed, fast-frozen relations, with their train of ancient and venerable prejudices and opinions are swept away, all new-formed ones become antiquated before they can ossify. All that is solid melts into air, all that is holy is profaned, and man is at last compelled to face with sober senses his real conditions of life, and his relations with his kind.

(1975: 37)

Marx brings us to that other aspect of modernity which I mentioned at the outset: the tradition of critique which is linked to the birth of the human sciences in the work of Wilhelm Dilthey and others, and which is reflected in such diverse thinkers as Friedrich Nietzsche, Max Weber, Émile Durkheim, Sigmund Freud, Theodor Adorno and Michel Foucault. That critique may begin with the Enlightenment attack on the 'ancient and venerable' prejudices of the past, but rapidly evolves into an analysis of modernity itself. In this critique, to put it baldly, modernity's emancipatory promises are never fulfilled, and instead it presents itself as a state of permanent crisis; it offers apparent freedoms, but is in fact linked to alienation, standardization and loss of individual autonomy – the diminution of experience which Weber labelled 'the disenchantment of the world'. Modern cultural industries, Adorno argued, offer a freedom which is illusory; and an increasing tension between the possessive individualism which drives capitalism and the tendencies of mass culture to commodify and standardize identity. What the Frankfurt School was to label 'repressive desublimation' – the expression and utilization of all forms of desire – simply becomes the artificial licence of Huxley's *Brave New World* (1932), a means of social control.

How does modernism, as a cultural expression of modernity, relate to this critique? In its own publicity, modernism is often depicted as a protest at the reign of instrumental reason and market culture which attempts to preserve or create a space for individuality, creativity and aesthetic value in an increasingly homogenous and bourgeois world. 'Preserve' and 'create' here suggest two quite different strategies, however. The former involves an anti-modernity rooted in the past – a nostalgia associated with a range of phenomena from the Arts and Crafts movement to Anglo-Catholicism and Fascism. This modernism is built on the ruins of both an 'authentic' or folk culture and an aristocratic 'high' culture, elements of which it attempts to resurrect: Yeats's attack on bourgeois Ireland and his celebration of the peasant and aristocrat; Eliot's conservative Anglicanism and nostalgia for the seventeenth century; Lawrence's hatred of rationalism and industry, and celebration of the chthonic powers of myth; H. D.'s Hellenism. The anti-modern, to put it cynically, can serve as a therapeutic abatement of the pressures of modernity, like the return to nature represented by the Boy Scouts or National Parks movements. But this itself is typical of the modern world, in which forms of mediation and technique constantly offer a return to the natural. Which is to say that modernity and anti-modernity as pathology and cure are bound together *within* the field of the modern.

The second response suggested above, that of *creating* an alternative ideological space, most readily involves what Adorno called negative critique – a refusal of coherent meaning and representation in the face of an unacceptable reality, a sometimes desperate declaration of 'autonomy'. The fragmentation and obscurity of the modernist text becomes, in this account, a programmatic alienation, exemplified by Kafka's investigation of the modern state in *The Trial* (1925) or Eliot's reduction of culture to a jumble of citation in *The Waste Land* (1922). Modernist formalism becomes a declaration of non-complicity; the preservation of a space which future generations might recognize as freedom. Or, in a more inflected form of this critique typified by the work of the Surrealists and the Weimar critic Walter Benjamin, the waste materials of capitalist civilization are investigated for the traces of hidden histories, startling juxtapositions, or alternative temporalities which might rupture the seamless totality and apparently inevitable flow which is capitalism, unsettling the reader or viewer.

The critique of modernity attributed to modernism must, however, be heavily qualified. One important strand of European, Russian and American modernism overtly identifies with the values of rationalization, technology and speed. Other modernist works register and incorporate the new sensory and epistemic regimes of the camera, cinema and phonograph; or incorporate, at the textual level, the economies of waste and excess intrinsic to modernity. The demand to 'make it new' places modernism and modernity in proximity, and often involves a violent rejection of the petrified values of 'art' in favour of 'life' or reform – whether the Suffragettes slashing paintings or Mayakovsky declaring that we must 'Destroy the old language, powerless to keep up with life's leaps and bounds . . . Throw the old masters overboard from the ship of modernity' (Lawton 1998: 101).

Modernism is in fact characterized by a series of seeming contradictions: both a rejection of the past and a fetishization of certain earlier periods; both primitivism and a defence of civilization against the barbarians; both enthusiasm for the technological and fear of it; both a celebration of impersonal making and a stress on subjectivity. It is both politically and sexually radical, and drawn to Fascism as an expression of a stability of social relations; both lofty in its cultural aims, declaring the autonomy of the artist, and preoccupied with self-promotion and market relations. Some of these issues can be untangled by attempting to discriminate different modernisms – for example the classical 'objectivity' and authoritarian politics celebrated by Wyndham Lewis versus the interiority and democratic merging he attacked in Bergson, Woolf, Joyce and others. But in many cases we need to seek more dialectical solutions: to see that the past celebrated by writers like Eliot and Pound is radically de-historicized by something akin to commodification, for example; or that modernist technophilia is typically founded on the Aristotelian notion of the tool or instrument – an extension of the body and will – rather than the Weberian idea of a social technology. We can begin our exploration of these contradictions with the notion of time.

HISTORICITY: SPLIT AND UNEVEN TEMPORALITIES

Still, this is the advantage of the new direction, that we do not anticipate the world dogmatically but that we first try to discover the new world from a critique of the old one. Until now the philosophers have had the solution of all riddles lying on their lecterns, and the stupid exotic world had only to open its mouth for the ready-roasted pigeons of absolute knowledge to fly into its mouth. Philosophy has become secularized, and the striking proof thereof is that the philosophical consciousness itself has been pulled into the torment of struggle not only externally but also internally.

(Marx 1979: 30)

The writer is Karl Marx, in a letter of 1843, expressing notions central to modernity: the present as a struggle to extract the future from the past; thought which cannot be extracted from temporality. Where did he get these ideas from? The answer is primarily from Hegel, for whom all human understanding is historical: the 'spirit which comes to consciousness of itself' is realized in the world, and in particular communities. History proceeds dialectically through a series of stages; each is specific; each born out of the collapse of its predecessor. From this view of time as a set of competing impulses, we can derive a view of modernism as involving a fundamentally *dynamic* temporality.

Historicism is a keynote of nineteenth-century thought: the tendency to see societies as evolving, and art as expressing a time-bound consciousness. Even Schopenhauer, though rejecting Hegel's idealism and progressivism – the idea that *Geist* was struggling to liberate itself – agreed on the absolute status of time: all we can know is the blind striving of the Will, immanent rather than transcendent, and which may as well be called Desire or Nature – hence a *Lebensphilosophie* or philosophy of life, for Schopenhauer best realized in the temporal art of music. In his *Einleitung in die Geisteswissenschaften* (Introduction to the Human Sciences), published in 1883, one of the origins of modern sociology, Wilhelm Dilthey separated the study of historical consciousness (anthropology, history, psychology, political science, literature, law) from the natural sciences. In later writings on literature, he stresses that 'poetry is the representation and expression of life', the particularities of an individual temporal experience rather than absolute truth: 'It is the nature of the present to be filled or ful-filled with reality in contrast to the representation of reality and its peculiar modifications either in memory or in the anticipation of reality and the will to realize it. This being ful-filled with reality is what remains constant in the advance of time' (1985: 225).

The notion of a *split* temporality needs to be explored a little further. For Hegel, dialectics involve a struggle between an 'accepted' view and its negation, a struggle from which the new is born. Certain individuals, pre-eminently poets, act as the vanguard: 'It is the world-historical individuals who first told men what they wanted' (Taylor 1975: 393). This is the cultural ground of modernity: modernists see, or open the path to, the future. At the same time, Hegel offers the possibility of uneven temporalities: some writers will have audiences in the future. Walt Whitman is an example of the resulting stance: 'Crossing Brooklyn Ferry' is passionately proleptic, reaching out to inhabit the future rather than the disappointing present:

Closer yet I approach you,
What thought you have of me now, I had as much of you – I laid in my stores
    in advance,
I consider'd long and seriously of you before you were born.

(1982: 311)

Whitman's late interest in Hegel confirmed an increasingly idealized sense of his audience, an America he could only prophesy and haunt.

The notion of uneven or competing temporalities can be applied in different ways. It is present in the temporally divided *self* depicted by Darwinism, inhabited by 'vestiges' of earlier stages. For Henri Bergson and others, cultural evolution produced a split time, human experience increasingly divorced from the increasingly autonomous regime of technological modernity. Up to the middle of the nineteenth century, each town had a local time, set by the sun. The needs of navigation and of regularizing railway timetables across continents, and the possibility of sending time signals across distances by the telegraphs strung alongside them, led to British Railway Time and the time zones proposed at the International Meridian Conference in 1884. Time becomes exploitable, suffused with the values of capital; in the science of work invented by F. W. Taylor, it is segmented and commodified (Kern 1983: 12–15). The result is a technologized time, indeed a teletime in which temporalities generated in the metropolitan centre are transmitted elsewhere. The Eiffel Tower broadcast radio time-signals from 1913; Big Ben chimes the hour in Woolf's *Mrs Dalloway* (1925), providing a formal and political metaphor. Conflicting understandings of time include the time of the West versus that of the East, explored by Conrad; the time of the reverie versus that of the clock; even the arrested time of the dead versus that of the living. The passing of the Newtonian world-view, with its notion of the disembodied, atemporal observer, also disrupts universal time.

Implicit in Hegel is the idea that uneven development applies to societies (peoples, nations): some societies are 'backwards', others progressive. The Futurist diagram of the Great War depicts the allies smashing, wedgelike, into the stagnating mass of the Austro-Hungarian and Ottoman empires. In the Marxist tradition, the notion of uneven development is elaborated by Trotsky and others, proposing that different temporalities exist in different places, producing a combination of emerging and developed ideologies. Christopher Prendergast puts it well when he suggests that modernity should not 'be identified with a "completed" form . . . of industrial and technological modernization, which is, rather, a feature of postmodernity. Instead, modernity is tied to a situation of "incomplete" modernization. It is a structure of hope, fear and fantasy invested in an emergent formation and a possible future' (2003: 103). T. J. Clark similarly proposes that it is the uneven temporality of modernism which makes it hard for us to read, in a later era of 'modernity's triumph': modernism involved wresting the past that mattered from the ashes of tradition, in order to create a vital future.

Ernst Bloch's formula 'the simultaneity of the non-simultaneous' points to the way that divergent temporalities can be visible within one text. An example is Willa Cather's *My Ántonia* (1918). Modernist in form, despite a realist narration, Cather's novel about Bohemian pioneers in Nebraska has a complex, cross-gendered narrative frame mediating the question of narrative desire directed at its central character (related by recent critics to Cather's lesbianism and the novel's autobiographical elements); it is unevenly episodic with 'gothic' inserts (a folk tale about a bride thrown to the wolves; the violent story of the Cutters), and refuses the expectations of the 'well-shaped' novel in terms of marriage and consistent focus on one character. It describes technological modernity: the view from the train; the role of the photograph in memory; but it is also suffused with nostalgia for pioneering days, childhood, and femininity defined as race-motherhood.

The result is a temporal and geographical dissonance exemplified by the description of the grave of Mr Shimerda, the cultured exile who cannot abide the new country and kills himself. His Catholic relatives want him placed, as tradition dictates, on the grid-map (a representation of Enlightenment origins) at a proposed cross-roads. But,

Mrs. Shimerda never saw the roads going over his head. The road from the north curved a little to the east just there, and the road from the west swung out a little to the south; so that the grave, with its tall red grass that was never mowed, was like a little island; and at twilight, under a new moon or the clear evening star, the dusty roads used to look like soft gray rivers flowing past it . . . I loved the dim superstition, the propitiatory intent, that had put the grave there; and still more I loved the spirit that could not carry out the sentence – the error from the surveyed lines, the clemency of the soft earth roads along which the home-coming wagons rattled after sunset.

(1994: 114)

This text written into the landscape can be related to an episode during the narrator Jim's study at the University of Nebraska which evokes the *translatio*, the notion of the carrying of classical ideas westward, from Homer to Virgil to Dante. This enables Cather to explore her own ambition to be 'the first to bring the Muse into my country' ('country' meaning locality here, as the classics teacher Cleric explains); a context related both to the decorum noted by early readers and resonant images like the plough against the sun. The novel thus explores the temporal dislocations produced in America – new literature being produced from engagement with the old, but imagined as a writing in virgin soil.

My Ántonia also gives an important role to the photograph as a mnemonic device: the photographs in the Shimerda family album and the postcards of their home town in Bohemia which Jim sends match the text's eidetic images. That images can be mechanically detached from the flow of time and stored is an important factor in the discontinuous histories of modernism. As early as Hawthorne's *The House of the Seven Gables* (1851) and George Eliot's *The Lifted Veil* (1859), the uncanny eruption of different temporalities – the past or the future – into the present is described in terms of haunting images akin to the photograph. The modernist critic Walter Benjamin's Marxist historiography, closely linked to his thinking on technological modes of reproduction, reflects this possibility: it is founded on the flashing up and redemption of a fragmentary *image* of the past – seen in his 'Theses on the Philosophy of History' (1940) as 'a memory as it flashes up in a moment of danger' (1973a: 257) – rather than on a sense that the flow of history might be seized and redirected in its totality.

There are more personal implications of the split temporality we have been discussing. For what Hegel called 'the Unhappy Consciousness', the fact that we are not self-created becomes a burden. Identity can only be formed from a struggle, and what emerges from that struggle is contradictory and unstable, since it believes it cannot be both 'true to itself', its immutable identity, and at one with the constantly changing world. The result of this unresolved contradiction is that the subject identifies with the contingent and changeable – with modernity – and projects the unchangeable onto a 'beyond' – which can never be achieved, remaining 'a hope . . . without fulfilment and presence'. Being and Time are split. This is an account of modernity as melancholy which Hegel shares to some extent with Freud: the self mourns a lost unity which for Hegel is best represented by Christianity, a religion of an ideal being, Jesus, who has been killed. In modern art, the corresponding situation is written into the aesthetics of the fragment, the incomplete picture, or the text whose unity is constantly deferred or subordinated to the play of desire: think of *The Turn of the Screw* and its battle to the death between the immanent (the world of the everyday, of 'clues' and psychology) and the absolutes of truth; between desire and imputed innocence.

Modernism works, then, with notions of temporality which overlap, collide, and register their own incompletion. As suggested above, the *dynamization* of temporality is one of the defining features of modernism: past, present, and future exist in a relationship of crisis. This suggestion – the central thesis of this chapter – can be explored in different aspects of modern literature: its depiction of historicity; the experience of time described by Bergson and others.

First, the past. The idea that the past is a burden is central to the avant-garde. The words of Mrs Alving in Ibsen's *Ghosts* (1881) echo through later literature: 'It isn't just what we have inherited from our father and mother that walks in us. It is all kinds of dead ideas and all sorts of old and obsolete beliefs . . . There must be ghosts all over the country' (1980: 62). Or as Apollinaire said in 1913, 'You cannot carry around on your back the corpse of your father. You leave him with the other dead' (Kolocotroni 1998: 263). A *Lef* manifesto of 1923 agrees: 'we will fight against the transfering of the working methods of the dead into today's art' (Lawton 1988: 196). Early twentieth-century literature often takes the forms of a *Götterdämmerung*, rage directed at those towering Victorian figures, the parents, a torrent of Oedipal anger including Edmund Gosse's *Father and Son* (1907), Lytton Strachey's mocking *Eminent Victorians* (1918), May Sinclair's bitter *Life and Death of Harriett Frean* (1922), and Woolf's family romance in *To the Lighthouse* (1927). Attacks on moralistic mothers, foolish fathers and incompetent generals culminate in Christina Stead's acidic *The Man Who Loved Children* (1940), a novel describing literal matricide and artistic patricide. These efforts are supported by a philosophical tradition intimately bound up with modernism. In the work of Max Stirner and of Nietzsche, Freud, Vaihinger, Marx, Kropotkin and others, the dissolvents of scepticism are directed at established knowledge.

To be sure, the complete rejection of the past is unsustainable, since as Paul de Man points out, without a past there can be no identity or intelligibility. Indeed, it is in the interests of overcoming modernity's flattening of experience that many modernists idealize earlier periods. A 'useable past' is realized in Yeats's Byzantium; in H. D.'s engagement with antiquity; in Pound's translations. Nevertheless the historical recovery in Yeats, Pound and Eliot is selective, a fetishization of particular moments and sites: the court of Malatesta, the age of Webster and Lancelot Andrews. The result is histories peculiarly isolated from any dynamic context – as in the vanished southern Chinese kingdom celebrated by Pound in the late *Cantos*, or the flattened historical parade of *Orlando* – or offered up simply as reified artworks, detached from their context: Byzantium *is* a golden bird. History as a dialogue of artwork with artwork is what Eliot describes in 'Tradition and the Individual Talent' (1919), and the result is a static version of temporality in which the question of historicity per se can never be raised: the question of how meaning is extracted from events; of whose voices are heard. In this, the modernists differ markedly from their Victorian forebears.

It must, however, be recognized that the rejection of the past, as an expression of a sense of the predicament of the modern subject, is part of the power of modernist texts, creating characteristic patterns of disavowal in which the denial of the historical object involves its reinscription as form. The drafts of *The Waste Land* include abject material – women, popular reading, Jews – whose haunting presence at the edge of the text is intrinsic to its meaning. Section IV, 'Death by Water', is a suggestive ten lines on the drowned Phlebas the Phoenician, a body which the poem understands as sacrifice. What Pound jettisoned was an eighty-three-line account of a cod-fishing voyage into the north Atlantic, ending with wreck on the ice. Eliot's draft is a fairly paradigmatic version of a narrative hugely popular in the previous 150 years, a genre which explored the costs of commerce and empire. In slashing it, Pound disrupts not only narrative but historical connection, part of the poem's preoccupation with empire, profit and loss. The suggestively fragmented form of the poem is, then, founded on buried histories which, because of the refusal of formal integration, remain in the 'real'.

There is a further question about the rejection of the past: how long is it before the 'new' is itself rejected? How stable can modernism be? If a generational model is applicable, must modernists be attacked in their turn?

The career of Pound raises such questions, with his restless movement through styles and programmes; but also with his obsessive chronicling of periods in such essays as 'Date Line', and his attempts to negotiate his inheritance among the Objectivists and others. One nodal point for the generational aesthetics of modernism, demonstrating their complexity, is May Sinclair. For the modernists she seems to have represented a figure of established authority who could be co-opted to bolster positions. Considerably older – she made her name with *The Divine Fire* (1904), published when she was over forty – she was enlisted by Pound, writing a defence of 'Prufrock', appreciations of Dorothy Richardson, Katherine Mansfield, H. D. and Pound himself. She also wrote a novel, *The Tree of Heaven* (1917), in which Vorticism's war-like aesthetics are evoked by name – a tale of family life on the brink of war without which, one wants to say, *To the Lighthouse* might not have been written.

Sinclair was highly conscious of the issues involved in declarations of modernity, as the following discussion from *The Tree of Heaven* demonstrates. The poet Morton Ellis insists that the old art and its 'parasites' must go:

'They must be scrapped and burned if we're to get rid of the stink. Art has to be made young and new and clean. Here isn't any disinfectant that'll do the trick. So long as old masters are kow-towed to as masters people will go on imitating them. When a poet ceases to be a poet and becomes a centre of corruption, he must go.'

Michael said, 'How about *us* when people imitate us? Have we got to go?'

Morton Ellis looked at him and blinked. 'No', he said. 'No. We haven't got to go.'

'I don't see how you get out of it.'

'I get out of it by doing things that can't be imitated.'

There was a silence while everybody thought of [his latest acolyte] Mr. George Wadham.

(1917: 240–41)

Sinclair's version of the 'Vortex' is, as Suzanne Raitt suggests, applied both to the Suffragette movement and Ellis's grouping; it suggests a critique of intellectual dependence and the crowd-mind, rather than a celebration of modernity. When this critique threatens to involve the collective enthusiasm of the war, which Sinclair supported fervently, she saves the situation by suggesting that the best reasons for enlisting are person and local – timeless – rather than collective and historical: death in battle is a personal fulfilment; a mystical or even artistic act. Sinclair thus wraps modernism into mourning – an early version of what we will see is a more general trend.

A struggle to reject or subsume the past is, then, one element of the sense of dynamic temporality associated with modernity. A second element is an anxiety about the future associated with rapid change, and a desire to wrest agency from modernity's appearance as an inevitable flow. Futurology as a mode of speculative writing begins with H. G. Wells's *Anticipations* (1901) and was promoted in the 'To-day and To-morrow' series published by Kegan Paul between 1924 and 1931; over fifty short books with titles like *Halcyon, or the Future of Monogamy* by Vera Brittain and *Cain, or the Future of Crime*, by G. S. Godwin, as well as volumes on more obvious issues like morals, sport, leisure, language, poetry, food and politics. J. B. Haldane's *Daedalus, or Science and the Future* (1923) went through seven impressions in three years; John Rodker wrote *The Future of Futurism* (1926). A number of topics (science, technology, eugenics, women, war, America, music, sex) had more than one book attached to them, positing alternative futures. At the end of this period Wells's novel *Things to Come* was made into a high-budget film (1933), initially planned with art direction by the Bauhaus designer Moholy-Nagy, promoting the message that a technological elite must run the world, replacing wasteful economics and nationalism with rationality. Exhibitions like 'Machine Art' at MOMA in New York in 1934 and Norman Bel Geddes's 'Futurama' at the 1939 New York World's Fair extrapolated technological modernity. More pessimistic futures like that in Storm Jameson's *In the Second Year* (1936), on the other hand, responded to the threat of fascism in the 1930s. A desire to stabilize the future is visible in Pound's pronouncements on the Enlightenment ideal of 'a science, almost a mathematical science of history' in Quincy Adams (1973: 149), and in Yeats's elaborate mathematical scheme of historical cycles in *A Vision* (1925) – a diagrammed version of his sense of crisis.

In a parallel way, politicized poetry of the 1930s is characterized by an intense temporal instability: time as loss; time as action; time the radiant future. The best-known example is Auden's 'Spain', with its likening of the movement of Spanish civil war volunteers to the drifting of seed; followed by its jerky separation of the inert, everyday past from the 'now' of action. Similar structures appear in Claude McKay's 'The International Spirit' (*Crisis*, 1928), and in Edwin Rolfe's 'These Men are Revolution' (*New Masses*, 1934). The latter begins by asserting that 'These men are revolution even as / trees are wind and leaves upon them', depicting the energy of change as sweeping across America, before falling into a blighted present in which prophecy is the only possible stance. The result is a broken temporality:

> Clear-eyed, alert, the stalwart legion grows
> to recognize the imminent bright hour,
> inevitable now. And time can but delay –
> never impede – the winning of the world
> by men for mankind. See approach the day
> when millions merge and banner is unfurled!
> Now the army moves, marks time . . .
>   (North 1972: 60)

Time here is at once apocalyptic, inevitable, impeded, arrested or stopped; at once flow and interruption – it exists in a state of crisis.

THE EXPERIENCE OF TIME

We have seen how notions of dynamic temporality are central to the understanding of modernity, and briefly considered the past and future. We now need to consider the issue of the present and the flow of time itself. Two recent approaches have stressed what seem radically different issues. In one, represented by Ronald Schleifer's *Modernism and Time* and Michael Tratner's *Deficits and Desires*, modern time poses the problem of 'too much': an abundance linked to consumer culture, flows of knowledge and information; creating problems of selection, apprehension and storage (see chapter 5). In the other, the issue is trauma, memory and ruptured temporality. The first is 'economic' in the broad sense; the second more to do with the adequacy of symbolization and the folding of one time onto another.

What the two have in common is a fascination with the embodiment of time in human experience. Schliefer argues that time moves from being the 'atemporal formalism' of Newton and of Marx's theory of labour – a simple quantity – to being a thicker medium indissociable from human action. Time becomes biological, vitalistic. This conception of time is expressed above all by Henri Bergson, whose work had such a marked impact on modernism. Bergson destroys both the absolute time of philosophy (the time of eternity) and the notion of the *moment*, the 'now' which he renders a scientific abstraction, a point on a graph or a technological construct (the photograph). Human time is always a rolling accumulation of traces of previous time, taken up into the body and bound up with intentions directed at the future, in what amounts to a psychologization of the dynamic field which we have been discussing.

This understanding of time is reflected in the work of Proust, Woolf, Ford, Joyce and even Eliot, despite his official anti-Bergsonism (Gillies 1996). Lawrence in his preface to the American edition of *New Poems* writes that 'One great mystery of time is *terra incognita* to us: the instant. The most superb mystery we have hardly recognized: the immediate, instant self. The quick of all time is the instant. The quick of all the universe, of all creation, is the incarnate, carnal self. Poetry gave us the clue: free verse. Whitman. Now we know' (Kolocotroni 1998: 411). In the novel the account of the present is touched by the accumulation described by Bergson. Although *Ulysses* does have a time scheme, it is never absolute and external, but rather physically and linguistically embodied, shot through with recollection and fantasy; discontinuous and ambiguous. What Conrad and Ford called *progression d'effet* involves the projection of temporality – progress, movement – onto the ticking of the narrative itself:

In writing a novel we agreed that every word set on paper – *every* word set on paper – must carry the story forward and, that as the story progressed, the story must be carried forward faster and faster and with more and more intensity. That is called *progression d'effet*, words for which there is no English equivalent.

(Ford 1924: 210)

This does not mean that the 'pace' of events speeds up; it is the narrative which has a life. The modernist split between story and narration (between the events as they might appear on a timeline and the charged order of telling) is implicit in Bergson's account of time, in which the workings of what he called 'involuntary memory' are fundamental to creation, storing up whatever of the past is needed.

For the Marxist critic Georg Lukács, the split temporality of modernism represented a fetishization of bourgeois alienation, rather than a unity of subjective and historical time (the lost 'totality' of epic). 'Time', he writes,

appears as no longer the natural, objective and historical medium in which men move and develop. It is distorted into a dead and deadening outward power. The passage of time is the frame within which a person suffers degradation. It turns into an independent and remorseless machine which flattens, levels and destroys all personal plans and wishes, all singularity, personality itself.

(1965: 79)

For Lukács, modernism involves subjectivism concretized as style, and thus a false consciousness divorced from social reality: the modernist is trapped in a solitary and sensuous nightmare. Yet Lukács's own style, for example in his essay 'The Ideology of Modernism', is itself fragmentary, and his career subject to revisionism which contradicts notions of objective history. And the time-distortions of modernism are, in any case, highly self-conscious about their status as trauma:

He sat down and tried to make sense out of what Homer had told him. A great deal of it was gibberish. Some of it, however, wasn't. He hit on a key that helped when he realized that a lot of it wasn't so much jumbled as timeless. The words went behind each other instead of after. What he had taken for long strings were really one thick word and not a sentence. In the same way several sentences were simultaneous and not a paragraph. Using this key, he was able to arrange a part of what he had heard so that it made the usual kind of sense.

(West 1957: 399)

This is Nathanael West's *The Day of the Locust* (1939). The character whose first name refers to the foundation of western discourse, Homer Simpson, is a hysteric. William Faulkner's *The Sound and the Fury* (1929) similarly investigates temporal pathologies: a world without time (the idiot Benjy's consciousness); time as it deforms itself through incest and suicide; time as endurance; simultaneity.

At the limit, the temporal perspectivism of modernism can threaten incoherence. In Ford's *The Good Soldier* (1915) the narrator, Dowell, tells a story of his own blindness in which the main events seem clear, despite his convoluted exposition: he has been deceived by his wife, Florence, who has faked a heart condition to avoid sex and taken as her lover the serial philanderer Edward Ashburnham. But on closer examination nothing is clear: the time-scheme is incoherent and seems to conflate the two central events of the novel; Dowell says he loves Leonora, Edward's wife, but he also hates her; he seems to identify with the figure, Edward, who has most wronged him; he tells us he is relating stories told to him, but he cannot have had access to all of what he tells; he says he is blameless but betrays touches of sadism – most clearly in saying casually that he has 'forgotten' to narrate

Edward's suicide. Divergent histories swirl through the novel, in particular the divide between Catholicism and Protestantism: hinging on the difference between a king who wanted six successive wives and another who wanted three at once; enabling the exploration of what René Girard calls 'mimetic desire' flowing between characters. The narrator's anti-modernity, his claims of narrative ineptitude ('It is so difficult to keep all these people going'); his desire for a 'shock proof world' – all are contradicted. It has even been suggested by one deliberately perverse reader, Roger Poole, that Dowell has concocted the story in order to hide his *own* cold machinations: he inherits a fortune, buys Edward's ancestral home, and has chaste care of the girl he loves. If this is right, the text has only ever had *one* true reader.

The fragmentation of temporality thus forces the modernist into formal strategies designed to focus the reader's attention on the construction of narrative. Lukács's time as 'the frame within which a person suffers degradation' is a fair description of John Dos Passos's *U.S.A.* (1937) – a trilogy which aims for epic scope, but which also confronts the technologically-mediated nature of modern experience. The four narrative modes of *U.S.A.* are the effect of that fragmentation: the third-person discourse of the classical novel; the 'topicality' of the newsreels (history as a cacophony); the subjective, memory-tinged voice of the 'Camera Eye'; and the journalistic biographies of great men, lives embodying 'progress'. The third-person narrative, which seems relatively traditional, is particularly interesting. For Marshall Berman, modernism can often be equated with a 'cultural despair' which sees the individual as locked into a world devoid of inner freedom (2001: 28). In *U.S.A.*, most readers notice the way the narrative sections, with their relentless flow of inconsequential events described in hard-boiled style, produce claustrophobia. Jean-Paul Sartre suggested that the key to the 'sad abundance' of this narration is that it narrates what is experienced as the present *in the past tense*: it intimates a future which is always closed off from foreknowledge and genuine causality, forcing us to experience time as a locked-in continuum. The reader becomes a 'reluctant accomplice', full of 'shame and uneasiness' at their lack of power (Sartre 1995). For Sartre, abundance is catastrophe, an unstoppable flow with no future – a perception which we will return to when we discuss the wasteful narrative of Stein and others in chapter 5.

FROZEN TIME: THE LEGACY OF WORLD WAR I

In July 1919 the German novelist Thomas Mann wrote in a letter that 'One must take a contemplative, even a resignedly cheerful view, read Spengler and understand that the victory of England and America seals and completes the civilizing, rationalizing, pragmatizing of the West which is the fate of every aging culture' (1970: 97). The German surrender was expressive, Mann implies, of a modernity confirmed by the decisive entry of America into the war. Indeed, it was the culmination of a history: imperial ideologies; the rigid timetables of mobilization plans; years of anticipation in the press and in spy novels like Erskine Childers's *The Riddle of the Sands* (1903).

At the same time, Mann's view of the Great War as a part of a continuous process seems strange, given its catastrophic proximity. The war punctures time, upsetting the dynamic relationship between past, present and future which constitutes modernity: locking its protagonists in the present; rendering the past a mythic 'before'; and displacing the hopes invested in the future. Its effects reverberate beyond its dates, often as a temporal and spatial dislocation: in notions of shock, trauma and flight; in the idea of the 'lost generation'. Stephen Spender's remark on the aftermath of the war captures this dislocation, at least in terms of middle-class life: 'People resembled dancers suspended in mid-air yet miraculously able to pretend that they were still dancing' (1951: 2–3). As the heroine of Ethel Mannin's *Sounding Brass* comments,

We live in an age of futilities . . . The war – can you think of anything more futile than that? . . . Theoretically we ought to have come out of it better and finer – purged by ordeal, isn't that the expression? Instead, we emerge into a reactionary world of cynicism and vulgarity, with all the old standards shattered and nothing to replace them. An age of sex and saxophones. Needing the bread of a new renaissance, we are given the stone of a new decadence.

(1925: 132)

This is one of the central myths of the war: nothing could be the same; politicians and generals and the rhetoric of sacrifice and patriotism would never again be believed.

We can begin with the present moment of the war itself, rather than its aftermath. If the German mobilization plan, the Schlieffen Plan, embodied a modernist fascination with speed, trench warfare quickly tended to costive compression. As Stephen Kern points out, it was experienced by those at the front as both utterly disconnected from previous experience and as arrested time – waiting, immobility (1983: 293). We can link this sense of paralysis to notions of trauma via Freud's introduction to the Wolf Man case, which refers to the situation in 1914–15, using entrenched positions as a metaphor for psychic resistance:

The length of the road over which an analysis must travel with the patient, and the quantity of material which must be mastered on the way, are of no importance in comparison with the resistance which is met with in the course of the work . . . The situation is the same as when today an army needs weeks and months to make its way across a stretch of country which in times of peace was traversed by an express train in a few hours and which only a short time before had been passed over by the defending army in a few days.

(1990: 238)

In a letter written in December 1914, when he was moving from the Wolf Man to the series of metapsychological papers which the case inspired,

Freud writes: 'I have fared in this matter as the Germans have in the war. The first successes were surprisingly easy and great, and they thus tempted me to continue, but now I have arrived at such hard and impenetrable things that I am not sure of getting through' (1987: 77).

The idea of the war as rupture, as the shattering of a world – associated with Samuel Hynes, Paul Fussell and other cultural historians – has recently been challenged by Jay Winter, who points out the importance of continuity in memorialization. Not least, the war contributed to a return to forms of neoclassicism in literature, music and sculpture. But it is often a neoclassicism frozen in place by the weight of mourning: 'By ushering a future characterized by instability,' Geoff Dyer writes, 'it embalmed forever a past characterized by stability and certainty' (1994: 5). The pre-war era becomes a lost landscape, forever obliterated. Two of the greatest novels of European modernism, Thomas Mann's *The Magic Mountain* and Robert Musil's *The Man Without Qualities* work by slowing and even suspending time on the verge of war, producing the 'general lull' into which Musil's prose expands and into which Mann's characters endlessly talk. T. S. Eliot's essay 'Tradition and the Individual Talent' (1919) has often been seen as a response to the war of this kind: his declaration that 'the existing monuments [of literature] form an ideal order among themselves', marginally displaced by new work, speaks for continuity after catastrophe.

One can also consider the war in relation to the future, which Mannin suggests has dissolved into cynicism. One of things that the war undoes is the avant-garde itself; the aggressive rhetoric of renewal of pre-war movements like Futurism. What could one do with a hatred of the 'masses' and the 'crowd' when they have become the dead? With war on established forms when war is a reality? With the rhetoric of activism and attack? Henry James hinted that what was involved was also a fraying of the power of language, and a haunted discourse:

The war has used up words; they have weakened, they have deteriorated like motor car tyres; they have, like millions of other things, been more overstrained and knocked about and voided of the happy semblance during the last six months than in all the long ages before, and we are now confronted with a depreciation of all our terms, or, otherwise speaking, with a loss of expression through increase of limpness, that may well make us wonder what ghosts will be left to walk.

(1999: 144–5)

This was a perception shared by many: by Ezra Pound, for example, whose turn to a poetry of the image was designed to signal a break from the discursive; from voices crying war.

To speak of haunting as James does is to evoke a trauma in which effects are carried forward. One reason that we need to understand the war as trauma is, of course, the dead and what they represent: a lost promise; a future never realized. 'There are so many dead' Lawrence wrote in 'Erinnges', 'Invisible, trooping home, the unassuaged ghosts / Endlessly returning on the uneasy sea' (1972: 739) – no doubt remembering Hardy's restless ghosts in his Boer War poem 'The Souls of the Slain'. The legions of the dead appear everywhere: the 'army of ghosts' (a spent division) which Siegfried Sassoon sees returning from the front; in Abel Gance's film *J'accuse* (1919), where the dead march into France to berate the living; and in post-war spirit photography (Winter 1995: 15, 75).

The mass death of the war presents a challenge to representation. The horror of a sacrifice for which there is no proper recompense enters war poetry with Whitman's 'Drum Taps' – praised by Isaac Rosenberg as 'unique in War Poetry' (1984: 267) – and is taken up by Wilfred Owen in his travesty of the biblical story of Abraham in 'The Parable of the Old Man and the Young': 'But the old man would not so, but slew his son, / And half the seed of Europe, one by one' (1983: 174). In the tropes of classical epic from Homer to Milton, the legions of dead in war are said to be name-less, like the leaves of autumn. But in the memorials which sprang up every-where in towns, workplaces and even streets across Britain and its dominions, we see a powerful counter-impulse: an insistence on specifica-tion. Cypress Street in London's East End has such a memorial: in one hundred houses, twenty-six deaths are listed. Even the unknown soldier must be symbolically accounted for. World War I could in this respect be seen as involving the birth of a particular kind of tension between death and mourning: on the one hand the mechanized, anonymous death of Owen's poetry; on the other an intensification of the demand to remem-ber. A sense of losses as dislocated, uncertain in status sent many to spirit mediums in the years after 1915. In the literature of the post-war period there is a similar sense of unresolved memory: the dead and the maimed haunt the texts of Pound, Eliot, Woolf, Faulkner, Rhys and others.

One novel in English does explore the kind of 'Rip Van Winkle' alle-gory of temporal suspension described at the beginning of this chapter. In Rebecca West's *The Return of the Soldier* (1918), Chris Baldry has amnesia produced by shell shock, and can only remember events which happened well before the war and his unhappy marriage. He returns to memories of an earlier love, Margaret, whom he insists on seeing, and finally reconciles himself to his wife only by an act of traumatic memory. When Margaret sees a photograph of Chris's child who died five years earlier, as her own child had done, she 'pressed it to her bosom as though to staunch a wound' (1980: 96). This displaced war-wound marks the traumatic depletion which Freud describes in melancholia. If Chris cannot confront it, Margaret and Jenny (the narrator, Chris's sister-in-law) can; indeed, in the final moment at which the two women embrace before Chris's 'cure', Jenny says 'We kissed, not as women, but as lovers do; I think we each embraced that part of Chris the other had absorbed by her love' (1980: 109) – embraced, that is, their losses, since neither 'has' him. The paired children who 'had half a life' (as Margaret puts it) represent the war dead as seen from a mother's perspective; the self-serving Edwardian wife Kitty the blindness of the public; Jenny and the psychotherapist who appears at the end for a more enlightened but helpless response to the madness of war. The war marks, in such texts, the entry of notions of trauma as temporal dislocation and anamnesis (lost memory) into western consciousness.

What is produced in the post-war world is, then, a disrupted temporality in which the dynamic relation between past, present and future which we saw as intrinsic to modernity is forced to co-exist with elements of 'frozen' time: a lost past; a traumatic present; a blighted future. The result is a reconfigured modernism, shot through with contradictory forces: mourning, hysteria, paralysis and delirium; a dwelling on mutilation and abjection; reconfigured gender relations; as well as the bitter critique of those in power typified by texts like *U.S.A.*, a curse on the war, its sponsors and the culture it created. Mourning becomes a major problem because modernity is founded on the ability to stabilize and subsume the past (Hegel's *Aufhebung*). Freud's 'Mourning and Melancholia' (written 1915) can be seen as a response to the war: separating pathological from 'normal' mourning; insisting that the dead might finally cease to haunt. One way in which Freud differentiates mourning from the pathology of melancholy is in the fact that the former is described in economic terms: he suggests that with a series of presentations of stimuli associated with the dead, and with the reality principle constantly asserting itself ('they *are* gone'), the subject will gradually dissipate the energy invested in its lost object (Freud 1991: 253, 265). But melancholy, in contrast, involves a traumatic puncturing of the psyche: 'the complex of melancholia behaves like an open wound, drawing to itself cathetic energies . . . from all directions, and emptying the ego until it is totally impoverished' (1991: 262). Freud adds that melancholia, like mourning, does dissipate; but via a more violent process in which the ambivalence attached to the love object is worked through in terms of aggression and denigration (hence, one could say, the bittersweet description of the pre-war world in texts like Ford's *Parade's End* trilogy). If, as Freud also suggests, the lost love object might include countries or even systems of belief, he is giving voice to a widespread sense of cultural crisis.

SHELL SHOCK AND FETISHISM

One effect of the war was to produce a huge number of wounded and maimed bodies – bodies which appear in the paintings and etchings of Otto Dix and in post-war literature, matched by the depictions of minds disturbed by war experience. In what Mark Seltzer calls 'wound culture', identity and trauma are bound together by a series of technological 'shocks'. This is Rifleman Giles Eyre at the Somme, 14 July 1916:

My pulses beat quicker and even our own trenches shook and quivered and rocked about at the shock of this tremendous burst of fire. One's being shrunk back appalled at this display of ferocious destructive might. I could sense the thoughts of those around me as if this wave of blasting sound had destroyed the material world and bestowed on me telepathic powers. Most of the men were gripped by unplumbed horror, and yet at the same time uplifted to the extent that space and time ceased to have any meaning. We were living in a world where flames, pandemonium and death held undisputed sway and our living bodies were as nothing.

(Powell 1996: 55)

The contradictions here – the obsessive presence of the body and its transcendence; the constriction and expansion of being – reflect, in their ambivalence, more general responses to the technologies of modernity.

The diagnosis of shell shock which emerged during the war involved a complex debate as to the status of wounding, the body, psyche and trauma. Some of its origins lie in the 'railway spine' controversy of the late 1860s, in which it was thought that railway accidents could produce hidden damage. Shell shock was typically explained, early in the war, by the idea of physical changes brought about by shelling: early diagnoses required the proximity of a shell, an explosion (certified on Army form W.3436). But as the numbers affected rose, such explanations became increasingly dubious. By the end of the war psychological factors had to a large extent replaced physical: shell shock was seen as an extreme state of mind affecting thousands, explicable not as malingering or cowardice but in terms of trauma. Chris Feudtner comments, 'as the psychological theories of shell shock elevated unconscious mental forces to the status of "social actors", they concomitantly established the unconscious as a new "social location"' (1993: 395).

In order to explore these new 'actors', I will take three examples, all short stories: Wyndham Lewis's 'The French Poodle'; Mary Butts's 'Speed the Plough'; and Lawrence's 'The Blind Man'. The first, published in March 1916, describes a strangely doggy world: the central character is Rob Cairn (a cairn is a kind of terrier), back from the front with a nervous disorder (Tait 1995: 167–73). He blinks 'dogmatically'; his girlfriend Dolly is also 'dogmatic' and has a pronounced 'lurch' (a lurcher is another dog). The story's plot hinges on his purchase of a poodle, Carp, which takes 'the place that some lady should have occupied in his heart'; and which he shoots before his return to the Front and death two weeks later. When his friend Fraser last sees him, Cairn is 'exhausted, and faintly bad-tempered', lurches himself, and sobs 'in a deep howling way'. Cairn argues that humans and animals should remain in proximity in order to keep the distance between them clear. But the confusion of human and animal (humans, dogs, fish), suggests a wider disruption, and a reversal of the logic which holds the 'human' in place. Geoff Gilbert brilliantly suggests an outrageous subtext: sexually-transmitted rabies; an interpretation which would nicely figure the war as a contagious madness, and suicide as self-medication. But the general point is that trauma in the story produces problems of readability centred on the body.

In 'Speed the Plough', Butts depicts a soldier with shell shock and traumatic amnesia, unable to sustain 'any sequence of thought'. He is sent to the country in order that nature might effect a cure. But throughout the story he refuses that cure, attaching himself to the materials of fashion: 'velours and organdie, and that faint windy stuff aerophane' become the 'unstable delicate things by which he might be cured'. Replacing the killing aeroplanes with aerophane, seeing nature as a series of aetheticized objects ('Each straw was brocaded with frost'), the protagonist cleaves to a visiting actress rather than the 'female animals' he milks. At the end of the story, his memory seemingly restored, he is a dressmaker in London, his eyes kindling at the remark of a beautiful client: ' "When the war starts interfering with my clothes", she said, "the war goes under . . ." ' (Butts 1991: 9–16; Tait 1995: 45–51). The suggestions of homosexuality and the celebration of the values of 'show' rather than 'use' make the story a subversive exploration of gender-ideologies. As in the zoot suits with which black and Latino Americans defied economy regulations in World War II, the 'waste' associated with femininity serves a political purpose – one could compare Gwendolyn Brooks's zoot suit poem, 'The Sunday of Satin-Legs Smith', which cattily reduces the war to 'your late trouble' (Gates 1997: 1585). The fetishism associated with Butts's protagonist – preoccupation with fabrics; his final suggestive stance 'on his knees, vertical in black cloth' – renders desire individual and perverse rather than natural and national.

My third example, Lawrence's 'The Blind Man', was written in 1918 and published in 1920 (1990: 46–63). It describes Maurice, a blinded soldier living in mysterious intimacy with his pregnant wife, Isabel, and with the animals with whom he sits in his darkened barn. For Maurice, who moves on the 'flood' of being 'in a sort of blood-prescience', the distance implied by sight has collapsed; touch replaces seeing. 'He did not try to remember, to visualize. He did not want to. The new way of consciousness substituted itself in him.' In fact, consciousness is scarcely the right word, as his state is described in terms of mindlessness. When the intellectual Bertie, vaguely posited as his rival, comes to visit, they have the following exchange:

'But what is there in place of the bothering? What replaces the activity?

There was a pause. At length the blind man replied, as out of a negligent, unattentive thinking.

'Oh, I don't know. There's a good deal when you are not active.'

'Is there?' said Bertie. 'What, exactly? It always seems to me that when there is no thought and no action, there is nothing.'

Again Maurice was slow in replying.

'There is something,' he replied. 'I couldn't tell you what it is.'

This is beyond language: knowledge of the dark. In the astonishing climax Maurice touches Bertie's face, asks him to describe his wounds, and then to place his own hands in his seared eye sockets. As Trudi Tate comments, 'Lawrence uses the idea of war injury to transform the terror of castration, blindness, or any other kind of physical damage into a source of power' (1998: 109). Forcing his rival to confront trauma as the site of both wounding and occlusion, Maurice paradoxically asserts his own masculinity (he is described constantly in terms of blood and erect stance), while Bertie is unmanned.

Fetishism and hints of perversion are central to all these stories. The mechanism of this refusal seems to parallel Freud's account of fetishism, in which (for a time) the man refuses to acknowledge the reality that his mother does not have a penis – refusing, therefore, the possibility of castration and lack – and sets up a surrogate object to which desire is attached. But there is more in Freud: his insistence that what is denied (woman's supposed 'lack of a penis') is a 'fact of perception' actually disguises a cultural judgement (Laplanche and Pontalis 1988: 120). So we could say that what is denied in these stories includes war's gendering (men fight, and 'for' women) and a refusal of the 'official' terms in which desire is imagined.

In contrast, for some women writers the war provided the possibility of refiguring nation and community around the notion of masculine sacrifice. Sinclair's *The Tree of Heaven* (1919) and Willa Cather's *One of Ours* (1922) provide good examples, their seemingly anti-feminist angle seems at odds with the more radical allegiances of their authors. Here, as in *The Magic Mountain*, sectional debates on modernity (in terms of gender, politics, locality) are finally laid aside in the name of action and history. But in each case, there are troubling elements which complicate this story. Sinclair's novel is forced to describe femininity as a multiple relinquishment; Cather's war story is disturbed, Sharon O'Brien argues, both by its vision of the dismembered body and by a guilt associated with the fact that the war actually empowers women (Cooper 1989: 184–204). Which is to say that even where the war seems to stabilize gender, it too becomes trauma.

In the post-war world, the effects of the war in memory are long – enduring as far as Fitzgerald's *Tender is the Night* (1933) and beyond. Indeed, one writer has suggested that the failure of literature to 'process' or even properly represent the traumatic dead of the war, or allow them into the modernist canon, is one of the cultural facts which 'allows' the second world war to happen (Norris 1996). This is overstated – and ignores the horrific depictions of mutilation and dismemberment in the paintings of Otto Dix, in John Rodker's 'War Museum – Royal College of Surgeons', and elsewhere. But one can say that the temporality of the post-war world is a product of the war, and this 'therapeutic' view – which suggests memory must be worked over and over, that trauma must be unlocked – is itself a product of the world the war made.

2 Mapping Modernism

Where does modern literature begin? Many recent accounts of modernism have begun with the metropolitan centre: Paris in the 1840s, the detached and ironic gaze of the masculine walker, the *flâneur*, and Baudelaire's essay on 'The Painter of Modern Life'. From that point, one can trace a trajectory through Flaubert, Mallarmé, Rimbaud, Laforgue and others to the Symbolists and early Eliot; a trajectory in which the stress is on an oppositional stance expressed in aesthetic terms, and the opening of a rift between 'bourgeois modernity, on the one hand, and aesthetic modernity on the other' (Kolocotroni 1998: 7).

But consider another point of origin: Edgar Allan Poe's letter to Charles Anthon in 1844, in which he writes 'I perceived that the whole energetic, busy spirit of the age tended wholly to the Magazine literature – to the curt, the terse, the well-timed, and the readily diffused, in preference to the old forms of the ponderous & the inaccessible' (1948: i.268). Situating the short story in the context of the rapidly expanding American print market, Poe describes an art conditioned by commodity status and by an audience whose attention span is limited, rather than seeking to place itself 'beyond' bourgeois modernity.

Looking to America for a point of origin means two things. Firstly, it involves attending to the periphery rather than the centre of Empire: a route into modernism recently explored by Robert Crawford. Secondly, it involves focusing on a turbulent mass culture and politics, informed by fierce debates on nationhood and slavery. The American Renaissance produced work which was consistently dissident in terms of both style and stance: the sublime style of Emerson and Whitman; the linguistic complexity and refusal of Dickinson; the reformulation of allegory in Hawthorne. Melville is a consistently experimental writer, offering a restless expansion of the possibilities of genre in the novel (the encyclopaedic *Moby Dick*), allegory (*The Confidence Man*), romance (*Pierre*) and short story; constantly exploring his own failure in the market. The rediscovery of Melville's work by Lawrence and others in the 1920s is an important moment for modernism. The Trinidadian radical C. L. R. James's works on Melville and Whitman – *American Civilization* (written in the 1940s) and *Moby Dick, Mariners, Renegades and Castaways* (1952) – represents these authors as the first moderns, offering a rupture with European tradition and a critique of modern individualism. To begin modernism at this point is to highlight issues of nation, market and politics.

VERSIONS OF MODERNISM

The aim of this chapter is to reflect on how we map literary modernism. At its broadest, modernism can be defined as a series of international artistic movements in the period 1900–40, characterized by their sense of engagement with ideas of the 'new'. Within that period, further divisions are often made: a politically-engaged, radical avant-garde modernism before 1918 is distinguished from the more conservative 'high' modernism of the 1920s (Bürger 1984); a 'late' or second-wave modernism is proposed with various periodicities; and the politicization of literature in the 1930s suggests a separate understanding of that decade.

The specific question 'what is *literary* modernism in English?' is a hard one, for a number of reasons. First, modernism is usually seen as a transnational phenomena characterized by cultural exchange, exile and displacement; a series of flows between cities and continents. Its sites include salons and galleries (Bloomsbury homes; the Paris flats of Gertrude Stein and Natalie Barney; the Arensberg apartment and Alfred Steiglitz's 291 gallery and its successors in Manhattan); specific exhibitions like the Post-Impressionist show in London (1910) and Armory Show in New York (1913); publications and presses (Chicago modernism centred on *Poetry* magazine; the *New Age* grouping in London); and places outside the West (Mexico, Africa, Bali). Translators, in contrast to many Victorian counterparts, were named and influential: William Archer as advocate of Ibsen; Constance Garnett in relation to Russian culture; Eden and Cedar Paul; Edwin Muir, poet and critic, and his wife, Willa, translators of Kafka. Pound was a prolific translator; like him, Dorothy Richardson was influenced by books she translated. However, as we will see, nationalism is also important for modernism.

Secondly, what is or is not counted as 'modernist' depends, in circular fashion, on one's sense of what modernism is: the question is bound up with the historiography of the subject. Though the period had its own notion of modernity – Pound's reference in 1922 to *The Waste Land* as 'the justification of the "movement", of our modern experiment, since 1900' (1951: 248) – 'modernism' was not a term much used. The object of literary study called 'modernism' is a retrospective construction, largely American, post-war and academic; linked to a 'winner's history' associated with the New Criticism and a narrow canon.

To illustrate that point we can look at two accounts of the period. The first was published in 1935 (revised 1938) by Frank Swinnerton, novelist and critic, and is entitled *The Georgian Literary Scene: A Panorama*. It covers only part of the period and literature in England, but nevertheless includes

sections on Henry James, George Bernard Shaw, H. G. Wells, travel litera-
ture (Norman Douglas and others), George Moore, Arnold Bennett,
Somerset Maugham, Ford Madox Hueffer (later Ford), Katherine Mansfield,
the satirist Max Beerbohm; on the Sitwells; a chapter on Virginia Woolf,
Roger Fry and other Bloomsbury writers; essays on novelists May Sinclair,
Dorothy Richardson, Aldous Huxley, Wyndham Lewis, James Joyce; on W.
B. Yeats, the 'Georgian Poets', Charlotte Mew and the war poets; on recent
writers including the Australian novelist 'Henry Handel Richardson' (Ethel
Robertson), Compton Mackenzie, and Mary Webb. The final chapter, which
points most clearly towards our understanding of modernism, is labelled 'T.
S. Eliot and the New Academicism'. The name Ezra Pound does not appear
in the index.

The second book was published in 1971, Hugh Kenner's *The Pound Era*;
an impassioned 600-page study which placed at its centre the person whom
Swinnerton does not mention, and those whom Lewis labelled the 'Men
of 1914': Pound, Lewis, Eliot and Joyce. For Kenner these writers and some
precursors and outriders (James, Yeats, H. D. and Williams) are central to a
heroic story in which Pound, armed with a philosophically and historically
informed vision of the reform of language and technique, and against the
grain of English cultural conservatism, creates the London Vortex from
which flows the monumental works of 'high modernism': the *Cantos*, *The
Waste Land*, *Ulysses* and *The Human Age*. Kenner's influential accounts of
modernism have little time for Virginia Woolf (he has described Bloomsbury as a provincial literature); he writes little on Ford or Lawrence, let
alone the broader list in Swinnerton's survey.

What explains the difference between these books is, in part, their very
different aims: Swinnerton is a participant mapping a broad field of con-
tenders whose work he read as it appeared, and resisting the trend represented by Eliot; Kenner aims to capture a group at the point of its vanishing
(he had been able to meet Eliot, Pound, Lewis and George Yeats; a year
after *The Pound Era* appeared all were dead). But Kenner's 'strong' version
of modernism, which derives its aggressive exclusions from Pound's own
sense of literary history, has considerable costs in terms of its exclusions. So
does the picture of the English 1930s associated with the myth of the
'Auden generation' (Deane 1998: 5–11).

There is, then, a need to be suspicious of the story of 'Modernism
Triumphant', as Michael Levenson describes it, and the established modernist canon. Rewriting the canon of modernism has, in recent criticism,
involved a number of tasks. Firstly, providing 'thicker' contexts, returning to
the original ground in all its density. One example is Steven Watson's *Strange
Bedfellows: The First American Avant-Garde* (1991), with its cast of hundreds
and diagrams illustrating salons, little magazines, alliances, flows of influence,
money and desire in New York, Chicago, London, Paris and Florence.
Much work has been motivated by a desire both to reclaim particular
neglected areas – the Harlem Renaissance; a woman's modernism in

contrast to the masculine line associated with Pound, Lewis and Eliot – and to examine the way in which the canon was shaped. In this context return-ing to a critic like Swinnerton helps us see a variety of positions compet-ing for attention, including genres marginalized by canonical modernism: satire; travel; futurology; middlebrow and popular literature. The same point can be made in the American context, for example in relation to lost radical traditions (Nelson 1989: 16–19).

Since the canon is centred so heavily on the 'epic' production of a core of male modernists, re-writing the canon means modifying our notion of the literary career. How would one fit the following examples, chosen fairly randomly, into modernism? All were well known in London in the 1920s and 30s; all are now well below the 'line' of canonical visibility. First, Ethel Mannin, a byword for emancipated youth: ILP member, pacifist, later anar-chist, and finally Catholic. She began writing popular novelettes 'at a guinea a thousand [words]', and subsequently wrote novels of working-class life, of London society, and politics. She wrote non-fiction, travel books, children's literature and poetry. She was a lover of Bertrand Russell, Yeats and others, hinting at her experiences in racy autobiographies. Her novels explore such difficult topics as homosexuality (*Men Are Unwise*, 1934) and relations with the enemy (*The Dark Forest*, 1946). Secondly, Robert Nichols, a shell-shocked World War I poet; a film-maker in Hollywood in the 1920s; a nov-elist, playwright (including the futurological play *Wings Over Europe*), broadcaster and critic. He lived in Japan and America in the twenties; Germany and France in the thirties. He was briefly the lover of Nancy Cunard and a friend of Eliot, Huxley and others. Thirdly, Len Lye: born in New Zealand in 1901, he lived in Samoa and Australia before arriving in London in 1926, quickly becoming a part of the avant-garde circle around Laura Riding in Hammersmith. He produced batiks and paintings for the London Surrealist exhibitions, published automatic writings, and became a radical film-maker and theorist at the experimental GPO film unit, pio-neering 'direct' images painted directly onto film stock. In 1944, perhaps sensing a shift in the cultural climate, he moved to New York, working with I. A. Richards on films promoting basic English. In America he became a kinetic sculptor, as well as promoting his theory – a classic piece of mod-ernist reform – of 'Individual Happiness Now'. Lye is close to invisible in histories of modernism, partly because of his mobility and tendency to switch modes – indeed, it is only when one starts to think about the mechanical registering of *motion* as a central problematic (outside the narrow parameters of film studies) that he comes into focus. All three figures had varied careers, exploiting new media and crossing genres – refusing the model of incarnation, maturity and late career associated with 'major' writers and epic works (Lipking 1981).

For such reasons, histories of modernism need revision. Take Hope Mirrlees's *Paris: A Poem* (1919), one of the first works published by the Hogarth Press – a hand-corrected pamphlet crudely bound in arresting blue lozenged paper. It owes a good deal to Apollinaire and Cendrars in its collage of city-fragments, but also offers much that Eliot would develop in *The Waste Land*: a descent underground, a cacophony of classical, biblical and demotic voices (adverts, street cries, songs); a cock cry; memories of the war; ghosts and dreams; endnotes. Mirrlees's poem differs from Eliot's in simply pre-senting fragmenation as an aspect of modern experience: there is no implicit 'state of mind', nor is there the overlay of a mythic journey. In terms of its poetics, the opening description of metro signs is interesting: 'I want a holophrase' followed by a list of Metro advertising signs for 'ZIG-ZAG', 'CACAO BLOOKER' and other products. Holophrasis is the condensation of a whole phrase or set of ideas by one word – a procedure often attributed to 'primi-tive' languages, and a key element of modernism seldom labelled as clearly as here. (It is central to Pound's understanding of the ideogram, for example.) Mirrlees's signs stand as a forgotten marker in the history of modernism.

Taking notice of this poem involves rewriting literary history: not arguing simplistically for 'priority', but noting that the monumentality of Eliot's masterpiece, achieved even as it was published, comes at the cost of the suppression of a broader discursive world. It has been argued, for example, that hand-setting the type for Eliot's poems nudged Woolf towards the spaced pages of *Jacob's Room* (1922) and a looser, more fragmented style. Should *Paris* be part of that story? Mirrlees vanished from poetic history – she published three odd novels and a translation in the twenties, and a few slim volumes late in life – while Eliot constructed a critical and editorial hegemony. With this series of caveats in mind, we can begin an outline of modernism: not one which displaces Pound and his friends, since the myth of the 'Men of 1914' is clearly important in the period as well as in later accounts; but rather one which (in the chapters which follow) attends to competing claims for attention.

EARLY MODERNISM IN ENGLAND AND AMERICA

Early modernism takes a rather different trajectory in England and America, involving different sets of key issues: in the first case temporal; in the second spatial. These differences are produced by the way in which modernity and modernism are configured in each country: in England, a sense of economic and imperial decline produces a split temporality of the kind discussed in the previous chapter, a sense of a need for renewal as well as an impulse to engage with the past. Modernism in England is inspired by European models, but takes a relatively independent path. In America on the other hand, we see a fracture (sometimes an internal fracture within a single corpus) between a 'native' modernism initially associated with the Midwest and a European modernism channelled through New York.

The years between 1909 and 1914 represent a crucial period for the development of English modernism and its aesthetics. The first date is important because it sees the founding of Italian Futurism, the first of the

European avant-garde movements, by Filippo Tommaso Marinetti. Futurism quickly spread through Europe and Russia; and in England, publicized by Marinetti's provocative London performances in 1910–14, it lay behind the Imagist movement announced in 'A Few Don'ts by an Imagiste' in *Poetry* magazine in March 1913. While there are earlier publications which represent an 'Edwardian' modernism – Ford Madox Ford's *English Review* (founded 1908) and A. R. Orage's *New Age* (1907) – it is with Ezra Pound and Imagism that the sense of a programmatic avant-garde begins.

Pound is central to any account of modernism in England: arriving in September 1908, ostensibly to work on Provençal poetry, he seems to have quickly forged a role as self-appointed organizer, lecturer, agent provocateur, editor, agent, impresario. For the next twelve years in London he cultivated connections, pouring out letters, reviews and translations, as well as his own poetry. In May 1909 he finally met W. B. Yeats, to whom his early poetry is heavily indebted. The acolyte quickly registered what he called 'the grain of hardness' in Yeats's new verse – the poems which became *Responsibilities* – and in their winters sequestered at Stone Cottage in Sussex from 1913 to 1916 the two poets solidified their friendship, reading and working on *Noh* plays. Imagism was proposed as a programme by Pound and T. E. Hulme in late 1912, its aesthetics centred on notions of instantaneity, immediacy, the elimination of waste, and a plasticity of style based on the 'prose tradition'. Its tenets were formulated in *Poetry* under F. S. Flint's name:

1   Direct treatment of the 'thing', whether subjective or objective.
2   To use absolutely no word that did not contribute to the presentation.
3   As regarding rhythm: to compose in sequence of the musical phrase, not in sequence of a metronome.

(P. Jones 1972: 129)

Imagist aesthetics will be discussed in detail later, but it is worth noting that for Pound it was essentially 'a movement of criticism rather than of creation' (1916: 95): it begins as an attack on existing style, a renewal born of negativity. Like all forms of Protestantism, it leads to further fractures: Pound attacked both the 'Impressionism' of Ford and Conrad and Futurism, which had clearly influenced him; and he was to attack Imagism itself in the name of the more dynamic art of Vorticism. Vorticism was succeeded by a turn to music and metrics (the period of the Pound and Eliot quatrain poems including 'Hugh Selwyn Mauberley', 1919–20), and by the epic project of historical recovery which was the *Cantos*.

By 1914–15 Imagism had achieved some public notice, with special issues of *The Glebe*, *The Egoist* and other journals devoted to it. The anthology *Des imagistes* was published in March 1914, but that represented an endpoint for Pound: the American poet and heiress Amy Lowell descended on London that summer and courted its contributors, wrenching the movement from his control. There were more anthologies (with a more mainstream publisher, Houghton Mifflin) and volumes like Aldington's *Images of War* and *Images of Desire*. But Pound was already investing his hopes in T. S. Eliot, whom he met in 1914, and gathering the artists Wyndham Lewis and Gaudier-Brzeska into the fold to form a more broadly aesthetic movement, Vorticism, with its aggressive journal *Blast* (1914–15).

The avant-garde in England had thus built up a certain momentum by 1914–15, a density of effort focused on a few small magazines and the anthologies which collected their work (*Des imagistes*; Pound's provocatively-titled *Catholic Anthology* in 1915; Harriet Monroe's *Modern Verse* in 1917; as well as the *Others* anthologies in New York). To read modernist texts as they first appeared in the little magazines is to quickly gain a sense of culture as a communication system; a network of connections and flows. Take the first three issues of *The Egoist* (formerly the feminist journal the *New Freewoman*), published fortnightly from 1 January 1914, with Pound acting as mentor. All open with editorial essays by Dora Marsden, in her radical 'individualist' mode. The first issue has an essay on 'France To-Day: A Group of Thinkers' by Edgar Mowrer, discussing Bergson, Poincaré and others; French influence is also represented by Remy de Gourmont's story 'The Horses of Diomedes'. Wyndham Lewis writes on Cubism, there are poems by the Imagist F. S. Flint, including 'Tube', a caustic comment on those who travel 'lulled / by the roar of the train in the tube / content with the electric light'. There is a piece on nudity in sculpture, a report of experimental theatre in Paris, and a review by Richard Aldington of Violet Hunt as a novelist representing a new generation of women. Issue 2 carries an account of Joyce's problems with censorship over *Dubliners*; issue 3 begins the serialization of Joyce's *Portrait of the Artist*. Also in issue 2, Storm Jameson writes on 'The Drama of Ideas since Ibsen', attacking a realist tradition in decline; there is Aldington on modern art and his poem 'Xenophilometropolitania', a parody of Sandburg, Pound and others which ends with an in-house joke, a version of Imagism's most famous couplet: 'The apparition of these poems in a crowd: White faces in a black dead faint' (Pound's 'In a Station of the Metro' had appeared in the same journal the previous August). Issue 3 includes Pound writing as 'Bastien von Helmholtz' on Synge and Yeats, poems by H. D, and Aldington's account of the occasion on which Yeats, Pound and six others visited the elderly poet W. S. Blunt in Sussex to present him with 'a carved reliquary of Pentelican marble, the work of the sculptor Gaudier Brzeska' – an act of homage formally marking the passing of the Victorian era.

Here, in embryo, is a full range of modernist concerns and tensions. Firstly, literary history in the making: an obsession with periodization, with what is dead and what newborn, and with influences from abroad; coupled with both the beginnings of canonization and a tendency to see the modern as – at the point of its inception – already in decay. Secondly, aggressive attacks on prudery and censorship; a championing of sexual candour, women's emancipation, and the values of the self over those of the machine-like crowd. Broadly speaking, these correspond to the two currents which Michael Levenson sees as informing early modernism: formalism and stress on abstraction on the one hand; an anarchic and more political declaration of the self's rights on the other.

Within the network described above, Pound worked to marshal a definable group. If one moves forward to *The Egoist* for September 1917, the assistant editor, installed by Pound, was Eliot; the issue contained work by Eliot, Pound, Aldington, and continued the serialization of Lewis's *Tarr*. Looking across from the contents page in the bound volumes one sees the advertisements on the back of the previous issue: for Joyce's *Portrait* and Eliot's *Prufrock*, available from *The Egoist*; for the *Little Review* ('EZRA POUND, London Editor') guaranteeing that 'Contributions by WYNDHAM LEWIS appear in all of the numbers', with work by Yeats and Eliot listed; for *Poetry* magazine (Pound was still its foreign editor). But this appearance of busyness must be qualified: the advertisements were mostly free exchanges, and the circulation of *The Egoist* had fallen off markedly as it became a literary rather than feminist magazine, to below 750 subscribers. In fact, the London Vortex was on the point of collapse. By the end of 1920 Pound had departed for Europe. Pound's Imagist associates splintered and scattered; many (H. D., Lawrence, Rodker, eventually Aldington) left England; some wrote histories or satires of the years of revolt.

Why does the English avant-garde appear to come into focus only at the point of fracture and collapse? The usual answer is the war. Imagism was, it is often pointed out, a mild version of the European avant-garde, shorn of its politics. Vorticism was, because of the influence of Lewis, more radical. The first (June 1914) issue of the Lewis–Pound journal *Blast*, the 'Review of the Great English Vortex', insists that the stagnation of England is 'the reason why a movement could burst up here, from this lump of compressed life, with more force than anywhere else' (Lewis 1997: 32). With its puce cover, violent typography and lists of 'Blasts' and 'Blesses', *Blast* aims to elicit what the second number calls 'rage or peevishness'. But *Blast* 2, the 'War Number' dated July 1915, allies itself to war-aims, and indeed claims that 'While all other periodicals were whispering PEACE in one tone or another . . . "BLAST" alone dared to present the actual discords of modern "civilization", DISCORDS now only too apparent in the open conflict between teutonic atavism and unsatisfactory Democracy' (Lewis 2000: 85–6). The danger of this position, as Lewis was later to see, was that the journal fades into the background, overcome by the literalization of its aggressive headlines in the tabloid press.

The war represented, of course, a general crisis. It curtailed the activities of publishers, and writers were absorbed into its aims – those who worked for the wartime cultural committee; those who like Lewis and Aldington served at the front. For Lewis, the war was an interruption, a fatal loss of momentum. In wartime Pound's stance shifted, as Levenson suggests, towards a stress on the 'sanity' of art and the monumentality of modernism's achievements (1984: 140–3) – an incipient classicism which asserted cultural continuity. Consider Pound's letter to Harriet Monroe in early 1915: 'My problem is to keep alive a certain group of advancing poets, to set the arts in their rightful place as the acknowledged guide and lamp of civilization' (Pound 1951: 90) – a statement which nicely suggests the contradictory position of an avant-garde: both a warring body (Pound as platoon leader) distinct from the mass, and an art which might aim for general recognition. 'Keeping alive' was another issue, and after the death of Gaudier-Brzeska in June 1915 Pound displays a more troubled and haunted stance.

However the war by no means offers a complete explanation for the decline of the avant-garde. In some respects, it could have stimulated it. In contrast to *Blast*, for example, *The Egoist* was not hostile to German writing: Alec Randall wrote on German poetry in 1914–15, and in a piece on 'Poetry and Patriotism' (Feb. 1916) praised Stefan Georg as offering a more nuanced response to the war than the conventional verses flooding the press. The war poetry of Guillaume Apollinaire, Isaac Rosenberg, John Rodker (written later) on one side, as with Georg and August Stramm on the other, represents a decisive step towards modernism.

In this light, it is necessary to consider the weaknesses of the image itself. With its stress on the instantaneous and the presence of the 'real', Imagism claims an aesthetics of presence. But that presence is, as Daniel Tiffany remarks, constructed on a regime of elimination and prohibition – an 'objectivity' constructed on a fear of pollution, a deathliness which must constantly be voided and avoided; an engagement with the symbolic which has its roots in a poetics of mourning (1995: 156; cf. Nicholls 1995: 170). Moreover the aesthetics of the image must contain *both* those currents which Levenson identifies in modernism: on the one hand Pound often depicts himself as a surgeon or hygienicist, cutting away the dead matter to reveal the real; on the other hand what is produced by this operation is highly sculptural, plastic and abstract. Such complex contradictions make Imagism difficult to sustain, for Pound at least. As we will see in chapter 6, one crucial element of Vorticism is the introduction of temporality – an addition which Pound came to associate, later, with the importance of music and metrics; but which we might also see as an animation of the dead matter of the image. The vortex, in Pound's formulae, is akin to a turbine, sucking in 'all the energised past', 'the past that is vital'. This recalls Bergson's vitalist conception of the moment as a kind of processing-machine which drives the past forward. On that conception of an art including history, the characteristic works of high modernism are founded.

Early modernism in the United States takes a somewhat different course from that in London, with multiple centres (the circle around *Poetry* magazine in Chicago; Manhattan's galleries, salons and Greenwich Village bohemia; the Wharf Theatre in Provincetown), and with, somewhat paradoxically, both a greater initial emphasis on European input and a more distinctly national cast than in England. Alfred Stieglitz's 291 gallery (1905–12) and its successors over the next two decades were central to the dissemination of European modernism, showing work by Picabia, Brancusi and others, as well as African art. The International Exhibition of Modern Art held in early 1913 (usually called the Armory Show, after its venue) introduced contemporary art to many Americans, and the beginning of the war saw a range of exiles from Europe arriving in New York. At Walter and Louise Arensberg's apartment in Manhattan Duchamp, Picabia, Mina Loy and others – the central figures of New York Dada – mingled with Americans: Man Ray, the painters Demuth and Stella; writers like Marianne Moore, William Carlos Williams and Wallace Stevens, creating a potent mixture expressed in short-lived magazines like Alfred Kreymborg's *Others* (funded by Arensberg), *The Blind Man* and *Broom*. Those magazines are marked by a greater emphasis on graphic work than more mainstream journals, and by a linguistic experimentalism indebted to European Dada. One exemplary figure was the Baroness Elsa von Freytag-Loringhoven, often seen as the first performance artist: she brought the decadent modernism of Vienna to New York, deploying her body in a bizarre critique of bourgeois style; decorating herself with coal-scuttles, light-bulbs, paint; threatening Williams with syphilis; and publishing cryptic poetry in the *Little Review* (Gammel 2002). Something of a critical myth has sprung up in recent years which portrays New York Dada as a radical, democratic style which anticipates postmodernism, in contrast with the conservative, authoritarianism of 'high' modernism. But this risks parodying both entities: New York Dada was a short-lived, expatriate movement; 'high' modernism is both less homogeneous than this suggests and more sustained.

What was equally important in early modernism in New York was an indigenous movement: nativist modernism. Steiglitz's 291 showed Brancusi; it also promoted the work of Georgia O'Keefe, John Marin, Arthur Dove and other Americans. The literary equivalent of this movement was stimulated by an influx of writers from Chicago modernist circles into the salons of Mabel Dodge and others – Floyd Dell, Sherwood Anderson, Vachel Lindsay, all of whom represented a distinctly Midwestern cultural inheritance derived from figures like William Dean Howells, the novelist and critic who promoted both Russian literature and American realism. The Chicago writers were complemented by the arrival in New York around 1915 of a generation of radically minded Harvard students, inspired by the teaching of William James and George Santayana. They included Walter Lippmann, Van Wyck Brooks, John Reed, and Harold Stearns: Lippmann edited the *Harvard Monthly*; Randolph Bourne the *Colombia Monthly*; both were later associated with the *New Republic* and the *Seven Arts*. They formed connections with a group of influential scholars at Colombia including John Dewey and Franz Boas. Collectively they were to launch a critique of American culture and propose a renewal typified by Randolph Bourne's *Youth and Life* (1913).

The revolt of youth represented a broad-based attack on inherited values: on sexual puritanism, the genteel New England tradition; and a brash commercial culture which seemed to have little time for the arts. The work of Waldo Frank (*Our America*, 1919) and others fuelled a debate on pluralism and nativism – in particular the idea that American identity is distinguished by its ethnic diversity – and a number of journals attempt to foster a distinctively American rather than Eurocentric modernism. *Contact*, started by William Carlos Williams and Robert McAlmon in 1920, was designed to counterbalance *The Little Review*, to which Pound fed material from Europe. Their manifesto declared: 'We will be American, because we are of America', the name of the magazine suggesting 'the essential contact between words and locality that breeds them'. Williams quoted John Dewey's essay 'Americanism and Localism' (1920), which stressed the pragmatic needs of the immigrant to deal with their immediate surroundings rather than an abstract 'American' identity (Kadlec 2000: 138). Later *Pagany*, the 'Native Quarterly' edited by Richard Johns from 1930 to 1933 with Williams as its presiding spirit, proposed a similar programme. Such debates stimulated interest in modernism: a number of publishing houses founded in this period – Knopf (1915); Boni & Liveright (1917); B. W. Huebsch (1905) – promoted both American and European modernism. At the same time, the contradictions within American modernism – its simultaneous nativism and debt to Europe – remained in place, nowhere more visible than in Williams, for whom Europe was both the threat of infection (the baroness's syphilis) and stimulus. We will return to that contradiction shortly.

'HIGH MODERNISM', CLASSICISM AND THE EPIC

'High' modernism emerges with *The Waste Land*. Eliot's poem, in part the record of a personal breakdown, was handed to Pound as a chaotic draft in January 1922. Pound then edited it substantially, with Eliot's help, and managed its publication. The poem was rapidly accepted as a classic. *Ulysses*, already trailed in the *Little Review*, appeared in the same year, Pound again having a hand in its publication: at an extraordinary dinner in Paris on 3 January 1922, Horace Liveright agreed to undertake American publication of both *The Waste Land* and *Ulysses*, paying Pound a retainer (Rainey 1998: 82).

The year 1922, having been declared modernism's *annus mirabilis*, began to make its way into the mainstream. It is instructive to compare 1922 with 1925: the latter year saw Woolf's *Mrs Dalloway*, Ford's *No More Parades*, Yeats's *A Vision*, Pound's *A Draft of XVI Cantos*, Fitzgerald's *The Great Gatsby*, Dreiser's *An American Tragedy*, as well as Kafka's *The Trial* and Stein's *The Making of Americans* (written 1903–11) – works already different in specific ways from those of 1922, suggesting a more established activity (these were mostly not issued in limited editions nor smuggled across borders). Most offer a critique of the values associated with post-war society which is more pointed and programmatic than Eliot's generalized anxiety; most are mid-career works.

On the whole, then, Pound's monumentalization of 1922 succeeded, particularly in America (in London, resistance to modernism remained a feature of reviewing throughout the twenties). Pound constantly projected his work into a future history, moving his perspective from literary revolution to a retrospective accommodation. Eliot too in his criticism began to wrap literary history around his own form, providing a critical genealogy for his work via such notions as 'minor literature'. His return to Harvard to deliver the Norton lectures in 1932–3, and the publication of *Ulysses* by Random House in the USA, consolidated the acceptance implicit in earlier moments such as Yeats's Nobel Prize (1923), and E. M. Forster's Clarke Lectures at Cambridge in 1927 (published as *Aspects of the Novel*).

By the early 1930s the first monographs on the modernists were appearing. Edmund Wilson's *Axel's Castle* (1931) was an insider's account of modernism and its origins in the 1890s. The Chatto & Windus 'Dolphin Books' included studies of Eliot, Aldington, and Proust; F. R. Leavis's *New Bearings in English Poetry* (1932) concentrated on Yeats, Eliot and Pound. The 1930s and 40s saw the developing alliance between Eliot and the American New Criticism (especially in its Anglo-Catholic guise represented by Allen Tate and Cleanth Brooks); and the canon-building efforts of critics like R. P. Blackmur (who championed Stevens) and Leavis (who incorporated Conrad, Lawrence, Eliot and Joyce into the 'Great Tradition'). By the end of the 1930s there would be a Wallace Stevens number of the *Harvard Advocate*, and anthologies like Roberts's *Faber Book of Modern Verse* (1936) began to map the new field. Brooks's exegesis of *The Waste Land* in *Modern Poetry and the Tradition* (1939) – in terms of its status as a modern revivification of religious ritual, a sacred book of the arts with an underlying unity – represents the culmination of that process.

Around high modernism, the notion of a modernist classicism forms, crystallizing in Eliot's declaration in 1928 that he was 'classicist in literature, royalist in politics, and Anglo-Catholic in religion' (1929: vii). Classicism is best seen as an ongoing set of possibilities within a field of different modernisms. It includes Baudelaire's insistence on the self-sufficiency of art; T. E. Hulme's rejection of Bergson and espousal of a new classicism in the columns of the *New Age* in 1912, under the influence of Worringer and others; Apollinaire's late essay 'The New Spirit and the Poets'; the musical neo-classicism of Ravel during the war; Picasso's move towards monumentalism in 1917; Eliot's turn towards the metaphysical poets and Dante. In 1920s France classicism was associated both with an anti-Romanticism and a romantic notion of French national identity. The work of Charles Maurras influenced Eliot and Lewis; Eliot saw it as confirming the anti-Romanticism he derived from the American critic Irving Babbit. John Middleton Murray wrote in rather different terms of a 'classical' revival in the *Adelphi* in 1926 – in terms of Augustanism, a fascination with the human as marionette, a scepticism which points towards Lewis's idiosyncratic return to the Augustans in the late 1920s. This represents a more formalist classicism, centred on non-moral satire and notions of artistic autonomy, in contrast to Eliot's stress on the 'orthodox'.

In the works of the 'high modernists' Pound, Joyce and Eliot, classicism centres on what Eliot, in his 1923 essay '*Ulysses*, Order, and Myth', labelled the 'mythic method' – Joyce's use of classical epic as a structuring device in his novel, for Eliot 'a way of controlling, of ordering, of giving a shape and a significance to the immense panorama of futility and anarchy which is contemporary history' (Kolocotroni 1998: 373). Eliot's easy slippage between 'structure' (which may be a contingent and arbitrary imposition in *Ulysses*) and 'significance' reveals a respect for the classics as models for revision. But we can find other ways of describing the simultaneous ambition and fragmentation of texts like *Ulysses* and the *Cantos*. In what Pound formulated as early as his 1911–12 essays 'I Gather the Limbs of Osiris' as the 'method of luminous detail', the collage-poem becomes capable of incorporating heterogeneous fragments which can, in the wake of *The Waste Land*, incorporate widely divergent materials and registers. The divergent possibilities Pound offered for understanding the *Cantos* – epic, metamorphosis, musical structure, poetic *Bildungsroman* – testify to the tension between copiousness, inclusiveness, subjectivity and contingency on the one hand, and the desire for structure and objectivity on the other.

We can also turn to Walter Benjamin's essay 'The Crisis of the Novel' (1930) for an explanation of the modernist 'epic'. Benjamin situates the origins of the novel in an individualism which cuts the writer off from the collectivity of the oral voice and epic (1999: 299–304). But he also sees (he is reviewing Alfred Döblin's *Berlin Alexanderplatz*) a return to epic, formulated on the principles of montage and the document which 'explodes the framework of the novel', incorporating the materials of mass culture and everyday life. Modernism is notable for the number of novels which aspire to create a totality which enfolds history, contemporaneity and a representative self into what Fredric Jameson calls 'The Book of the World'. There are nineteenth-century precursors – *Moby Dick* and Balzac's multi-volume *Comédie humaine* – but such works as Joyce's *Ulysses*, Proust's *Remembrance of Things Past*, Dos Passos's *U.S.A.*, and Musil's *The Man Without Qualities* are striking for they way they seek an expansion of the generic limits and documentary scope of the novel.

LATE MODERNISM AND SURREALISM

The emerging hegemony of the 'Men of 1914' created a problem for those who followed: the problem of belatedness. What cultural space was available to 'make it new' *again*? Writing in *The Future of Futurism* as early as 1926, John Rodker commented that 'the time has come to widen our definition of the classical, for futurism only exists as a state of flux, immediately it is accepted becoming the classical of its own generation and posterity. Picasso for example in painting, Stravinsky in music, and in literature let us say Joyce' (1926: 21–2). The historical concretion of modernism meant, then, a problem of literary moder*nity*. One often finds a sense of lassitude and historical uncertainty in work of the early 1930s. An example is Louis MacNeice's 'An Eclogue for Christmas' (1933), very oddly placed, with its 'jazz–weary' stance, as a representative of *new* poetry in Yeats's *Oxford Book of Modern Verse*. MacNeice's references to Picasso, 'broken facets' and modernist abstraction suggest the exhaustion of a style. In 1949 Wallace Stevens wrote that 'Somehow modern art is coming to seem much less modern than used to be the case. One feels that a good many people are practising modernism and therefore it no longer remains valid. It is odd how quickly the experimental becomes routine' (1966: 630).

Some of the fiercest battles over the developing canon emerge from the central groupings of the 'Men of 1914'. Wyndham Lewis went 'underground' after the war, publishing little between *The Caliph's Design* (1919) and *The Art of Being Ruled* (1926). When he re-emerged it was with a satirical stance, that of 'The Enemy', often directed against modernism and its aesthetics: Bergson, Joyce, Stein, Woolf, Eliot and Huxley are attacked in *Time and Western Man* (1927) and *Men Without Art* (1934). Arguing for a world of objects rather than psychology, and attacking the commodification of art and other targets including political art, Lewis saw himself as a dissident in relation to most of the trends of his period. Historicity is for Lewis, as for Nietzsche in *On the Advantages and Disadvantages of History for Life* (1873), a dangerous temptation: if history enters consciousness it paralyses the self.

A revisionist canon-formation is also central to Yeats's *Oxford Book of Modern Verse* (1936). Drawing on what he calls the 'privilege' of achievement, Yeats arranges Pater's prose into verse, plays down Eliot, debates obliquely with Pound, and includes poetry by friends like Dorothy Wellesley. Notoriously, he excludes Wilfred Owen and other war poets on the grounds that 'passive suffering is not a theme for poetry' (1936: xxxiv). The collection writes the history of modernism as a descent from Pater and the poets of the 1890s – 'We were the last romantics – chose for theme / Traditional sanctity and loveliness' – but it also shows an anxiety about its canon-building: Yeats admits that 'certain poets' included but not discussed in his introduction, like Robert Nichols and Hugh MacDiarmid, 'might have confused the story' (1936: xli).

Second-stage modernists use a variety of strategies for clearing cultural space. These include direct attack and satire or parody. The former is represented by Rebecca West's essay 'What is Mr T. S. Eliot's Authority as a Critic?' (1932) and, more ambivalently, Delmore Schwartz's 'The Literary Dictatorship of T. S. Eliot' (1949). A more satiric relation to the works of 'high' modernism characterizes a number of novels of the 1930s: Lewis's *The Apes of God* (1930) violently parodies Bloomsbury; Djuna Barnes's

Nightwood (1936) scarcely contains its own satiric energies, directed at Barnes's Paris milieu and at Joyce. Samuel Beckett's novel *Murphy* (1938) includes a satire on Yeats's legacy in the episode in which Neary bashes his head against the buttocks of the statue of Cuchulain in the General Post Office in Dublin; there is also a vicious attack on Austin Clarke ('Austin Ticklepenny'), who represented that legacy. Balso's journey up the anus of the Wooden Horse of Troy in Nathanael West's *The Dream Life of Balso Snell* (1931) is laden with parodic moments – Jane Goldman is surely right in seeing the cry 'O anus mirabilis!' as a joke about 1922. Tyrus Miller argues that late modernism, seeking a new aesthetic, extrapolates tendencies that were present but overshadowed in high modernism: a desire to investigate the figural (or non-semiotic) rather than the systemic and discursive; the exploration of forms of disassemblage and fetishism; a savage humour directed at the formal preoccupations of earlier texts.

An early response to the problem of belatedness was in fact one of the first to use the term 'modernist', Laura Riding's and Robert Graves's *A Survey of Modernist Poetry* (1927). Riding and Graves clearly resent the hegemony of Eliot, and attempt to circumvent the notion of the avant-garde by conceiving (as Arnold had done) the 'modern' as a principle of perpetual opposition rather than a historical dialectic. Modernism becomes not a historical moment, but a possibility perpetually renewed; and is contrasted with a mere time-bound preoccupation with fashion and newness. They seek, that is, to de-periodize modernism even as they accept the period label. 'I put religious trust in the predictiveness of poetry as an immediacy, not a future in the making', Riding wrote in the introduction to her own poems (1980: 3). Michael Roberts's *Critique of Poetry* (1933) is similarly complicated in its attempt to criticize the grounding of modernist classicism in the work of Hulme and Eliot and to introduce a more open, Darwinian notion of poetic progression which would make space for the Auden generation, Hart Crane and other second-stage modernists. The 1930s in general see a range of polarized debates – on politics, on 'pure poetry' (the French movement associated with Henri Bremond) in which different aspects of the modernist inheritance are developed.

One strategy is that represented by the journal *transition*, run by Eugene Jolas in Paris 1927–30 and then in the Hague 1932–8. *transition* disseminated a late modernist style associated with the 'revolution of the word', publishing segments of Joyce's 'Work in Progress' (*Finnegans Wake*), Stein's work, and forging links with Dada and Surrealism. It also published the work of emerging writers including Riding, Beckett and Zukofsky. Above all it concerned itself with the idea of the cultural interface, publishing writers from dozens of countries; sending a questionnaire around American writers asking why they were expatriates; seeking links between different cultural modes: painting, writing, photography, cinema.

Surrealism, the Parisian movement founded by André Breton and others around 1919, with its first manifesto in 1924, itself had a major influence on Anglophone modernism in the 1930s, in part because of the impact of art exhibitions in London (from 1936) and New York (1932 and 1936). In London, a range of artists registered the impact of the movement: the painters Roland Penrose and Paul Nash, the theorist Herbert Read, poets David Gascoyne and Dylan Thomas (who offered cups of boiled string to audiences), the film-maker Norman McLaren (Rémy 1999). The Surrealist exhibitions in New York in 1932 and 1936 introduced first the figural art of Ernst and Dali, and then the more abstract and automatic work of Masson, Miró and others, influencing a range of American painters including Gorky, Motherwell and Pollock. The arrival of the Surrealists themselves at the end of the 1930s both solidified that influence and opened the path to Abstract Expressionism as a dominant late modernist style. In literary terms, surrealism offered a revision of modernism away from the developing monumental, epic style of Pound and Eliot towards notions of spontaneity, infection and excess. Surrealism also suggested that the detritus of commercial culture might be reclaimed, suffused with desire – as in the boxes constructed by Joseph Cornell.

A number of American writers consciously allied themselves with Surrealism, especially Charles Henri Ford, friend and lover of Djuna Barnes, and his friend Parker Tyler in their magazine *Blues* (1929–30). Nathanael West's Surrealism, founded on his years in Paris, is most clearly expressed in his investigation of anality, dreamscapes and metamorphosis in *The Dream Life of Balso Snell*. Mina Loy's novel *Insel*, a portrait of her lover the Surrealist Richard Oelze, uses Surrealist technique. But the most compelling encounter, in part because it represented a way of strengthening his own modernist dissidence, and in part because it offered a theory of literary influence related to the dialogue between America and Europe noted earlier, was that of William Carlos Williams. Williams's engagement with Surrealism includes writings in the mid-1920s, his translation of Philippe Soupault in 1929; his links with Ford in the early 1930s and later with the Greek Surrealist Nicholas Calas. For Williams the question of the *influence* of Surrealism – the translation of the movement into America – takes on a particular importance: he was, after all, the American most strongly associated with a nativist version of modernism; with the rejection of Europe and the past.

Why was Williams attracted to Surrealism? In *The Embodiment of Knowledge* he describes it as returning reality to language, not simply by a linguistic operation like metaphor, but by a cognitive twist which produces a skewed relation to the real: 'In Surrealism the distortion of the emotion, the object, the condition, makes the words (the true material of writing) real again' (1974: 19). Linking Surrealism and Stein, he stresses that Surrealism collapses the space between words and the 'object depicted' by a process of deformation or distraction which bypasses perceptual and linguistic habits. What is not involved is Surrealism simply as a source of material, of striking images from the unconscious; it is always a *practice* which renews language; a practice like translation, which works through dissonance and transports material from elsewhere, renewing the native context.

Surrealism thus supported Williams's poetics of renewal. He quickly saw Surrealist automatic writing practices as a way of explaining the experimental prose which he wrote between 1918 and the early 1930s (collected as *Imaginations*). In *I Wanted to Write a Poem* (1958) he writes in terms of Dada, but the real referent is its successor, Surrealism:

> The pieces in this book [*A Novelette and Other Prose*] show the influence of Dadaism. I didn't originate Dadaism but I had it in my soul to write it. *Spring and All* shows that. Paris had influenced me; there is a French feeling in this work. I returned to a more placid style than in *Spring and All* but it was still a tremendous leap ahead of conventional prose. An American reader would have been lost entirely. I had abandoned all hope of getting American readers of a special sort. I wrote for personal satisfaction. This was automatic writing. I sat and faced the paper and wrote. The same method as in the IMPROVISATIONS but the material has advanced; it is more sophisticated.
>
> (1967: 60)

There is the issue of priority: Paris influenced him, but Dada is in the 'soul'. There is the 'leap ahead' of an American audience – a leap which, implicitly, carries him across the Atlantic. Automatism is associated with the new, but is subject to temporal skewing: both anticipated in the figure of influence, and claimed for the self as priority – since here and elsewhere Williams dates his automatic writing to *Kora in Hell* (1918), *before* Surrealism.

In *A Novelette* – written January 1929, as he translated Soupault's *Last Nights of Paris* – Williams found his clearest response to Surrealism. In this text, its epidemic status is literalized, as Tyrus Miller points out, in terms of the flu epidemic of early 1929. Williams describes the epidemic as both distraction and the refocusing of attention; he even finds a physiological basis for the equation of epidemic and the release of static constellations of knowledge, since the toxins of flu create a state of fatigued dissipation. Infection comes from abroad, even as it locates itself in American actuality:

> It has the same effect – the epidemic – as clear thought. It is like the modern advent of an old category supplanting a stalemate of information. A world of irrelevancies in the doing of one thing. . . . And they have added a new brick front to the old brick house, coming out to the sidewalk edge for a store. Writing should be like that, like the world, a criticism of ideas; a thought implied in trees, the storm grown vocal: One thing supplanting all things – the flu, summing all virtues. A lardy head – new bricks joined to the old – the corner of the street in a wind that's driven them all indoors.
>
> Take the Surrealists, take Soupault's *Les Dernières Nuits de Paris*, take . . .
>
> (1970: 279–80)

The epidemic is a distraction like that which generates the automatic text. Surrealism is the literary reference, and it *is* an epidemic. Or to complete the circle, influenza *is* influence – a hoary etymological pun which the text repeatedly implies, an example of what Breton called 'objective chance', the coincidence of the external world and the operations of mind. In America the figure of automatism (rupture) becomes, via the influenza epidemic, the influence, of the far-fetched. (A further set of American puns links the notion of the automatic and the automotive.) What Williams labels 'automatism' thus allows *contact*, the term enshrined in his early journal.

There were attempts elsewhere to wrest new potentials from modernism. Ireland is a particularly interesting case because of the dominating presence of Yeats, a Protestant, in the literature of the new Catholic state. Thomas MacGreevy, poet, critic and art historian, wrote studies of modernist writers Eliot and Aldington in which he attempted to formulate an aesthetic which would avoid the contempt for the masses within Yeats's work. Turning to the idea of a more inclusive and explicitly Catholic aesthetic, he seeks a middle way between disengagement and populism, abstraction and 'reality', high and mass culture. Accordingly in his critical study *Richard Aldington* he defends a specifically *bourgeois* art against modernist writers who reject it. The bourgeoisie has, he suggests, carried the responsibility for tending the 'Great Tradition' for only a century, and needed more time to produce an art of 'revolutionary humanity' (1931b: 11–12). Louis MacNeice, located in the Protestant north, was more ready to consider the ironies of an Irish modernist inheritance, offering a bridge between the personal style of Yeats and Auden's influence. And Samuel Beckett's 1934 essay 'Recent Irish Poetry' represents the conscious continuation of a modernist position in a situation in which radicalism must now be directed against (rather than allied to) the state. In attacking those whom Beckett sees as Yeats's followers, 'twilighters' and 'antiquarians', and praising those like MacGreevy, Coffey, and Devlin who link themselves to other influences (Eliot, Joyce, Surrealism, Hart Crane), Beckett produces an aesthetics of dislocation which is not simply exilic, but in which identity and language are disarticulated. He writes of 'the breakdown of the object, whether current, historical, mythical or spook' (1983: 74).

Finally, it is worth noting the afterlife of modernism. It is remarkable how many late-modernists had interrupted careers, going underground for decades between the 1930s and the 1960s: George Oppen, abandoning poetry for politics and exile in Mexico; Basil Bunting; Thomas McGreevy, becoming an art critic before a small late flowering; Brian Coffey, becoming a schoolteacher in America before returning with such poems as 'Missouri Sequence' and *Advent* (1975), arguably the greatest religious poem of its period. The English Surrealist David Gascoyne, deep in breakdown in the late 1960s, reportedly emerged after a hospital visitor (later his wife) read out a poem only to hear one of the inmates say 'I wrote that'. The revival of the careers of these poets represented both a rediscovery of modernist histories – many were prompted to write again by younger writers – and a question mark for the emerging narrative of modernism as the period style of the inter-war years. They thus began to write again out of a discontinuous history into which they were already written; the discontinuity produced by the power of the late work, and by the question of what is 'beyond' modernism – an attenuated continuation or a separate periodicity.

MODERNISM AND GENDER

A further issue in relation to the canon is gender. What is at stake includes both the question of women's exclusion from the canon, and of the gendering of modernist aesthetics. The possibility of an alternative 'women's modernism' is implicit in both these questions.

It is undoubtedly true that the canonical narrative of modernism, focused on the 'Men of 1914', neglected women writers. While Pound's post-war career included a concerted effort to rescue him from a treason trial and sustain his tradition, women prominent in the inter-war period – Mina Loy, Zora Neale Hurston, Nella Larsen, Laura Riding, Mary Butts – often vanished. To some extent this exile (to use Loy's term) was elective, as in Riding's choice not to reprint work or be labelled a 'woman poet'. But the point is that the ideological context which enabled Pound's 'professionalism' was difficult for women writers. It was only with a new generation of feminist critics in the eighties, and the efforts of presses like Virago in publishing reprints, that modernist women began to receive systematic attention.

One reason for that disappearance from visibility is the fact that women often played supportive rather than agonistic roles. Many of the editors and patrons of modernism were women. Harriet Shaw Weaver is the heroic example: heiress, publisher of *The Egoist*, lifelong supporter of Dora Marsden; sponsor, publisher and literary executor of Joyce; settlement-worker in the East End and fundraiser for a women's hospital in London; communist. If we conceive modernism in terms of the network rather than iconoclasm, women move closer to the centre: Harriet Monroe, Mabel Dodge, Bryher, Amy Lowell, Nancy Cunard, Gertrude Stein, Jessie Faucet and many others. Women's networks include the predominantly lesbian world of Paris in the 1920s, with intricate links between Stein, Barney, Barnes, Loy, Beach, Bryher and others (Benstock 1987) – lesbian women often had a freedom, in terms of space and support, unavailable to heterosexual women. Other sites include both the permanent (Bloomsbury) and temporary (Hayford Hall in Devon, rented by Peggy Guggenheim in the summers of 1932 and 1933).

As suggested above, a second set of problems surround the gendering of modernist aesthetics, and the often explicitly masculine rhetoric of 'breakthough' associated with the avant-garde. The doctrine of 'paedomorphism' was a commonplace of biological thinking: women were more conservative and 'primitive'; the extension of human capacities was a masculine activity. Pound, Williams and others understood creative activity in terms of masculine aggression and spermatic fecundity. Other aspects of femininity can be added to the mix. In the wake of Andreas Huyssen's *After the Great*

Divide, it is often suggested that modernism is founded on the confluence of two associated hate objects: women, and the sentimental mass culture they are said to passively consume. Domesticity itself is often the object of attack in the literature of the inter-war years: in Orwell's *Coming Up for Air* (1939) the female body, fat and the spreading suburbs are equated.

However the idea that modernism was pervasively misogynistic, or that it can be characterized by its opposition to mass culture and commercial art, does not bear close scrutiny (Huyssen's evidence is skeletal). Undoubtedly, male modernists display misogyny: a vein of offensive comments runs through the correspondence of Pound, Lewis, Eliot and John Quinn; Hemingway, in such stories as 'The Snows of Kilimanjaro', depicts women as trivial and castrating. But the issue is often complicated by the fact that it is a cultural construction of femininity that is at stake. In the case of Italian Futurism, 'hatred of women' served as a shorthand for an attack on sentimentality and a conservative Victorian inheritance – the Futurists in fact supported women's rights, and women were active within Futurism. Pound, despite his fulminations, supported and enlisted a number of women writers; and even the masculine *Blast* praised the Suffragettes and included a short story by Rebecca West (though one which figures gender as a battleground and implicitly condemns masculine weakness). The actual gender positions adopted by modernists could be complex: Duchamp and Woolf explore cross-dressing; Stein describes her genius as 'masculine'; Rebecca West criticizes sentimentality; Joyce hinges his epic on the shift from the stern modernist Stephen Dedalus to the 'feminine' Bloom; Williams centres his aesthetics on identification with feminine figures as well as on virility; Robert Graves writes a study of the mother goddess.

Our third question was: given women's position and the gendering of modernist aesthetics, does it make any sense to posit a women's modernism? Such a modernism need not be separatist; indeed, it must be seen in terms both of identifications with women and dialogue with the masculine public sphere. Virginia Woolf provides a complex example. She was powerfully affected by her identifications with women: Vita Sackville-West; Katherine Mansfield, whose rivalry she read as directly sexual (the 'civet cat' smell). At the same time, she constructs her aesthetics by attacking Arnold Bennett, and despite her distaste for the scatology of *Ulysses*, it informs her account of a day in *Mrs Dalloway*. The notion of a feminine aesthetic is implicit in Woolf's analysis of women's work and pleasure, and in a utopian notion of an androgynous being containing both genders. This is complicated by a certain hostility towards mothers epitomized by the treatment of Mrs Ramsay in *To the Lighthouse* – not only her death, but the representation of her tendency to see children as part of the bargain with patriarchy which Freud described, in which women give up any claim to the 'phallus' (power) in return for children. By the time she wrote *Three Guineas* (1938) Woolf could only see that as a violent silencing epitomized by 'the wireless of the daily press' and its obliterating, technologically-amplified voice calling for women to remain at home: 'it takes the words out of our mouths' (1993b: 269). The technological reference both anticipates the chuffing gramophone and public-address systems of *Between the Act*s (1941) and recalls the earlier reference in *Three Guineas* to 'the old worn ruts in which society, like a gramophone whose needle has stuck, is grinding out with intolerable unanimity' (1993b: 231).

What does this grinding? Woolf equates the masculine ego with both the machine and an authority associated with a kind of prosthetic privilege: the bolt-on armour of education, profession, public recognition and military prowess. As Ann Banfield observes, citing *Moments of Being*, for Woolf 'castration is the removal of a hard covering, "the outer crust of the self, one's personality"' (2000: 169). This seems to point towards Lewis's formulation of an armoured, prosthetic self as the masculine ego – a self punctured by Mina Loy in her satires on Futurism. Compare Stein's meditation on penetration in 'THIS IS THIS DRESS, AIDER' in *Tender Buttons*:

> Aider, why aider why whow, whow stop touch, aider whow, aider stop the muncher, muncher munchers.
> A jack in kill her, a jack in, makes a meadowed king, makes a to let.
> (1971: 176, corrected)

The 'to let' (toilet), at once desecration and possession; the cry for help and the pun on 'distress' in the title; the jack becoming a king which is masculine succession, perhaps even 'meadowed' becoming the 'mad old' king George III – the poem hints at both critique and an alternative sexual rhythm which might 'aid her', the release of lesbian desire.

To imagine a woman's language in this way is to rethink modernism. In her 1923 review of H. D.'s poems, Marianne Moore wrote of 'a martial, an apparently masculine tone to such writing as H. D.'s', in contrast to the retiring stance H. D. adopted in private. But she qualifies that: 'There is, however, a connection between weapons and beauty. Cowardice and beauty are at sword's points and in H. D.'s work, suggested by the absence of subterfuge, cowardice and the ambition to dominate by brute force, we have heroics which do not confuse transcendence with domination and which in their indestructibleness, are the core of tranquillity and of intellectual equilibrium' (1987: 82). One might compare her comments on Pound: 'apropos of "feminolatry", is not the view of women expressed by the Cantos older-fashioned than that of Siam and Abyssinia?' (1987: 272). In these formulae, Moore hints at an aesthetic in which the modernist shibboleth of the 'hard' and accurate style is divorced from notions of masculine force, and reattached to notions of openness, accuracy and modesty – a poetics expressed in successive appreciations of Stein's *The Making of Americans* and Hardy's late poems which she wrote in 1926.

Finally, in Woolf and others the possibility of a woman's writing involves the question of language as such: a language of classical knowledge and masculine expertise which the woman writer cannot share; a language which she must resist. The one-scene tragedy which the adolescent Louie writes for her father, Sam Pollit, and her teacher in Christina Stead's *The Man Who Loved Children* (1940) exemplifies the strategy of linguistic resistance. It is written in a kind of Esperanto, and performed by the children with Louie translating. 'Tragos: Herpes Rom' (Tragedy: The Snake-Man) describes a murderous and incestuous father, Anteios. 'Why isn't it in English?' Sam asks. Louie's reply 'Did Euripides write in English?' covers her lack of learning (she 'would have written it in French, but doesn't know enough grammar', Ernie explains) (1970: 408). Nevertheless this language has the power to uncover the scandal of Oedipal domination, in Megara's cry 'Ia ocen ib esse volid prin men aten men atem, men jur' (translated: I see you are determined to steal my breath, my sun, my daylight). Sam, throughout the novel, is the master of a copious and corny patois (or pa-toise, one might say, from the French *toise*, a measuring instrument). The play ends with the children 'oddly excited' and Sam unable to 'find words' before he shouts Louie down with a 'barbarian chant' (1970: 411). Order is restored when Louie's teacher, Miss Aiden, comes to dinner and Sam monopolizes her and jokingly declares he will marry her. But the seeds of rebellion – of Louie's attempt to kill Sam and departure – are planted. The paternal plot begins to fracture.

NATIONALISM AND MODERNISM

We can conclude with a comment on modernism's geography. The earlier discussion of nativist modernism in America suggests that the view that modernism is an inherently international cultural entity must be qualified: modernism is in fact inextricably linked with the emergence of the modern nation-state from late Victorian imperialism. Yeats's nation-building and its plot of struggle, violence, identity and disillusionment is one keynote here: a progress in which the notion of an imagined community is constantly invoked and revised; in which notions of sacrifice (Parnell, the Easter Rebellion, Yeats himself) are used to forge national identity. The discourse of national 'character' was, Pericles Lewis suggests, one of modernism's inheritances from Victorian thinking, though in a form in which it appears as crisis; in which the author must abandon distance and plunge into the effort of building a self-conscious community. That discourse is apparent equally in Stein's obsession with nation and racial types in *The Making of Americans* and *Three Lives* (1909) and in Stephen's desire to forge the conscience of his race in Joyce's *A Portrait of the Artist as a Young Man* (1916). In *Ulysses* this is tempered into a less racially-marked and more dialectical notion of Irish anticolonialism and cosmopolitanism, founded on the joking interplay between Bloom's Jewishness, the text's Irish nationalists, and representatives of British authority.

In England, at the centre of the (decaying) Empire, issues of national identity are also important, though domesticated and subject to anxious scrutiny. *Blast* emerges, in its second ('War') issue, as stridently nationalist. Woolf's *Mrs Dalloway* is darkly and satirically preoccupied with the comings and goings of Empire, with its monuments and rituals: 'an absurd statue with an inscription somewhere or other' in Regent's Park; the 'little crowd waiting at the gate' of Buckingham Palace 'to see the king drive out'; the photograph of Lady Bradshaw in 'Court dress' on Sir William's desk; Lady Brunton's 'ramrod bearing' at the thought of Empire; the 'some one in India' Peter wants to tell Sally about – from these fragments Woolf assembles a virtual empire. In the 1930s nation is a recurrent topic: in Auden's poetry, for all that it is preoccupied with frontiers and travel, the condition of England is a constant issue – for example in the obscurely hilarious rituals described in his drama *The Ascent of F.6.* (1937), in which the clichés of sacrificial mountaineering are spouted by characters who 'behave in general like the Marx brothers' (1958: 91). It is no accident that the radio features so strongly in the play, since it is in this period that the BBC formulates a rhetoric of nationhood.

The link between modernism and national identity is perhaps most apparent in the way in which a 'delayed' modernism becomes linked to cultural nationalism in its emerging temporal and spatial self-consciousness, and to forms of local epic in which geopolitical struggles are enacted. A short-list would include the Scottish modernism of Hugh MacDiarmid; African-American modernism – *Invisible Man* in 1952; and such texts as Robert Hayden's historical montage poems 'Runagate Runagate' (1962) and 'Middle Passage' (1941–66); Native American modernism – N. Scott Momaday's *The Way of Rainy Mountain* (1969). There are antipodean versions: the 'Angry Penguin' group in Australia; the modernist nationalism of the 1930s in New Zealand which Stuart Murray labels 'settler modernity', involving such works as A. R. D. Fairburn's fragmentary and polemical epic *Dominion* (1936) and John Mulgan's novel *Man Alone* (1939). In the Caribbean, Aimé Césaire's Surrealist-influenced poem *Notebook of a Return to My Native Land* (1939) and the work of E. K. Brathwaite are both revisions of the modernist tradition.

A notion of community even more tightly focused on regionalism was also an important component of nativist modernism. If Pound declared 'Provincialism the Enemy' in 1917, there are localisms built into his own work – the resonance of place. In America, the small town was explored in Sherwood Anderson's collection of stories *Winesberg, Ohio* (1919) and Edgar Lee Masters's *The Spoon River Anthology* (1915). Many later American writers explicitly founded their work on a locality which could be re-imagined or subjected to an imaginative archaeology: Williams celebrated Paterson, New Jersey, the industrial city on the Passaic river; Stevens located his work, for all its abstraction, firmly in New England. Faulkner's Mississippi, and his imagined Yoknapatawpha county and Frenchman's Bend, is perhaps the most striking example of the imagined community, since it is depicted in Darwinian terms both as a polis in which Southern

degeneration is explored (*The Sound and the Fury*); and as stable community invaded by dangerous incomers (Joe Christmas, the Snopes). In the
UK, there are parallels in the west of England and Wales celebrated by the
Powys brothers, David Jones and Mary Butts; in MacDiarmid's Montrose;
and in the general interest in vanishing regional identities in the travel
writing of H. V. Morton and others. These represent not just a regionalism
self-consciously distinct from modernist internationalism, but an attempt to
create new cultural and political affiliations, temporalities and spatialities
within modernism – MacDiarmid's linkage of Scotland and Lenin's USSR,
for example.

The sketch of the shape of modernism offered in this chapter has been
necessarily rapid and selective. It should be emphasized that the historiography of the subject is in a state of flux, with the scholarship needed for
a more comprehensive sense of modernism's history only just beginning –
and this is the case whether we are speaking of producing an edition of
the *Cantos* which would make the complexities of the poem's composition
clear, or of the canonical 'promotion' of writers like Loy. The canon is a
powerful construct, and any revisionist history of modernism must necessarily account for the emergence of the myth of high modernism within
the period – a story which the next chapter continues.

3 Modernism, Mass Culture and the Market

Most magazines are worthless a month after their appearance. Transition is the one review whose back numbers increase continually in value.

Advertisement, 1928

In order to gain a fuller sense of what modernism *was*, we need to return to the scene of its emergence, and attempt to understand something of the difficulties and resistances involved. This means examining institutions of cultural production and reception – editing, publishing, criticism, anthologizing – and the way in which modernist writers negotiate their audiences, teaching them how to read its texts. In this chapter I will consider particular cases, including the short story and little magazines. At its centre is a discussion of the way modernist texts seem to divide imagined readerships into 'insiders' and 'outsiders', an issue which leads us to the problem of modernist 'difficulty', and to a final topic, the modernist hoax.

First, a comment on mass culture. Modernity is constituted by mass activity, cutting across work, leisure, politics and intellectual life: the rows of the typists' pools or Ford factories; the massed limbs of exercisers ('4000 legs lifted towards the ceiling') and the Tiller Girls; 7,000 masons sitting down together for dinner; 10,000 boy scouts at a Jamboree; marching songs of Suffragettes or Fascists; the massed readers of the Left Book Club; the massed diners of the Lyons Corner House; Hitler's rallies; the readers of the tabloid newspaper; the Mass Observation project. Flicking through images of these occasions, it can seem as if the energies of life are marked by a mimetic impulse, a desire for sameness stamped on identity of the kind described by Gabriel Tarde in *The Laws of Imitation* (translated into English in 1903). Tarde suggested that a form of unconscious mimesis underpinned social action; and that crowd phenomena were a regressive form of that behaviour. This was a perception confirmed by the crowd psychology of Gustave le Bon: forms of mass expression seemed susceptible to both atavism and manipulation. For many in England, it was Lord Northcliffe who represented the powers of the new mass-market press. With his use of the *Daily Mail* to support militarism, conscription and an anti-Suffragette line; with his close involvement with government propaganda (he and Beaverbrook served as ministers), he was accused of debasing language and promulgating a new 'mobocracy' (Kibble 2002).

If we turn to the more specific issue of modernism and mass culture, a more ambivalent set of relations are apparent. We can begin with Norbert Elias's suggestive 1935 essay 'The Kitsch Style and the Age of Kitsch', a pioneering attempt to grapple with modernity and formal issues. Elias argues that with the passing of a dominant court style in the eighteenth century, the relation between form and formlessness altered: all works needed to be 'wrested from the abyss', creating an 'incessant interpenetration of structure and disintegration', and often an obsessive formalism (Elias 1998: 28). At the same time, the artist became increasingly distanced from the taste of mass society, a specialist whose detachment is rendered by the word 'kitsch' – from 'sketch', paintings made for tourists. But the situation is more complex. The rejected detritus of mass culture was ripe for a fascinated reappropriation; the process Elias calls *verkitschen*, turning into kitsch, in fact describes a circulation of materials through the modernist text, not least because kitsch accurately represents, as Elias puts it, 'a state of the soul engendered by industrial society', in which creativity is exiled to the margins of life, to the status of 'leisure' activity.

This is an argument which more accurately reflects the modernist relation to mass culture than simple-minded suggestions that modernist texts reject it. There are many links between the European avant-garde and mass culture, including an enthusiasm for music hall, cinema, jazz and popular music. In America Gilbert Seldes and others consciously attempted to bridge what Andreas Huyssen misleadingly calls the 'great divide' in the name of a vigorous, demotic culture. Ford claimed he edited *English Review* in the music hall; *Ulysses* is suffused with cinematic references. *The Waste Land* itself was seen in terms of 'the jazz of the music halls', as Edmund Wilson put it. Stein works detective fiction into her prose. To be sure, while admiring the vigour of working-class amusements, modernists often directed their scorn at the new middlebrow culture: best-selling novelists, literary pages. But many modernists also participated in that culture – Virginia Woolf giving talks for the BBC; Richard Wright toning down *Native Son* (1940) for the Book of the Month Club. Even the more virulent modernist attacks on mass culture – Ortega y Gasset's *The Revolt of the Masses* (1929) and Eliot's *The Idea of a Christian Society* (1939) – are balanced by an engagement with aspects of that culture. It is against the background of this ambivalence that modernism develops its complex sense of market relations.

THE MARKET

Is modernism to be understood as a phenomenon of the market? Competing accounts of this topic have recently emerged. According to Lawrence Rainey, modernism attempts to create a new niche market for an 'advanced' literature, structured by scarcity rather than abundance, and by patronage rather than direct commercial relations. On the other hand, Mark Morrisson claims that modernism is characterized by engagement with the public sphere and fascination with the techniques of advertising, even where it seeks to create a 'counter-public sphere'. What these two differently inflected accounts have in common is an understanding that the 'autonomy' often claimed for the modernist text is a strategic illusion, an advertising point rather than a philosophical absolute. To be sure, this hardly seems news: we are so used to saying that ideas are 'marketed' or 'sold' that the commodification inherent in these formulae goes unremarked. It is necessary to recall that the relation between the supposed autonomy of the literary text and its existence as a function of the market is itself part of the dialectic of modernity: only at the point where the mass market becomes ubiquitous must something be 'saved' from it.

Modernism originates in a period of considerable instability in literary production. For much of the Victorian period publishing existed in a relatively stable relation to established markets. In the UK the three-volume novel was sold at the inflated price of 31s 6d to the circulating libraries. By 1890 this arrangement was fraying and the triple-decker market collapsed as the libraries and new publishers combined to introduce cheaper one-volume novels. In an expanded market there were more novels and periodicals publishing short fiction. Factors behind this expansion include the increase in the reading public produced by the 1870 Education Act (solidified by the public library system), cheaper printing, and increased competition and professionalism in publishing, within the context of an expanded consumer culture. The resistance on the part of authors like Meredith and Hardy to the censorship associated with 'family' magazines created a more provocative approach to the novel.

One consequence was that relations between writers and readers became more direct, no longer mediated by the circulating libraries. In America, this had always been the case; one reason why America was early to see modern forms of authorship, characterized by a heightened commercialism, on the one hand (the columnist 'Fanny Fern' published arguably the first celebrity novel, *Ruth Hall*, in 1854); and a restless and alienated experimentalism both at odds with and fascinated by market culture on the other. In the UK, 'quality' literature increasingly became separated from popular taste: one could register cultural allegiances by purchasing the limp yellow covers of *The Savoy*, read stories in *The Strand*, or opt for the populism of the penny weeklies. Poetry became a less mainstream activity, associated with aestheticism.

Such developments might seem to point towards a split between 'high' and mass culture. Modernism, in this account, must separate itself from market culture, in the spirit of Joyce's 1901 remark (he is quoting Bruno) that 'No man . . . can be a lover of the true or the good unless he abhors the multitude' (2000: 50). But as already suggested, audiences cannot be so neatly separated into 'high' and 'low'. Peter McDonald argues that the late Victorian period sees 'the moment when instability became the most conspicuous feature of all cultural hierarchies, and new cultural spaces began to open up' (Bradshaw 2003: 226). Populist magazines like *T. P.'s Weekly* published literary material designed to improve their readers; cheap reprints of quality literature appeared; reading circles flourished. This may be ridiculed by Pound as 'the classics in paraphrase', but it is bound up with modernism's sense of edgy cultural demarcations and its cult of the expert. As Michael North argues, a shift towards a fractured public sphere is intrinsic to the crafts of advertising and public relations, accompanied by a psychology which sees the mass as driven by irrational desires (1999: 69–70). It is this sense of a contested public sphere which provides the context for modernism. Certainly, early modernism is less stratified by divisions between high and low culture than later modernism, hence the participation of James and Conrad in genres such as detective fiction. Nicholas Daly suggests that the genre of the romance – the adventure stories produced by Stevenson, Stoker, Kipling and others – constituted an early 'popular modernism', offering a challenge to realist fiction. In this account we need to see connections not simply between modernism and Symbolism, but also with genre fiction – while refusing the temptation to see modernists as distinguished by an 'ironic' approach to popular material.

Into the uncertain new spaces of the expanded literary culture described above, various cultural agencies inserted themselves. The professional mediation of market relations is a feature of late Victorian literary activity: the Society of Authors, the Publishers' Association; the rise of literary agents and syndication agencies; the use of publisher's readers; and the increased number of publications carrying book reviews. Such developments can be seen as examples of the regularizing processes intrinsic to modernity: literature is professionally processed, its values codified and rendered visible. One can even see the policing of cultural space in Britain in the new public libraries and library associations, endlessly worrying about the public's penchant for 'cheap' literature.

Authorship in the new century also became closely bound up with publicity: with interviews, photographs, gossip. The twenties consolidated this focus. Billie Melman notes 'the emergence of a new kind of personality cult characteristic of the burgeoning film industry' (1988: 67). Scott and Zelda Fitzgerald and Anita Loos had notorious lifestyles; Michael Arlen, author of *The Green Hat* (1924), pursued a life of extravagant self-display, purchasing a yellow Rolls-Royce to match the Hispano-Suiza in his novel. In America, publisher Horace Liveright, guided by one of his authors, the public relations expert Edward Bernays, pioneered the campaign selling the 'must-have' read. Modernists participated willingly in this culture: despite her ambivalence about the market, Gertrude Stein sold her own experience in *The Autobiography of Alice B. Toklas* (1932), remembering the world of Paris and Picasso before the war and celebrating her 'genius'. Henry Miller did little other than recycle accounts of his own bohemian existence, producing himself as a 'writer' in advance of any successful writing. This self-display is satirized in such texts as Fitzgerald's own Depression-era novel

Tender is the Night (1934) and Storm Jameson's satirical novella *Delicate Monster* (1933). The latter describes the neglected 'serious' writer Fanny, and her friend Victoria, the seamstress's daughter who becomes a popular novelist in the scandalous mode of Ethel M. Dell. Victoria poses naked and runs through numerous lovers, preaching a doctrine of 'reformed phallic worship' and becoming 'the first female novelist to have a public career equalling in interest the career of a Ziegfeld Follies girl' (1982: 15, 42). Fanny rejects this world, dwelling Flaubert-like on the purity of the word.

The modernist novel registers the way in which the market penetrates the modern self. In characters like Dreiser's *Sister Carrie* (1900) and Joyce's Gerty MacDowell in *Ulysses*, personhood appears as an effect of advertising – Gerty is a compendium of images associated with the 'seaside girl', reflexively aware that she is there to be looked at. The publicist is a central figure: Cowperwood in Dreiser's *The Titan* (1914) and the hero of Sinclair Lewis's *Babbitt* (1922) are self-promoting businessmen; Hurstwood, the PR expert, is the most prominent figure in Dos Passos's *U.S.A.* He and Ethel Mannin's hero James Ricard in *Sounding Brass* (1925) talk in capitals: 'American business has been slow to take advantage of the possibilities of modern publicity . . .' (Dos Passos 1937: 273); 'He was interested in Progress and Publicity, and the formation of that organization which would prove to the world the connection between the two' (Mannin 1925: 90). At the end of *Sounding Brass* the hero is enveloped in scandal, but unfazed: 'Ruined, indeed! Not with three wastepaper baskets full of Press-cuttings, and more to come . . . He was the most advertised man in London' (317).

As a kind of allegory of the literary marketplace, I will offer an example: the short story (earlier called the 'tale'), a genre developed most markedly by Poe, Hawthorne and other Americans. Its association with modernism derives from a formalist agenda which likens it to poetry. Poe's declaration in his review of Hawthorne (it exists in two versions) that the story must be directed towards a 'single effect' proposes an aesthetic which was to find an echo in Mallarmé and others: 'If his [the writer's] very first sentence tend not to the outbringing of this effect, then in his very first step he has committed a blunder. In the whole composition there should be no word written of which the tendency, direct or indirect, is not to the one pre-established design' (1984a: 586). The tale, Poe continues, demands a reader who 'contemplates it with a kindred art'; the 'unblemished' transmission of its central idea contrasts with the messiness and historical contingency of the novel.

The terms bequeathed by Poe, hovering on the edge of contradiction, had a pervasive influence. But equally important are the market relations bound up with the short story. A basic unit of production in the demanding world of the American magazine, it occupies a contradictory position: defined by the market and what Poe characterized as the short attention-span of the modern reader; and on the other hand recuperated in terms of an extreme formalism predicated on concentration of effect and intensity of reception. This is a contradiction central to modernism as a whole, since its criticism both emphasizes the detachment of close reading and borrows from mass culture a stress on the embodied, on the shock effect. Compare Woolf on *Ulysses*: 'Indifference to public opinion – desire to shock' (Scott 1990: 643).

More specifically, the 'cost' of literature, as magazine content, exists in fascinating relation to commodity culture in this period. As Richard Ohmann shows, in the 1890s the mass-circulation magazine took off in America, propelled by the rise of the professional-managerial class. An important commercial discovery drives this process: that if advertising was buoyant a magazine could be sold for less than production cost. 'Publishers mass-produced a physical product, which they sold at a loss, and used it to mass-produce an immaterial product, the attention of readers, which they sold at a profit' (1996: 346). By 1900 'advertising was running the publishing business. Sixty-five per cent of all the income received by magazines came from national advertising' (Goodrum 1990: 33). In the periodicals and illustrated magazines on both sides of the Atlantic: *The Strand, Black and White, Cosmopolitan, Munsey's* and *McClure's* stories served, putting it deliberately crudely, as the 'quality' filler in a sandwich comprised of aspirational copy aimed at the middle classes and matched advertising. Sally Stein's study of the *Lady's Home Journal* (1914–39) shows the evolution of the recognizable modern magazine format, with opening advertisements (usually in colour), a block of editorial material, and a long tail with run-over stories combined with ads, so that the reader is forced to repeatedly traverse the magazine. She concludes that 'the women's magazine in the twentieth century, though continuing to include literary texts, was becoming a predominantly visual experience, constructing an audience of spectators and, by extension, consumers' (1989: 146). Since it is bound to this commercial and visual regime, the status of literature is curiously detached: the carrier of value, yet also in a sense 'free' – reinforcing the autonomy of the literary, but paradoxically within a consumer nexus.

Henry James's relation to the short story illustrates these points. As Philip Horne argues, James's struggle with the 'compression' demanded by the commercialized form resulted in an aesthetic which stressed the literal and metaphorical 'costliness' of the product (the reserves of intention and meaning behind it) as an intrinsic part of its formal qualities. Initially failing to sell his stories or to succeed as a dramatist, James paradoxically achieved a position as the signifier of 'Art' which editors might purchase. By the time we arrive at the short fictions of Turgenev, Joyce and Mansfield, the short story has become definitional to modernism: epiphanic, ambiguous, formally perfect – but still a basic unit of magazine publication. *Blast* might aim to dynamite a cultural order, but it still includes a short story by Rebecca West. Introducing Jean Rhys's first collection of stories, Ford Madox Ford might praise her 'instinct for form', but he does so as the editor of the *Transatlantic Review*, telling us how he attempted to tailor them to the market (Ford

1987: 244). The position of the short story can be taken as emblematic of modernism as a whole: 'quality' cannot be dissociated from a consumer culture in which it identifies a particular audience.

LITTLE MAGAZINES AND PRIVATE PRESSES

If we turn to the little magazines which are the 'engine' of modernism, we find a story with many similar characteristics: a preoccupation with identifying markets; the association of art with cultural 'distinction' (as Pierre Bourdieu terms it). The ephemeral lives of modernist magazines testify to a restless search for audiences within a fragmentary cultural scene in which the middle ground sought by publications like Ford's *English Review* was hard to find. Avant-garde publications like *Others*, *The Egoist*, *Blast* lasted a few issues or a few years, aimed at a small selection of the educated population; subscription lists could range from a few hundred (*The Blind Man* in New York considered hand delivery) to, at most, the few thousands of journals like *Poetry* and *The Dial*. But limited readership and relatively high cover prices did not place them outside the advertising economy: they sold to middle-class audiences. As a suffragist magazine, *The Freewoman* made more money from advertising than subscriptions (Morrisson 2001: 91); the *Little Review* advertised Goodyear tyres. An issue of John Middleton Murray's *Adelphi* from the early 1920s, with work by Mansfield, Lawrence and others, advertises typewriters, lingerie (Debenhams), knitwear (Harvey Nichols), annuities and sea voyages; one could turn, in 1927, from the first printing of Yeats's play *The Resurrection*, with its Egyptian witness, to a tour of Egypt with P&O.

The awareness of literature as cultural capital is thus intertwined with modernism's official suspicion of the mass. Morrisson takes this argument further when he argues that the editors of little magazines, far from being indifferent to sales, were keen to borrow the publicity techniques of the mass market, assuring their purchasers that they were defining themselves as modern and daring. *The Egoist* sold itself as 'read by most of the well-known people in London'; the *Little Review* declared itself 'THE MAGAZINE THAT IS READ BY THOSE WHO WRITE THE OTHERS'. Even the radical *Masses* in America borrowed the techniques of popular magazines, including the cover girl. The Suffragette movement, with its demonstrations, parades and happenings – the slashing of paintings; the fatal dash in front of the Prince of Wales's horse – provided models for publicity to the Vorticists and others, expounded in such manifestoes as Mary Lowndes's 'On Banners and Banner Making' (Lyon 1992; Goldman 1998). Not only did *Blast* present itself as a series of advertising slogans, but the tenets of Imagism and Vorticism – immediate impact, absence of discursive prose, the image itself – anticipate post-war advertising (Dettmar 1996, 17: 36). Vorticism was an attempt to create a market for fine and decorative arts centred on the Rebel Art Centre; later Lewis proposed an edition of *The Apes of God* with advertisers for 'Steamship Lines, tooth-pastes, and lawn-mowers' allowed to invest in the 'permanent form' of the novel (1963: 196) – as always, it is hard to measure the depth of his irony. Artists like Delaunay and Charles Delmuth celebrated the billboard, and William Carlos Williams the neon sign in his poem 'The Attic Which is Desire'. Gertrude Steins's 'Advertisements', reading like a Berlitz phrase book translated from an unknown language, slyly undermine the anthropology of cultural exchange. In terms of this economy, certain writers had iconic status: Mina Loy was one emblem, appearing in the inaugural issues of three magazines, *Rogue*, *Others* and *Contact*. Her 'Love Songs' were published in the first issue of *Others* in July 1915, creating a scandalous success. This was a conscious gesture: Alfred Kreymborg, wanted to position the journal as outrageous, bohemian and linked to Futurism. The 'elimination of punctuation marks and the audacious spacing of her lines' (as he later described it) is a textual rendition of the sexual flows which signal free love, a visible language of the modern.

An awareness of publicity is among the attributes which make Pound so important. Grooming Eliot as the exemplary modernist, he chose 'Prufrock over 'Portrait of a Lady' for *Poetry*, 'as I wanted his first poem to be published to be a poem that would at once differentiate him from everyone else, in the public mind' (1951: 112). The publication of *The Waste Land* in 1922 was, in Lawrence Rainey's account, a classic case of market manipulation on Pound's part: playing off publishers including the mass-market *Vanity Fair;* selling it to the editors of the *Dial* as the representative poem of their period; arranging co-publication with Boni & Liveright (1998: 77–106). That the *Dial* editors were willing to award it their lucrative annual prize as part of the package, *before they had even seen the poem*, testifies to the status of the poem as token.

If the little magazine is bound up with commercialism and the exploitation of notions of cultural distinction, so too is the limited edition format in which so many modernist texts appeared – published by small presses which to some extent took over commercially risky materials from such publishers as Elkin Matthews: the Egoist Press, the Hogarth Press, the Hours Press, the Ovid Press and many others. As Rainey argues, private press publication could be a way of negotiating modernism's need to exploit a niche market. Texts were released in a managed series of formats: part-publication in periodicals; limited edition first publication; and trade. *Ulysses* was issued by Shakespeare & Company in Paris in three formats at different prices; many early copies were snapped up by dealers and collectors. For Rainey this involves a decision to define readership in terms of markets rather than reading, aiming 'to transform the reader into a collector, and investor, or even a speculator' (1998: 52–3). This is rather absolute: the private press could offer a mediated space in which the market has a part, but in which notions of intellectual community are also important. For Virginia Woolf, the Hogarth Press was, as Laura Marcus puts it, 'a space somewhere between the private, the coterie, and the public sphere' (Willison 1996:145) – a semi-private entity which as it became more successful moved towards the mainstream.

As modernism became more established in the 1920s, its styles were taken up by mass-market magazines. *Vanity Fair* published work by Eliot, Barnes, Langston Hughes and others; it included abstract photographic work by Edward Steichen in its advertising. *Smart Set* had dealings with Pound and others; *Vogue* and *Harper's Bazaar* adopted Surrealist styles. For Rainey this represents a shift from rebellious exclusion to a 'market economy' in which it gains 'a position of prestigious dominance' (1998: 91). One could simply see it as a confirmation of tendencies to commodification present from the start.

PATRONAGE

Patronage was the other factor insulating modernist writers from the market: a form of private sponsorship which barely exists in the Victorian period, and which most decisively signals the movement of literature firmly towards 'high art'. Modernists who existed, at least in part, on subsidy include Joyce (funded by Harriet Shaw Weaver), H. D., Dorothy Richardson and Robert McAlmon (Bryher), Pound (John Quinn), Eliot (Quinn and Lady Rothermere), Barnes (Peggy Guggenheim), and Zora Neale Hurston (Charlotte Mason). A majority of the little magazines and small presses were privately supported.

Patronage creates a cultural space set apart from mass culture, from commercial 'pressures', involving an understanding of community focused on a few privileged readers – though how that community is understood ranges from the fantasy of aristocratic, cultured patronage (Yeats and Lady Gregory) to an erotics of reading. This insulation has been interrogated by a number of critics, not simply because of the cultural elitism it implies, but because in the modern world the market and the public sphere are so closely bound together. Joyce Wexler suggests that removal from the market damaged modernist texts, enabling them to indulge in indisciplined play and obscurity – echoing James's claim as to 'that benefit of friction with the market which is so true a one for solitary artists too much seeped in their mere personal dreams' (Anesko 1986: 6). Rainey makes a similar argument about H. D., whose output was underwritten by Bryher in what amounted to private publication.

Such arguments are at least potentially tendentious, fetishizing the virtues of the market – how can market effects be quantified? Moreover relations between patrons and writers could be antagonistic and complex: charity, as Georg Simmel observed, involves an aggressive separation of giver from recipient. Patronage and its interaction with the market is a focus for both anxiety and fantasy. Pound attempted to distinguish good and bad patronage. Referring to his own support for Gaudier-Brzeska in a letter to Quinn, he writes: 'My whole drive is that if a patron buys from an artist who needs money (needs money to buy tools, time and food), the patron then makes himself equal to the artist: he is building art into the world; he creates.' On the other hand, 'If he buys even of living artists who are already famous or are already making £12,000 per year, he ceases to create. He sinks back into the rank of a consumer' (1951: 97). This attempts to separate speculation from investment construed in terms of a distribution of shared wealth, a bodily intervention (tools, time and food) which itself is a form of making. Pound's 'Bel Esprit' proposal of 1922, by which he hoped to raise money from subscribers to enable Eliot to leave his job at Lloyds Bank, alternates different ways of seeing readers: the idea of writers and those who care for literature 'releasing' Eliot (on the model of a mutual society); and the idea that 'the reader is a consumer' and Eliot an investment which will provide a return, a luxury product: 'It is a risk. So is an oil well' (1951: 242). The conflation of these two paradigms, society and market, reinforces the sense that consumption is a dangerous, depersonalized association, whereas patronage is a kind of idealized reading.

Pound's example of the anti-patron is the wealthy American poet Amy Lowell, who descended on London on the eve of World War I, taking a floor of the Berkeley Hotel and coaxing authors into contributing to her Imagist volume. Pound, with some justice, saw her as buying up the movement and bitterly criticized her self-publicity. Subsequent criticism has either followed Pound in mocking Lowell, or celebrated her as a pioneering lesbian poet. But what seems significant is the way the 'impure' mixture of backer and practitioner has always made it difficult to assess her status. Consider H. D.'s letters of support against 'E. P.' – letters in which thanks for money and polite praise of Lowell's poems mix with embarrassing assurances both that Lowell's wealth will not be mentioned in profiles, and that F. S. Flint (in a draft article breaking those rules) changed his copy willingly (Scott 1990: 135). The contradictions tell us a great deal about power relations.

The fact that a majority of the patrons of modernism were women is important. There is a utopian element to removal from the market, enabling writers outside cultural institutions dominated by male gatekeepers. But the gender of the holders of the purse strings also reflects a set of cultural assumptions. The career of Bryher (Winifred Ellerman) is representative: the millionaire daughter of a shipping magnate, Bryher wrote, supported H. D. (her lover), Marianne Moore and others; and funded the film journal *Close Up* and presses including McAlmon's Contact Editions. She sustained a coterie which could separate itself from the literary market, and allow the exploration of areas of experience seen by many as difficult. But in such cases women also represent the cultural arm of capitalist society (leisured conspicuous consumption, in Veblen's terms), and what is produced is a cultural sphere dependent on the labour of those outside its markets. The description of the monumental shopping spree of Nicole in Fitzgerald's *Tender is the Night* describes this role in terms inflected by the novel's pervasive misogyny: 'For her sake trains began their run at Chicago and traversed the round belly of the continent to California; chicle factories fumed and link belts grew link by link in factories; men mixed toothpaste in vats and drew mouthwash out of copper hogsheads; girls canned tomatoes quickly in August . . .' (1986: 51). The 'autonomy' of the modernist text is in this sense the product of surplus value.

For some modernists, the position outside the market was self-created; though here too the market generates anxiety. Gertrude Stein could, thanks to a stipend, write texts that did not sell. When her autobiographies did do well in the 1930s, she felt an awkwardness at re-entry – as well as a countervailing sense that her genius had finally been recognized: 'It is funny about money. And it is funny about identity. You are you because your little dog knows you, but when your public knows you and does not want to pay for you and when your public knows you and does want to pay for you, you are not the same you' (1938: 32). As Michael Szalay suggests, to think of money is to destroy an identity founded on a pure productivity.

A final form of patronage one might consider is state patronage, the Depression-era funding of the arts in America, managed by the Works Progress Administration (founded 1935). The Federal Writers' Project sponsored a *Guide to America* series and other projects. The WPA can be linked, Szalay argues, to a 'New Deal Modernism' in which the market as the focus for aesthetics is reconsidered, along with the relationship between formal innovation and the audience. The 'speculative' and 'luxury' status of modernism is rewritten: art becomes 'as necessary a staple as food and other daily essentials' (2000: 95), and the artist becomes a salaried professional rather than the focus of investment or speculation.

How well does Rainey's thesis that modernism can be understood in terms of market culture and scarcity hold up? He has been criticized for the conclusions he draws from a limited sample, and clearly there are many exceptions: Conrad's *Chance* (1914), for example, was the subject of a publicity drive which sold it to the female reader; relatively mainstream publishers showed an early interest in forms of modernism, particularly in America. Nevertheless, the analysis of the market as the mechanism for the negotiation of audiences, as in the case of the short story, opens up a dialogue between formal innovation and value in which the 'freedom' of modern art *is* linked to its peculiar forms of commodification.

MYSTERY: INSIDERS AND OUTSIDERS

For Q. D. Leavis in *Fiction and the Reading Public* (1932), the mediation of the supposedly pure activity of reading within a market culture is the problem with modernity: the magazine, book club and publishers package culture for a hasty, nervous age, and refuse the reader the concentration needed for real art. In fact, the necessity for mediation is written into modernism's self-construction, as her husband F. R. Leavis was demonstrating at the University of Cambridge. The discourse of professionalism was important to negotiating a public sphere which differentiated itself from the amateur status modernists associated with their cultural enemies.

As Thomas Strychacz argues, the formally difficult modernist text depends on the idea of a reader who shares this approach, collaborating in a reading culture founded on expertise. For Rainey the question of expertise might be a red herring: he focuses on the cultural cachet associated with *purchasing* a hard-to-get copy of *Ulysses*; and even (playfully) suggests that we cease reading modernist texts and read their context instead. In an earlier view which could be seen as mediating these positions, David Trotter argues that we should see modernist 'difficulty' in economic terms: the text 'raises the cost of processing a text in order to make us dig deeper into our mental and emotional resources, to mine our assumptions more extensively, and thus generate richer contextual efforts' (1993: 68). This is to see reading as a kind of intellectual training: it is not enough to buy *Ulysses*, one must get to work. The persuasive but highly metaphorical economy of 'effort' and 'return' threatens, however, to collapse interpretation back into the market – the very issue that is at stake. If Adorno suggests that the obscurity of the modernist text is designed to *resist* commodification, and to open a space in which the future reader might find some redemptive potential, Trotter suggests a pay-off.

What I want to investigate here is a related model of 'investment', psychoanalytically-inflected but nevertheless having some relation to the idea of the market. We can begin with the idea that modernism is a matter of insiders and outsiders, professionals and public. On its cover, *Poetry* had a quotation from Whitman: 'To have great poets there must be great audiences too.' Whitman had demanded a democratic reader who would wrestle with the poem. But to read the texts of modernism often seemed to require an insider's knowledge. Links with occult societies – Yeats and the Golden Dawn; the influence of Madame Blavatsky – suggest a 'secret' understanding, like that implicit in Pound's mysterious reference to 'a certain "Doctrine of the Image"' which did not concern the public.

Modernism's tendency to market itself in terms of exclusivity, insiders and outsiders, can be related to the central place of issues of readability and obscurity in its reception. Who exactly was supposed to understand *The Waste Land*? Was there a 'key' which would unlock *Ulysses*? In *The Genesis of Secrecy*, Frank Kermode offers a model for obscurity, Jesus's explanation of the parable of the sower in Mark 4: 11–13:

And he said unto them, Unto you is given to know the mystery of the kingdom of God: but unto them that are without, all *these* things are done in parables:

That seeing they may see, and not perceive; and hearing that they may hear, and not understand; lest at any time they should be converted, and *their* sins should be forgiven them.

And he said unto them, Know ye not this parable? And how then will ye know all parables?

This apparently savage doctrine suggests a hermeneutic paradox: only the insider who *already has* the knowledge can decode the message. Or, since Jesus goes on to explain the parable in terms of the sowing of the word, parables are really for outsiders; insiders get straight talk.

Mark's story suggests two interpretations, one of which could be called symbolist and the other modernist. The doctrine of reserve, so influential in the theology of the Oxford Movement, suggests that symbolic truth is veiled, unknowable; and must be carefully elicited by a priesthood. For modernism, on the other hand, it is the principle of inclusion and exclusion which is more important: do *you* have the key? Goram Munson suggested this predicament in an early article on *The Waste Land*, 'The Esotericism of T. S. Eliot' (1924), writing that its difficulty 'derived neither from abstruseness of subject nor from abstruseness of technic. It is artificially concocted by omissions, incompletions and unnecessary specialization in the assembly of those circumstances which ought to evoke in the reader the whole effect of the given emotion' (Clarke 1990: 126). Modernism's difficulty is not formal or symbolic, but constructed around a 'familiar mood' of melancholy which has been rendered 'inscrutable to all but a chosen coterie of his similars. . . . He constructs a mask for himself'. This is to say that Eliot's obscurity is enabled by a withdrawal of the self which nevertheless places the self centre stage. The poem can only be decoded by a key which Eliot holds and withholds.

Munson's argument about incompletion helps, I think, to pinpoint a defining contradiction in modernist texts. On the one hand, modernist writers are often all too happy to reveal their own practices. The most notorious example is *Ulysses*, for which Joyce managed the release of an elaborate structural scheme via two different sources. Stein's *The Making of Americans* includes comments on its own narrative problems, and later essays like 'How Writing is Written' elucidate her work. Eliot's notes to *The Waste Land* directed readers towards an anthropological reading, further developed in his 1923 essay 'Ulysses, Order and Myth'; and Eliot's staging of the poem's British debut in the inaugural issue of *The Criterion* can also be interpreted as offering a series of contexts: a fragmentary plan of a novel by Dostoevsky; reports on European literature. Yeats's *Per Amica Silentia Lunae* explained his doctrine of the mask and *A Vision* (1925) is consciously offered as the source of the symbolism of his late work. The preface continues to be a vehicle for aesthetic theory: from Conrad's preface to *The Nigger of the Narcissus* (1897) to Richard Wright's 'How Bigger Was Born' (1940).

At the same time, modernist texts often work through the evacuation of meaning, generating allegories of unreadability. Poe's 'The Man of the Crowd' (whose motto is *er lasst sich nicht lesen*, it does not permit itself to be read) is the model for later texts like Kafka's marvellous late story 'Josephine the Mouse Singer', in which there is no real answer to the question of whether the much-loved Josephine, the incarnation of her people's spirit, really sings at all. The loss of the object world of the Victorian and Edwardian novel might be seen as symptomatic: a world of scenes, interiors, streets, which in its density both guarantees a 'reality' and offers the reader a field of interpretation: which of these objects carries significance? The modernist text refuses that world or empties it of moral hierarchy. Ford Madox Ford protests mildly in 1927 that in recent work 'what, in my hot youth, used to be called atmosphere' – topography, locality – is eschewed in favour of psychology (1987: 244). Yet Ford himself had written, in his memoir-novel *No Enemy*, that the war effaced landscape and place: 'During the four years that the consciousness of the war lasted, he had noticed only four landscapes and birds only once – to know that he was noticing them – for themselves. Of course, one has memories of aspects of the world – but a world that was only a background for emotions' (1984: 23). To be sure, Ford constructs a book around these four landscapes; but the impoverishment of context and the enrichment of psychology is the point.

It could be suggested that the tantalizing dual status of the modernist text – explicable if one has the key; resistant and even empty – offers a formal correlative of the predicament which we explored in the short story: part of the market, but in some senses a blank token. It is a predicament intimately bound up with commodity culture. The commodity is characterized by the 'empty' desire it calls up (the desire for real exchange; for it to invest in us what we have invested in it). Commodity-fetishism – the allure of that which offers to complete the reader's desire – and notions of a privileged exchange based on identification emerges as an important component of advertising in the period, described in Walter Dill Scott's influential *The Psychology of Advertising* (1909). As David Kuna points out, two major schools of advertising competed. An older school espousing 'reason-why' ads and working with a rationalist model might be linked to the mode of realism. An emergent school represented by Scott and others, dominant by the second decade of the century, could be described as modernist, founding its practice on suggestion and symbolic capital. Roland Marchand suggests that the distinctive feature of post-war advertising was the emphasis on the personal, and on the acting-out of a dramatic situation in which the protagonist faces a choice or test before satisfaction is gained – with the advertiser acting as confidant. In this view, consumption is equated with the formation of identity, with a search for selfhood pursued via object-choice and what psychoanalysis calls 'investment'.

This is a situation we can see modelled in *The Turn of the Screw* (1898). In the prologue to James's ghost story, the larger audience represented by the country house is set aside in favour or a direct interchange between the narrator, Douglas, and his male friend, the unnamed frame narrator. The question is why the governess has kept the story secret:

'. . . You'll easily judge why when you hear.'
    'Because the thing had been such a scare?'

He continued to fix me. 'You'll easily judge,' he repeated: '*you* will.'

I fixed him, too. 'I see. She was in love.'

He laughed for the first time. 'You *are* acute. Yes, she was in love. That is, she had been. That came out – she couldn't tell her story without its coming out.'

(1992: 117)

This is homologous with the various stories of seduction told in the tale, positing reading as an intimate sales pitch: '*you* will'. The governess is seduced; Douglas is seduced; and the reader seduced in turn – though the secret, the precious item passed down this chain is unknowable. In a parallel way, modernist texts propose readings constructed in terms of an interchange between text and reader, creating circles of investment and inclusion under the heading of a privileged compact, within which uncertainty might be contained. This is Wallace Stevens's 'Of Modern Poetry':

> It has to face the men of the time and to meet
> The women of the time. It has to think about war
> And it has to find what will suffice. It has
> To construct a new stage. It has to be on that stage
> And, like an insatiable actor, slowly and
> With meditation, speak words that in the ear,
> In the delicatest ear of the mind, repeat
> Exactly what it wants to hear, at the sound
> Of which, an invisible audience listens,
> Not to the play, but to itself.
>
> (1997: 218–19)

This asks a lot: not simply that poetry respond to history, but that it construct the 'stage' which is the historical possibility of its enunciation, reflecting on its own procedures. The passive-voice incantation 'It has to . . .' is at once persuasive, like the voice of the advertisement, and self-reflexive. The aim, in terms of the audience, is the very opposite of obscurity; rather a version of Jesus's parable in which all might be saved by art. What such texts demand is a particular kind of reading, akin to that which Freud demanded of the analyst listening to a patient: an 'evenly-suspended attention' in which any detail might assume relevance and offer the gateway to hidden meaning. If this posits the analyst as a listening device, the theory of transference and counter-transference also suggests an investment at the level of hidden meanings – 'You'll easily judge . . . *you* will.' At once empty commodity and resonant token, the parcel which is meaning circulates within modernism's economy.

HOAXING

At the extreme end of anxiety about readability, the absence of meaning, and the literary clique lies the *hoax*. The history of hoaxes, from the South Sea Bubble in 1720, is linked to the uncertainties of market relations: a scheme is 'sold' to gullible investors; it creates a rolling effect in which consensus creates value, before a collapse. The uncertainties involved are intrinsic to modernism's self-presentation as a market phenomenon: in realist debates about the market, 'real' value is represented by the Gold Standard, and the idea that paper money can be cashed in. If the real is abandoned or dissolved into the 'speculation' in meaning intrinsic to the modernist text, value can appear a chimera.

In refusing readability, modernism in art and literature often seemed, to early audiences, to produce works which were spurious, empty; supported by a critical conspiracy. The 1910 Dreadnought hoax seemed to confirm that structure: members of the Bloomsbury circle including Virginia Woolf were escorted around HMS Dreadnought disguised as the Emperor of Abyssinia and his entourage, speaking an impenetrable 'language' made up on the spot. Anti-modernist hoaxes aimed to expose this structure, but paradoxically often reinforced its centrality, producing texts which mimicked the redolent 'emptiness' of modernist works. The absent centre as a product of modern publicity is nicely figured in Theodore Dreiser's novel *The Genius* (1915), in the property developer Winfield: 'Anyone who ever came to look at a lot in one of Winfield's perfect suburbs always found the choicest piece of property in the centre of this latest burst of improvement set aside for the magnificent house which Mr Kenyon C. Winfield, the president of the company, was to build and live in. Needless to say they were never built' (1954: 493). This proposes a constant excess of desire over possession, a useful formula for the reader's position in relation to the modernist text: meaning is not where it seems to be, but rather in the will-to-inhabit. The house never built: Pound's epic *Cantos*, the ongoing project of forty-five years, ends in the declaration of CXVI, 'I cannot make it cohere' and in rumours of recantation. Hermann Broch's novel *The Death of Virgil* (1945) is founded on the conceit that Virgil wished to destroy *The Aeneid*: the 'eternity-cry' which accompanies Caesar's retrieval of the poem and Virgil's insistence that the poem destroys 'perception' suggest the pain of completion (1983: 284, 343).

The hoax is also related to the question of value implicit in notions of genius; what Wyndham Lewis called the artist's 'credentials'. If the text is de-authored, value becomes uncertain. Gertrude Stein's early texts, often self-published, were often seen as an imposture; her claims to 'genius' seemed oddly impersonal; when she was accused by psychologist B. F. Skinner of using automatic writing techniques learnt at Harvard, suspicions were confirmed. But the accusation of 'mechanical' production was applied to others: Joyce in his construction of *Finnegans Wake*; Eliot in his assembling of citations, which many saw as a undergraduate trick whose high phrases concealed emptiness. Other modernist works (for example Yeats's *A Vision*, with its frame-narrative) incorporate formal elements of hoax.

The hoax exposes, then, the structures of meaning and valuation implicit in modernism and commodity culture generally. Modernist hoaxes include the 'Spectra' school, supposedly in Pittsburgh, and the 'Ern Malley' affair in Australia. Spectra was invented by Witter Bynner, Marjorie Allen Seiffert and Arthur Davison Ficke in 1916, and was circulated as a manifesto with attached works in the *Little Review*, *Others* and elsewhere (Smith 1961). The 'Ern Malley' poems are a fascinating case: written by two poets in 1943, and submitted to the Australian editor Max Harris with a biography of the melancholy and deceased Ern, they attempted to explode the pretensions of modernist obscurantism. But the tables were turned when Harris and others defended their value; indeed they have since been seen as classics of collaborative automatic writing, releasing the authors into a world of surreal imagery (Ruthven 2001). The movement from Guernica to Footscray (a Melbourne suburb), supposedly ridiculous, becomes an ironic confirmation of modernism's reach. Ern's 'Petit testament' makes a claim for linguistic freedom and the embodied text:

> There is a moment when the pelvis
> Explodes like a grenade. I
> Who have lived in the shadow that each act
> Casts on the next act now emerge
> As loyal as the thistle that in session
> Puffs its full seed upon the indicative air.
> I have split the infinitive. Beyond is anything.
> (Tranter 1994: 100)

The grenade and split infinitive is meant to be bathos in a world at war; but many readers have found in such lines an allusive, free-associative richness which is liberating rather than alarming.

This chapter has, to some extent, followed Rainey in taking a demystifying path through modernism's claims to newness, seeing it as a luxury commodity in the spirit of Veblen's analysis of conspicuous consumption. I have drawn parallels between texts and the commodity, and between modernist reading and the identification suggested in advertising copy. That is a suggestion which may help in relation to the institutions of literature, but it only takes us to the threshold of the internal negotiations on value conducted by texts. The formal criteria which govern modernist 'difficulty' can appear empty (the hoax) or irrelevant (the detail of a luxury object which is primarily desirable because of its price and aura). But it is significant that modernist texts themselves meditate self-consciously on the question of value and the market, reflecting on their own conditions of production, and opening that reflection to questions of reading.

4 Reform! Bodies, Selves, Politics, Aesthetics

The idea that modernism can be characterized by its opposition to the world of instrumental reason, or as a response to the failure of enlightenment, is a deep-rooted one, pervading the work of Adorno and still more or less axiomatic in later works such as Charles Taylor's *Sources of the Self* (1989). The purpose of this chapter is to further qualify that view, considering modernism as a mode of reform, and aligning it with what Jürgen Habermas has described as the incomplete project of modernity; the Enlightenment project of subjecting human affairs to the scrutiny of a reasoned public sphere, in which a central aim is the emancipation of the subject.

Necessarily, this chapter considers the politics of modernism, a spectrum from anarchism to fascism. But instead of dealing separately with these strands I wish to consider the extent to which a common reformist impulse energizes a cultural field – making problematic common distinctions between a 'political' avant-garde in which revolutionary form and action are united, and a later modernism in which politics and aesthetics are divorced. Links can be made between modernism and a range of political movements; between modernism and body-reform; and more generally between modernist technique and notions of efficiency and intervention. The aim is to move towards a description of modernism as not merely avant-garde in terms of *form*, while adopting a socially alienated stance, but conversely as knitted into traditions in which art and social and political life are constantly brought into relation. Those reform movements often see themselves as avant-garde, as struggling to create an oppositional public sphere in the face of entrenched interests and public inertia.

Reform traditions can be characterized by a few key terms: modernity, the fight against tradition, individualism, efficiency, hygiene, and the extension of human powers. One underlying doctrine is, as William James put it in 'The Energies of Men' (1907), that 'as a rule men habitually use only a small part of the powers which they actually possess and which they might use under appropriate conditions' (1988: 9). The aims included the release of physical, mental and social energies, either through the removal of blockages or the stimulation of new capacities. The deeper changes implicit in reform discourse include (as Foucault suggests) an understanding of the human subject as driven by the need to be true to its being; to calibrate performance against identity. In what follows, we will begin with the individual and move outwards to more collective programmes, before returning to aesthetics.

REFORMING BODIES AND MINDS

The body is central to modernism. The reasons for this lie in the intellectual and scientific shifts of the nineteenth century typified by the *Lebensphilosophie* of Schopenhauer, which focuses on Being or Will conceived in vitalist terms, rather than on detached consciousness (the Cartesian *cogito*) and abstract universals. Darwin confirms this trend; and for those who follow him it made sense to think, as Herbert Spencer and Nietzsche did, in terms of a physiological aesthetics. Rebecca West's description of Thomas Hardy in terms of 'a joy in the earth itself, in beauty, in strength, in sex, in the play of the body' (1987: 251–2) is typical of an attention to embodied thinking. To speak the truth about the body becomes, in the nineteenth century, an imperative for reformers like Ibsen. In *Songs to Joannes* (1917), Mina Loy wrote provocatively of 'Pig Cupid his rosy snout / Rooting erotic garbage' and of desire which is 'the daily news'. Abandoning 'petty pruderies', she writes, 'We sidle up / To Nature / – – – that irate pornographist' (1996: 63). Loy's sexual openness – reflected in her 'Feminist Manifesto', which advocates the '*unconditional* surgical *destruction of virginity*' (155) as well as eugenics – is emblematic of the spirit of reform.

One important point of origin is the work of the Viennese doctor Franz Anton Mesmer in the late eighteenth century. Mesmerism 'arrived' in Britain in the 1830s, postulating that the energy of life, 'animal magnetism', was a superfine fluid akin to electricity, which could be redistributed or unblocked by the mesmerist's hand (Winter 1998). Since that hand might often simply pass over the body, mesmerism invokes the theory of corpuscular bodies and the 'action at a distance' which Newton linked to gravity and magnetism. Mesmerism also influences notions of sympathetic reverberation central to the novel, entering the social theory of Schopenhauer and others as a way of understanding hierarchy, exchange and proximity; and in pathologic form informing the crowd theory of Gustave Le Bon, in which the crowd is a mesmerized mass. A neo-mesmerism is central to the revival of medical interest in hypnosis and hysteria after 1870, especially in the work of Charcot in France: science in which a male practitioner elicits a response from, displays and interprets a female (or feminized) subject – a paradigm informing *The Waste Land* (Koestlenbaum 1989).

Although attacked by the establishment, mesmerism remained popular and by the 1850s existed in a loose relationship to phrenology, free love and other radical movements including spiritualism. An example of the confluence of such traditions is Victoria Woodhull, the first person to publish the *Communist Manifesto* in America; the first woman to run for president (in 1872); a socialist, spiritualist and advocate of free love. America was fertile ground. The mesmeric 'body electric' which pulses through Walt Whitman's work enables him to see reading and writing as a flux of inherently democratic energy – best seen in 'The Sleepers', in which the poet-healer floats through the dreams of his compatriots, form becoming interpersonal drift. But mesmerism also produces dislocations like those in the terrifying final lines of Poe's mesmeric tale of 1845, 'The Facts in the Case of M. Valdemar'. Answering the question of whether he is in mesmeric sleep, Valdemar says: 'Yes; – no; – I *have been* sleeping – and now – now – *I am dead*' before collapsing into corrupt flesh (1984b: 840). Present; absent; telegraphically flickering on and off; Valdemar represents mesmerism's tendency to dissolve the self into flows of energy.

Mesmerism offered the possibility of a radical intervention in the body, deploying its most fundamental energy. Later bodily reform movements applied themselves in more specialized ways to the systems separated and mapped in nineteenth-century medicine. By 1900 health reformers promoted 'fitness' via a range of devices and cures: electric belts and probes; patent medicines and gland-treatments; mechanical devices which massaged and jolted (Zander therapy), or built muscle (the 'Health Lift'); stomach and dietary cures like the 'Culture of the Abdomen' and Fletcherism (extensive chewing aimed at complete digestion) which aimed to eliminate 'waste' and 'poisons' and release energy. The American publisher Bernarr Macfadden promoted the healthy (and naked) body in *Physical Culture*; spas and 'Institutes' flourished. Strongman Eugen Sandow's regime was heavily marketed, while later exercise and movement systems like those developed at the Hemenway gymnasium at Harvard and the Alexander Technique shifted attention to a 'balanced' body. The isolation of radium in 1902 even brought the radioactive body in the form of elixirs administered to patients in the period 1905–30, promising to flood the body with energy (Thomas de la Peña 2003). The new diagnoses and machines were targeted at the new professional-managerial classes – the over-tired businessman, his housebound wife. In one of the paradoxes of modernity, what Jackson Lears calls the 'therapeutic ethos' (1981: 47) offered a return to the 'natural' body which could only be achieved by *technique*.

One cannot simply dismiss such methods as representing a bourgeois modernity, anathema to modernist writers – for all that they are parodied in Sinclair Lewis's *Martin Arrowsmith* (1925), with its gadget-obsessed hero; or George Schuyler's *Black No More* (1932), which hinges on a medical technique for changing skin colour. Modernists were attracted in quite concrete terms to bodily reform. The Californian photographer Edward Weston provides an example of reformist eclecticism: his interest in ESP, nudity, helioculture, vegetarianism and curative fasting reflected in his work's rendition of the body perfected by abstraction, at once objectification and spiritualization. Fletcherism was practised by Henry James in the period 1904–10, and the prefaces to the New York edition suggest that 'chewing over' and digestion inform the massive revision project of those years (Armstrong 1998). Ezra Pound constantly intervened in bodies: his medical interests included Remy de Gourmont on sex, Berman on hormonal glands and Gould on eyes. He sought to have Joyce's deteriorating eyesight cured (linking it to what he saw as the myopia of *Finnegans Wake*); helped to arrange Yeats's marriage; worried about Valerie Eliot's hormones. Upton Sinclair promoted fasting and antisepsis; Dorothy Richardson advocated raw food and rational diet; Arnold Bennett wrote a mind-cure text; Mina Loy a manifesto on 'Auto-Facial Construction'; Aldous Huxley explored cures from colonic irrigation to the Alexander Technique. The Harlem Renaissance writer Jean Toomer was a body-builder and worked as a PE instructor; in one of the stories of *Cane* (1923), 'Bona and Paul', the American College of Physical Training founded by Macfadden is the scene for an exploration of self-construction (Whalan 2003). Toomer's later 'post-racial' thinking and his embracing of Gurdieff's extreme version of self-making is an extension of this practice.

Such techniques represent a complex and even contradictory mixture. At the same time as the body was plugged into modernity, rendered electric or efficient, modernity was a problem. Physicians suggested that moderns were subject to neurasthenia, blockages of energy, hyperstimulation, seminal depletion. In an 1893 article entitled 'Infelices Possidentes!' [Unhappy Dwellers], Georg Simmel suggested that even leisure becomes struggle:

Now . . . play has become feverishly excited, tensing all the nervous forces to the utmost – we not only expend the strength we have but also live, to a certain extent, on our future resources, consuming for the demands of the moment what should suffice for the future . . . The modern person is driven back and forth between the passion to win everything and the fear of losing everything. The competition of individuals, races and classes stages the feverish chase of daily work and also draws the person who does not work into that restless rhythm and self-consumption . . .
(1997: 260)

This nicely captures the ambivalence of such discourse: modernity is both a kind of Darwinian struggle ('natural') and a pathology.

If bodily techniques represent one strain in reform methodology, mental reform – the dynamization of thought and personality – is another. The idea that personhood might be 'improved', outside a moral and religious framework, was new. The shift from notions of character (engraved, fixed) to those of personality (assumed, malleable) has a long history, but intensifies in the late nineteenth century, with the marketing of techniques which aim to condition the intuitive processes of the mind, just as other techniques reworked musculature. Positive thinking manuals reach something of a climax in Depression-era America, with Edward Filene's *Successful Living in this Machine Age* (1931), Walter B. Pitkin's *Life Begins at Forty* (1932) – which suggests training in speed-reading – and Dale Carnegie's *How to Win Friends and Influence People* (1936). Underlying these texts is the idea of self as image, as in Frank Baum's *The Wizard of Oz*, with its under-confident, cure-seeking characters and Wizard who is an effect of publicity. Fitzgerald's Jay Gatsby is another constructed identity, signalled in his youthful mail-order exercise regimes and self-improvement charts.

There are traces of mind-cure within modernism. One point of entry is Christian Science, founded by Mary Baker Eddy and representing itself as a 'modernized' religion in which self-cure is central. Like spiritualism, a disavowed influence, the movement offered women authority: the modernist Dora Marsden was compared to Eddy in her visionary notions of cosmic consciousness (Clarke 1996: 122). Willa Cather's first book as a journalist was on Eddy, and for all her scepticism her understanding of civilization as depletion and the mystique of self-redemption in her war novel *One of Ours* (1922) has affiliations with the movement. Mina Loy's Christian Science can be seen in her convictions about the need to embody truth; in her religious notes in the 1940s she suggested that the illuminati would send 'Deific electricity coursing through a circle of mentalities' (Burke 1996: 397). Her friend the artist Joseph Cornell was another Christian Scientist, and his magical boxes share with her assemblages a sense of a dynamic universe, suffused with a materialized spirituality. But Loy's artworks with their dirty materials and Bowery poems like 'Hot Cross Bum' also retain some of the reformist impulse of her earlier work: the determination to present the abject and excluded.

The occult study and eastern religion which are an important component of turn-of-the-century culture can also be seen as an extension of the mind-reform tradition, replacing Christianity with a more direct access to truth. The influence of occultism on modernism has often been underplayed. Translations of the Upanishads and esoteric Buddhist texts were read avidly by Thoreau and others. Theosophy, the system of belief codified by the Russian émigré Madame Blavatsky in her *Isis Unveiled* (1877), influenced many modernists including Yeats, George Russell, Pound, and (via Jessie Weston) Eliot. Crucially, Theosophy informs the abstract art of artists like Kandinsky, Malevich, Mondrian and Bisttram: in focusing on higher truths, their art is released from representation; colours take on a symbolic weight and flood the eye with meaning (there are parallel influences on the composers Scriabin and Schoenberg).

In England, A. R. Orage, editor of the *New Age* from 1907, served as the centre of a nexus interested in Theosophy and spiritual revival. Orage helped popularize the work of G. I. Gurdieff, a distillation of reform tradition attached to eastern spirituality: arguing that people are 'asleep' and inauthentic, Gurdieff aimed to unsettle and revitalize. His Institute for the Harmonious Development of Man near Paris had as patron Lady Rothermere, funder of Eliot's *Criterion*; it was implicated in the dialogues on reformed religion in the *Criterion* and Middleton Murray's *Adelphi* in the 1920s. Katherine Mansfield died at the Institute; others including Huxley and Henry Miller expressed interest in its work. Gurdieff's anti-establishment thinking seems to have appealed particularly to those seeking self-affirmation outside social norms: there was a Gurdieff circle in Paris involving lesbian writers Jane Heap and Margaret Anderson; in New York Jean Toomer and other black writers were followers; Toomer's later writings, in the wake of his 1924 visit to the Institute, have a mystical cast centred on notions of universal brotherhood.

SEXOLOGICAL MODERNITY

Central to the drive towards wholeness in body reform movements is the insistence on the cleansing of sex and the expression of a unified being. 'My words are the unspoken words of my body' said Pound, citing de Gourmont (Pound 1954: 341). Michel Foucault argues that the idea that sexuality is central to identity, and that desire must be transformed into discourse, are nineteenth-century developments. Sexuality in Foucault's account floods individual and social life; important enough to stake one's existence on, as in the ecstatic *Liebestod* ending Kate Chopin's *The Awakening* (1899) or the climax of Lawrence's *Women in Love* (1920), in which Gerald attempts to strangle Gudrun in the snow: 'The struggling was her reciprocal lustful passion in this embrace, the more violent it became, the greater the frenzy of delight' (1960: 531). Foucault cites Lawrence – 'Now our business is to realize sex. Today the full conscious realization of sex is even more important than the act itself'– before commenting that 'people will be surprised at the eagerness with which we went about pretending to rouse from its slumber a sexuality which everything – our discourses, our customs, our institutions, our regulations, our knowledges – was busy producing in the light of day and broadcasting to noisy accompaniment' (1979: 157–8). Which is to say that the pursuit of the 'truth' of sexuality must be seen as a form of *production* rather than a release from repression; indeed a productivity linked to the consumer economy and its engines of desire (Birkin 1988).

The attack on 'repression' which Foucault portrays as historical myth was, nevertheless, important for the avant-garde. Many late Victorian radicals were free-love advocates, seeing marriage as an outdated constraint, and sections of the women's movement campaigned for sexual emancipation, likening marriage to prostitution. In the early twentieth century birth-control advocates like Marie Stopes in London and Margaret Sanger in New York offered advice on contraception and sex. A number of high-profile obscenity cases in the UK and USA served as rallying-points in the war against prudery: the pulping of Lawrence's *The Rainbow* in 1915; the suppression of an issue of the *Little Review* over Lewis's story 'Cantleman's Spring Mate' and the trial of its editors for publishing parts of *Ulysses* in 1921; the 1928 trial relating to Radcliffe Hall's lesbian novel *The Well of Loneliness*; the banning of *Lady Chatterley's Lover* the same year. In America the *Masses* mocked Anthony Comstock, self-appointed censor and guardian of public morals, for his campaigns against vice, pornography and birth control. The exploration of sexual licence in modernist texts works in dialogue with these debates, for example in the focus on young women which runs from Dreiser's *Sister Carrie* (1900) to West's *The Day of the Locust* (1939) – novels evoking sexual panics about actresses, prostitution and disease.

Where Foucault's suggestions about the productivity of sex are most obvious is in the discourse of sexology. The sexologists who began to investigate and codify sexuality in the late Victorian period, including Kraft-Ebing, Havelock Ellis, Magnus Hirschfeld and Freud, inherited from Darwin and Schopenhauer (who influences both Nietzsche and Freud) a universe in which desire is the motor. In the 1920s, the World League for Sexual Reform organized conferences in London and elsewhere to discuss their findings, with a number of writers involved. In Ellis's six-volume *Studies in the Psychology of Sex*, and especially in the appendices with their autobiographical case studies, sexual experience moves to the centre of life stories and gives birth to new identities: the homosexual; the fetishist (Bryher and H. D. consulted Ellis on the 'normality' of lesbianism). Consider the rapid alternation between sexological discourse and excited response in the following, taken from the account of a man who describes his marriage and encounters with servants:

I had lately heard about *cunnilingus*. I now did it to her. I soon found I experienced very great pleasure in this, as she did . . . I also had intercourse *per anum*. (This again was an act I had heard about, but had never been able to regard as pleasurable. But books I had been reading stated it was most pleasant both to man and woman.) She resisted at first. Finding it hurt her much, it excited me greatly; and when I had done it in this way several times she herself seemed to like it . . .

(Ellis 1926: 245)

Book in hand, this experimenter – whose account is appearing in another book on sex – takes his pleasures in Latin. Lawrence prefers the Anglo-Saxon in *Lady Chatterley*, but is driven by the same desire to name (and indeed to explore) the anus. The body produced by sexological discourse is necessarily a reformed body, its truth rendered visible, and this drive to expose is paralleled in modern literature: Bloom's masturbation and shitting in *Ulysses*; Mellors's erection; Betty's breasts in West's *Miss Lonelyhearts* (1933). All acts are human, as Propter argues in Huxley's *After Many a Summer* (1939):

Among men and women, even the most apparently bestial acts of eroticism were associated with some or all of these non-animal factors – factors which were injected in every human situation by the existence of language. This meant that there was no one type of human sexuality that could be called 'normal' in the sense in which one could say that there was a normality of vision or digestion. In *that* sense, all kinds of human sexuality were strictly abnormal.

(1962: 229)

Implicit here is the assumption that sexuality can only be explained in terms of developmental *narrative*; that the course of desire is never obvious.

The interventions practised by sexology could be very literal: Huxley's novel was a satire on popular rejuvenation treatments using monkey glands. Yeats's related Steinach operation in 1934, a fashionable surgical procedure, was designed to flood his body and his poetry with energy by shifting the testes from semen to hormone production. The operation can be linked to the thematics of self-insemination and the obsession with aged desire in the poet's late work: to work on the body is to work on the *corpus*. Speaking of 'ductless [hormonal] glands', as John Rodker does in two of his *Hymns* (1920), becomes the common currency of modernism. Rodker is interesting because, as Andrew Crozier comments, his work in the 1920s represents a 'turn towards a biological understanding of human motive and behaviour' (1996: xviii). 'The Pale Hysterical Ecstasy' depicts all bodies, even the sexually repressed, suffused with hormonal energy (the brackets below are the author's):

> glands flash open [though ductless]
> a black draught for blood stream,
> the spate boils on the dams.
>
> Perceptions smash through brain –
> a ball in a skittle alley
> thrown by a drunk.
>
> (1996: 85)

This is consonant with Rodker's obsession with dolls and puppets: the bio-mechanical self is assailed from within and without, driven by the heat of desire or freezing into deathly stasis – but never achieving a fixed designation as 'machine' or 'self'.

The exploratory literature which reflects the concerns of sexology includes both popular and highbrow. The 'sex novel' thrived at the turn of the century, though what was meant by the term ranged from scandalous best-sellers like *The Blue Lagoon* (1908) to the work of Wells and Lawrence. Sex novels presented readers with fictions in which desire and fantasy are more important than realism; especially feminine desire. A fine example is Marjorie Bowen's *Black Magic. A Tale of the Rise and Fall of Antichrist* (1909), a novel best read in the spirit of Rebecca West's comment that Bowen's method was to think of a historical period and double it. It uses the legend of Pope Joan to weave a complex tale of black magic, transsexualism, betrayal, murder and Church politics. At the climax the hero Thierry receives a suicide note from the Pope, who loves him and whom he now realizes is his old friend Dirk (aka Blaise or Ursula). The letter expresses a startling fluidity: 'If I be a devil I go whence I came, if a man I lived as one and die as one; if a woman I have known love, conquered it and by it have been vanquished. Whosoever I am I perish on the heights, but I do not descend from them'. (1909: 388–9). Thierry discovers his lover's body, and moves to resolve the ambiguity about gender; but as he uncovers the breast it crumbles to dust and he dies as well.

This is extreme. But equally, to open the flaming purple covers of Elinor Glyn's best-seller *Three Weeks* (1907) was to enter a fluid world in which a man could be an athlete and a passive baby; in which a woman could be a femme fatale and a politician; in which sexual perversity leads to moral awakening; in which English empiricism is replaced by ambiguity – the world of Rider Haggard's *She* repackaged for the female reader. Paul, the kind of young Englishman of good family who was the staple of the adventure story, enters an exotic scene like a harem; is read to from *The Golden Ass* in Latin; and has caresses whispered in unknown tongues before consummation on the notorious tiger skin. Sexual knowledge operates as knowledge in general, as his father suggests: 'They were only together three weeks . . . And during that time she contrived to cram more knowledge of everything into the boy's head than you or I have got in a lifetime' (1907: 237). The mass-cultural plot of sexual initiation informs more highbrow texts, from Lawrence's *Women in Love* and subsequent writings to Aldington's narrative poem *A Dream in the Luxembourg* (1930). Lawrence can, with his focus on the dark mysteries of the phallus, alienate readers today, but many women readers undoubtedly found his stress on feminine desire liberating.

A more oblique example of the uncertainties of sexual knowledge is provided by Katherine Mansfield's story 'Bliss'. The protagonist, Bertha, is filled with indescribable feeling, ostensibly related to her dinner party and husband, and finding its symbol in a 'lovely pear tree with its wide open blossoms' (1962: 100). She feels a perfect communion with the guest Miss Fulton, a rush of new passion for her husband, but at the end of the party seems to find that he too desires Miss Fulton. In theory sex is discussable – 'They were so frank with each other . . . That was the best of being modern' (1962: 108), but at the party conversation is trivial or concealing, and desire is conveyed by the mysterious 'sign' Miss Fulton gives, by contradictions and glimpses. Passion flows between characters, incorporating adultery, lesbianism, orality, and even, in the cat associated with the guest, animalism. This tradition finds its consummation in Djuna Barnes's *Nightwood* (1936), a novel describing lesbianism, a transvestite doctor masturbating in church, and a scene in which a woman seems to sexually mesmerize a dog. Desire in Barnes's text hollows out and fragments subjects; it is impossible to stabilize.

For an account of the vagaries and hidden structures of desire in such texts, we need to turn to Freud. Psychoanalysis has been given a privileged place within histories of modernism, and arguably this has made the broader field of sexology harder to see. But it too can be seen as a reform movement, albeit qualified by Freud's pessimism and uncertainties. Freud aimed to describe the deep structure of the self in terms inherited from Victorian psychology and reform discourse: the flow of energy, blockages, hygiene; the need to bring the dark places of the self to light. What he provided, in the face of the timeless obscurity of the unconscious, is a narrativization of the course of desire – a detective story, in his most compelling cases, in which the analyst pieces together evidence and uncovers a hidden history. Or, to turn to another pair of the many metaphors Freud provided, the analyst tunes her own psyche to that of the patient, becomes a synthetic object of desire, and enables a kind of psychic theatre: a staged re-enactment of childhood trauma and conflicts.

The influence of psychoanalysis begins with the impact of *The Interpretation of Dreams* (1900). Translations of this and other texts and Freud's 1909 visit to America confirmed that impact. The historical importance of America for the psychoanalytic movement has to some extent obscured the role it played in England: writers like May Sinclair, John Rodker and Dorothy Richardson were among the first to read and absorb Freud's work; analytic writers like Wilfred Bion, Melanie Klein, Ella Freeman Sharpe and Adrian Stokes (the latter linked to Pound) engaged with the arts; Barbara Low applied psychoanalytic thinking to film and education (Stonebridge 1998).

Psychoanalysis can appear in literal forms: characters called 'Id', 'Ego' and 'Superego' in the German Expressionist Iwan Goll's play *Methusalem* (1922); in the family romance of Eugene O'Neill's posthumously produced *Long Day's Journey into Night*. It could also be a vehicle for self-understanding, as in Woolf's comment that in writing her parents into *To the Lighthouse* 'I did for myself what psycho-analysts do for their patients. I expressed some very long felt and deeply felt emotion' (1976: 94). But perhaps the most decisive legacy of Freud for aesthetics lies in the notion of over-determination in the meanings attached to psychic and bodily symptoms and linguistic utterances. Among the riches of his case histories, one might pluck out 'A Child is being Beaten' (1919) – an analysis in which the utterance which forms the title is interpreted as a multi-layered fantasy. Briefly, Freud's account runs like this. In its adult form, it is an anonymous expression of concern: 'A child is being beaten.' However the origins of the fantasy lie in a different situation: sibling rivalry. The very young child fantasizes a pleasurable scene in which 'that other child, the bad child' is being beaten. The middle stage is the one which is repressed: the child expresses its love for its parent via a fantasy ('I am being beaten'). The punishment expresses a dual and contradictory purpose: as a displaced expression of desire, and as punishment for that desire: if one desires one's parent one deserves to be punished, but the punishment is also a pleasure. In the final stage the fact that the child is oneself is repressed, and the fantasy again superficially resembles the first stage: 'A child [any child] is being beaten' – though that situation has a sexual charge whose origins are forgotten. Across this trajectory, there is no fixed position for the self; at different stages it is present and non-present; guilty and innocent. The beating fantasy is sadistic (aggressive) and masochistic (passive): its aggression comes from its origins in sibling rivalry and in projection; its masochism from the desire to be punished for a transgressive fantasy. Finally, late in the paper Freud comments that the fantasy may have no 'real' origin but may (like the 'primal scene' itself) be a fiction borrowed from literary sources. One of his examples is *Uncle Tom's Cabin* – a book which Harriet Beecher Stowe reported as coming from her vision of a slave being beaten to death, a masochistic fantasy. Literature and psychoanalysis find a strange intimacy.

EUGENICS

Like sexology, the study of human populations can be regarded as part of the modern regime which Foucault describes as 'bio-power'. The idea that humans might be describable in statistical terms has its origins in the Enlightenment: in the study of death rates; in insurance. The work of Darwin placed species and environments in a dynamic relation, attempting to explain changes across time, and opening up the possibility of the manipulation of those changes. But Darwinism also, for this reason, produces a pressure on the human: a sense of the insignificance of the individual, the collapse of the self into the statistical or the 'type', characterized in terms of identity rather than acts.

One element of Darwinism which received increasing attention at the turn of the century was the anti-teleological suggestion that evolution may be non-developmental; that there may be no clear analogy possible between individual or cultural development and the evolution of species. Darwin implicitly supported developmental views in relation to racial thinking, ideas buttressed by a Lamarkian tradition which asserted that cultural and familial achievement might be passed on via inherited superiority or organic memory. Edward Carpenter's essay 'Exfoliation: Lamarck *versus* Darwin' (1889) is a typical expression of the desire to escape the Darwinian story of random variation and statistical survival, substituting an account of evolution which allows for agency. This was important because the spectre of evolutionary reversal, of degeneration, haunted the late Victorian consciousness, feeding into depictions of the poor, the slum, and Empire. As William McDougall put it in 1921, 'the superior half of the population is ceasing to produce children in sufficient numbers to replace their parents, while the lower half continues to multiply itself freely' (1921: 160). 'Race suicide' involved a failure to reproduce seen in class, racial and topographic terms: the inferior were the criminal and labouring underclass, Jewish immigrants located in London's East End. In America, fears of miscegenation and regression linked to southern European immigration produced a post-war upsurge in Klu Klux Klan membership and culminated in the restrictions of the 1924 National Origins Act.

The science of eugenics responded to these perceived problems, offering a social hygiene which would discourage or prevent the 'unfit' from breeding and encourage the fit. Eugenics aimed to produce a 'second nature', technologically engineered, which would compensate for the supposed lack of evolutionary pressure. Developed by Darwin's cousin Francis

Galton in London in the 1860s, it flourished in the period 1890–1940 through the efforts of the Eugenics Education Society, the work of Karl Pearson (Galton's protégé at University College London), the psychologist E. Ray Lankester, the journalist and campaigner Caleb Saleeby and others. Far from being the discredited entity which Nazi policies were to render it, eugenics was in the mainstream of social thinking, supported more readily by progressives than conservatives. Modernist eugenicists include Wells, Shaw, Lawrence, Huxley, Yeats, Sackville-West (Bradshaw 2003); others like Marianne Moore and T. S. Eliot produced work which engages with eugenics (Kadlec 2000; Childs 2001).

Eugenics answered different needs in all these authors. For Yeats and Eliot, it was part of a crisis-rhetoric, suggesting an imperilled inheritance. As Donald Childs shows, Yeats's eugenics may have begun as early as the 1900s, when he read American accounts of experimental living and 'race improvement'; works like *On Baile's Strand* (1903) show a concern for breeding (2001: 170–202). By the 1930s, reading R. B. Cattell's *The Fight for our National Intelligence* and joining the Eugenics Society, Yeats was on the extreme wing of a movement in retreat, cursing the decay of Ireland in plays, poems and his pamphlet *On the Boiler* (Bradshaw 1992). In part this was a response to populist Catholic nationalism in Ireland, which left Yeats celebrating the hybrid vigour of an abandoned Anglo-Irish tradition, and lamenting the failure of his own cultural 'race-building'. It also is related both to his Steinach operation, preformed by the sexologist and eugenicist Norman Haire, and to his extraordinary occult notion that his child might be the new Irish 'avatar'. Eliot too was exposed to eugenics in his Harvard lectures and in his reviewing. The influence of the Professor of Zoology E. W. MacBride is visible in his cultural pessimism; in his depiction of race and 'recessive' types like Sweeney; and in *The Waste Land*'s degenerating metropolitan civilization, middle-class sterility and working-class breeding.

Eugenics poses particular problems and opportunities for the woman writer, who bears the burden of the discourse's contradictory demands: that she be 'fit' and intelligent; and that she sacrifice career for reproduction. Eugenic mothers – Frances in May Sinclair's *The Tree of Heaven*, who chooses her husband for the bodies he will give her sons, aiming to 'drive out Morrie', her tainted brother; even Mrs Ramsay in *To the Lighthouse* (1927), whose care over children and guests, their development and marriage, combined with her social work, has a eugenic tinge – pay a cost which Sinclair spells out in her account of two sons killed in the war: they have a doomed attachment to the bodies of their children. Moreover in the discourse inherited from the nineteenth century, 'brain-work' is detrimental to motherhood. Bertrand Russell teased out the contradictions in 1916 when he argued, in what reads like a parody of eugenics (though Russell's eugenics were genuine enough), that the kind of independent women typified by the modern office worker would vanish; instead a 'placid maternal type' would reproduce itself (Childs 2001: 139). For Woolf motherhood is surrounded by anxiety related to her doubts about her own inheritance (her bouts of mental illness), and this is in turn bound up with writing. These conflicting demands are represented in the relation between Mrs Ramsay and the artist Lily Briscoe, whom she describes in terms which to the suspicious reader might recall F. G. Cruikshank's *The Mongol in our Midst* (1924): 'With her little Chinese eyes and her puckered-up face she would never marry; one could not take her painting very seriously; but she was an independent little creature' (1992b: 250). If we compare the 'Chinese eyes' of Elizabeth Dalloway in *Mrs Dalloway*, which, as Childs points out, her mother speculates may derive from 'some Mongol . . . wrecked on the coast of Norfolk', and remember the popular term for Down syndrome, mongolism, we see a eugenic complex latent in the text. But this is not to suggest (as Childs does) that Woolf passively subscribed to eugenics: in *Mrs Dalloway* the eugenicist Dr Bradshaw is savagely mocked as 'obscurely evil, without sex or lust'. The point of the 'Chinese' traces is surely that English 'purity' is a myth; that Empire produces diversity. At the end of *To the Lighthouse* Lily offers a symbolic completion of the dead matriarch's life in her final brush-stroke ('a line there, in the centre'), one which finally insists on a written rather than biological 'line'.

The difficulty of combining dynastic and creative roles is also suggested by Mary Butts's *Ashe of Rings* (1925), whose heroine Vanna is a dynastic defender, loyal to the patriarchal line represented by her dead father. In this novel, set against the background of the war, the men are traumatized, shell shocked and negative; it is Vanna who rejects a doctrine that would 'make pain valid for ever'. Much of the story concerns Vanna's defence of her Celtic inheritance, represented by the ring of stones on the family estate; in a climactic scene the sterile usurper Judy urges Vanna's neighbour Peter to rape Vanna as she lies semi-naked on the stones (he fails). The weakness of the male characters and the aggression directed at her mother – Vanna thinks 'What would it be like to have a mother who would stand the truth? There are no such mothers' (1998: 228) – makes it difficult to imagine a positive inheritance.

The suppositions of eugenics inform other texts in subtle ways: the idea of the relative fixity of social types, and their self-replication; a sense of threat surrounding social and national topography (seen in invaders like Dracula or Eliot's Bleistein); as well as the more general tendency to see individuals as emergent or superseded. Evolutionary thinking is visible throughout Faulkner's exploration of family and region, thematized in issues such as endogamy, exogamy and incest; in characters like 'the old couple named Hines' in *Light in August*, looking 'as if they belonged to a different race, species' living in a 'slack backwater' (1960: 256); and in the exploration of the 'taint' in the blood (a genetic fallacy of huge historical potency) and the invasive outsider (the Snopes family).

E. M. Forster provides an example of an author struggling with eugenic paradigms. In *Howard's End* the question of rightful inheritance which surrounds the country house is resolved via a complex plot in which an infusion of 'German' (that is Saxon) and of lower-middle-class blood is carefully managed against a background in which inter-class sexual relations remain traumatic. The point is that a feminine Schlegel line must be sustained, rather than the patriarchical, commercial and scientific world-view of the callisthenically-minded Wilcoxes. As William Greenslade points out, critique is associated with the neurasthenic Helen Schlegel, a figure who threatens the social body and is close to being labelled 'mad' – but whose bonds of affection with her sister finally overcome the patriarchal discourse of medical expertise (1994: 219–25). Racial thinking similarly pervades Djuna Barnes's texts, but in a way which suggests that the classifying, self-perpetuating work of eugenics is doomed to fail. Her 1917 short story 'Smoke' is a dynastic novel of twelve pages in which the Fenken family declines over five generations, from having 'iron in our veins' to a stillbirth and the remark 'Well, the Fenkens lived themselves thin'. The last husband, Misha, is man with 'that show of nervous expectancy that a man always betrays when he knows within himself that he is deficient – a sort of peering into the face of life to see if it has discovered the flaw' (1996: 143–54) – a distinctly eugenic anxiety. In *Nightwood*, Felix Volkbein's attempts to establish a dynasty produces only an idiot.

In America, racial thinking is closely related to eugenics. Toomer's *Cane*, as Laura Doyle points out, depicts women as the carriers of racial identity, susceptible to the enervating effects of civilized life (1994: 81–109). Racial and cultural inheritance are elided in the figure of the 'portly Negress' of 'Box Seat', whose unconscious roots flow south. We see it more subtly when Fern is described as having a 'Semitic' nose and the sound of a Jewish cantor, as if cultural attributes must carry a racial marking. The elision of race and culture is also important to the final section of *Cane*, 'Kabnis', which ends with the adolescent Carrie kneeling before the elderly Father John, who has finally stuttered out his message: 'O th sin th white folks 'mitted when they made th Bible lie' (1988: 117). The young girl literally 'carries' the hope of a cultural continuation, figured as birth in the 'gold-glowing child' of the sun at the end, born from 'Night, soft belly of a pregnant Negress'. Many readers find it difficult to understand the weight of John's declaration; Kabnis, the cynical northern intellectual, thinks it an archaic reversion to abolitionism. But that is the point. The story is located in the 1920s, when direct memories of slavery are vanishing (a slave of twenty at the Emancipation Proclamation would be eighty in 1923). At the moment where embodied memory becomes history, it is transmitted to somebody else. The equation of racial identity, memory and the female body typifies the way in which genetic thinking works through a syncretism which assimilates the cultural to the biological. Toomer's anxiety at the necessity for women to incarnate the process of cultural reproduction is symptomatic.

One wants to say that genetics and modernism should exist in a close formal relation. In the nineteenth century there is a general comparison between the evolution of life forms and those of art. As Heinrich Wölfflin argued in 1886: 'Progress in both realms takes place similarly: an evolution from dull, poorly articulated forms to the most finely developed system of differentiated parts' (Mallgrave 1994: 161). But the new genetic science of the twentieth century fits the parameters of modernity in that it eschews developmental models: the past is not relevant to the question of the present interaction of genetic variation and environment; the moment must be seized and the future shaped *now*. In Bergson's work, art becomes an evolutionary force, an opening to the future. For William James, similarly, evolution provides a model for the emergence of genius: 'Leaders give the form' which is then tested by society; they produce (in fairly random fashion) material from the morass of the everyday. Ideas are, in this account, close to what more recent biologists call *memes* – an observation taking us beyond the scope of this study.

POLITICAL REFORM: ANARCHISM, MUTUALISM, FASCISM

We have seen the reformist impulse working at the level of the self and the population. The ultimate sphere of its operation is politics. But here we are on difficult ground. Historians of the avant-garde like Peter Bürger have tended to see radical politics as associated with the 'true' (pre-1914) avant-garde in Europe, with some continuation of that impulse in Russia, followed by a split between aesthetics and politics and the emergence of more reactionary positions within 'high' modernism. For a number of reasons this view needs revision. In America a thriving radical culture continued to produce work which was often formally innovative (Nelson 1989). Elements of the European avant-garde, for example Surrealism, continued to unite political and aesthetic radicalism. British critics like Herbert Read (in 'What is Revolutionary Art?', 1935) continued to argue the necessity to 'discredit the bourgeois ideology in art' (Kolocotroni 1998: 528). And even where modernists rejected liberal democracy and what Charles Ferrall calls 'the emancipatory aspects of bourgeois modernity' and embraced the right (2001: 5), as the Italian Futurists, Pound and Eliot did, that could represent the continuation of a reformist stance – in Pound's case, obsessions rooted in progressive-era America (coinage, banks and 'interests'). Perhaps it is more accurate to say that the relationship between politics and aesthetics becomes progressively more complex with the decline of liberal individualism, amidst the pressures on the social contract effected by unemployment and inflation.

We can begin with the politics of the self and the self's emancipation: anarchism. Loosely defined as a stress on the absolute rights of the individual, an attack on the state, and an assertion of principles of mutuality and self-government, anarchism broadly considered also includes Nietzsche's attack on idealism and foundational thinking. The main line of anarchist thinking descends from Rousseau to Godwin, Bakunin, Proudhon and Kropotkin, taking on in the work of the last two an ethical dimension, opposing the savagely competitive world of Social Darwinism. Political anarchism represented by Emma Goldman influenced Margaret Anderson (editor of the *Little Review*) and others including the Dada leader Hugo Ball. But the form in which many modernists encounter anarchism is through the work of the 'egoist' philosophers Max Stirner and Friedrich Nietzsche. The American James Huneker's *Egoists: A Book of Supermen* (1909), lumps together Stirner, Nietzsche, Ibsen, Baudelaire, Flaubert and Huysmans as enemies of tradition. Translations of Nietzsche began to appear from 1896; he was championed by Havelock Ellis, Orage and others, and typically read as a prophet of a new type of human, a new aristocracy of free spirits. Stirner's *The Ego and His Own* was translated into English in 1907 and expounded in the polemical editorials of Dora Marsden in the *New Freewoman*, impacting on Pound, Williams, and possibly Lawrence (Clarke 1996; Kadlec 2000). The young James Joyce seems to have been attracted to egoism for its emphasis on self over the political (though in *Ulysses* the abandonment of Stephen's egoism signals a process of growth and potential community).

Egoist politics are closely tied to the history of two English literary magazines of the period, *The Freewoman* (founded 1911, relaunched as *The New Freewoman* in June 1913, and in December 1913 renamed *The Egoist*), edited by Dora Marsden; and *The New Age*. *The Freewoman* demonstrates the interconnections between various reform and cultural movements: originally a splinter suffrage magazine, it gave voice to anarchists, syndicalists and sexual reformers; the Blavatsky Institute provided office space in Bloomsbury. Its discussion groups continued the arguments pursued in its correspondence columns, on such topics as eugenics, household labour and divorce (Hanscombe 1987: 163–64). Marsden's militant suffragism in the period 1909–11 was supplanted by a radically individualistic politics derived from Stirner, in which all corporate activity was suspect: 'They are Egoists. They are Autocrats, and government in their autocracy is vested in the Self which holds the reins in the kingdom of varying wants and desires, and which defines the resultant of these different forces in the Satisfaction of Itself. The intensive satisfaction of Self is for the individual the one goal in life' (1913: 5). Recent historians have suggested that the change of title, accompanied by Pound's installation as literary editor, represents not a modernist 'takeover', but rather Marsden's conscious decision to shift the fight to the broader field of culture – a decision which again blurs distinctions between 'political' and 'formal' modernism.

At the heart of egoist philosophy as expounded by Marsden was a vitalism centred on the idea of will, or life force, as the expression of a restless individuating power, realized in the present moment rather than in the pursuit of an ideal. The self (as Bergson agreed) exists in a state of constant evolution; attempts to limit its autonomy via morality, religion, family or state, or even resolve its contradictions in liberal fashion, must be resisted. At a general level, egoism supports arguments for aesthetic autonomy and iconoclasm; for the destruction of realist forms in favour of the vital fragment. Indeed, David Weir argues that the move from the 'political egoism' of the early moderns to the 'aesthetic individualism' of modernism is the crucial step (1997: 177–9) – modernist aesthetics, in this formula, are an extension of the 'self-ownership' preached by Stirner.

For many, the cleansing of the self in the name of reform was also associated with both feminism and what we could call a 'northern modernism'. Feminism energized the work of modernist women in the inter-war period: Anna Wickham, Mina Loy, Rebecca West, Dorothy Richardson, Virginia Woolf and many others, in ways which find different expressions – Wickham's angry formalism; Loy's Futurist-style Feminist Manifesto; Woolf's passionate essays. Ibsen's individualist protagonists, often women, struggling against the dead weight of conformism and hypocrisy in the name of the integrity of self, provided a model for radicals including the young Joyce; George Egerton's independent-minded heroines in *Keynotes* (1893), living in Scandinavia, are typical. Ernst Bloch attributes this influence mysteriously to the landscape of the northern heaths – indeterminate roads, disconnected villages, iridescence – implying a loosening of human life; a shift towards the freedoms celebrated in the Wandervögel movement: 'the bourgeois ego . . . has become lighter' (Bloch 1998: 391, 402). Beside this we might place Christopher Caudwell's insistence, in 1937, that 'the *surréaliste* . . . is the last bourgeois revolutionary . . . What politically is this final bourgeois revolutionary? He is an anarchist' (Deane 1998: 125) – a claim which, for all that it is unfair on Surrealism, surely the most collectivist of modernist movements, persuasively links modernist aesthetics to a bourgeois politics centred on self-emancipation.

At this point in what is necessarily a sketchy account of the politics of reform we can turn to more mainstream politics, and in particular to forms of mutualism. The point of departure for any consideration of the politics of modernism in Britain is the period of rapid change following the Liberal victory of 1906, producing a Labour–Liberal consensus which continued after the war with the rise of the Labour Party and the development of the welfare state. The shift in class relations linked to these changes, famously figured by Virginia Woolf as the Victorian cook emerging from the depths of the kitchen into the light of the drawing room, is reflected in the uncertainties of the bourgeois novel, for example in the treatment of lower-middle-class characters by Forster, Woolf and others.

At the same time, the period after 1906 sees the birth of what one could call an anti-modern politics; that is a politics which opposes itself to the new mass public sphere, and to democracy. Many of the movements involved enter modernism's history through the pages of Orage's *The New Age*. They include Fabianism, Syndicalism, the Guild Socialism of G. D. H. Cole, Distributionism, the Co-operative Movement, Social Credit and

Kindred of the Kibbo Kift. They included both radical and nostalgic elements: the idea of a return to a less exploitative, pre-capitalist economic order; a stress on arts and crafts; and forms of economics designed to release social energies.

Syndicalism influenced a range of modernists, and in America was linked to the IWW and Rosa Luxemburg. A central component of syndicalist thinking as formulated by Georges Sorel is class antagonism, and the General Strike as a mass radicalization which would mark both a moment of rupture with the past and a response to modernity on the part of a deskilled and industrialized workforce. Sorel's *Reflections on Violence* (1908), translated by the Imagist T. E. Hulme in 1916, stressed the role of the charged image or 'myth' in imagining a historical break: a modernist politics which was to inform fascist thinking, but which could equally be applied to the political mode of the Suffragettes – revolutionary rather than reformist (Sorel envisioned violence as energizing and unifying the bourgeoisie as well as the workers). A version of this can be seen in Yeats's response to the Easter Uprising: even hopeless violence engenders a symbolic redemption, creating a national myth which is capable of breaking through history's surface and re-forming mythology: 'A terrible beauty is born' is at once an aesthetic and a declaration of political community. The British General Strike of May 1926 can be seen as the symbolic pivot of a turn towards more authoritarian positions, visible in the contrast between Lewis's Nietzschean scepticism in *The Art of Being Ruled* (1926) and the insistence on cultural tradition in *Time and Western Man* (1927); between the disintegration of *The Waste Land* and the conservativism of *After Strange Gods* (1933). The desire to seek authority outside the turbulent flow of history represents an attempt to master the threat of mass society. Descriptions of the General Strike by Woolf, Lewis and others stress waiting, interruption; the sense of a suspended temporality has even been linked to the 'Time Passes' section of *To the Lighthouse*, written during the strike.

Woolf's attendance at meetings of the Women's Co-operative Guild (WCG) and her friendship with the Fabian leaders Beatrice and Sidney Webb place her at the fringe of left-wing versions of mutualist politics – though she seldom fully committed herself to these causes. The politics of community, taking in self, other and language, is an important concern in her later work: the melding of individuals in *The Waves*, the concern with public discourse and community in *Between the Acts*. But the concern for connection and division in earlier texts, most obviously in *Mrs Dalloway*, also represents an engagement with the problems of class and nation. Jessica Berman reads *Orlando*, with its 300-year transsexual history, as the transposition of 'a political rhetoric like that of the WCG', registering marginality in a way which questions myths of national inclusiveness (2001: 131–9). *Three Guineas* represents the culmination of Woolf's political thinking: positing women as a class of permanent outsiders, she suggests that emancipation and enrichment will create a new harmony in which 'education', 'pleasure' and 'philanthropy' rather than accumulation and self-interest will govern human activity. Michael Tratner applies these ideas to *Mrs Dalloway*, suggesting that the shopping, parties and Sally's kiss represent 'an ecstasy of consumption and a release from self-abnegation imposed by the social order' (2001: 117) – though Septimus represents the point of blockage at which the circulation of pleasure is rendered pathological by society.

Woolf's emphasis on consumption as a component of mutuality is shared – though it may seem odd – with Ezra Pound. Outside a restricted Marxist tradition few novels deal with the key political problem of the inter-war years: unemployment, which in the UK never fell below a million. By the 1930s, in the wake of the Stock Market crash, the politics of work were more explicit. Ezra Pound in Canto 46, describing the '3rd year of the reign of F. Roosevelt' wrote of 'FIVE million youths without jobs' (1975: 235). Pound only slowly came to economics, but when he did he found another reform movement in Social Credit, the economic philosophy developed by C. H. Douglas around 1918. Social Credit thinking has its origins in the money-reform debates pervading American Populism, focusing on the Gold Standard and the limited availability of money. Simply put, it sought to replace an economy of scarcity and hoarded capital with one of abundance and circulation. Douglas argues that money-power always lags behind goods produced, and proposed a 'National Dividend' distributed to all members of society which would close the gap between the money controlled by bankers and the actual potential of a society. For many Social Credit thinkers, this would create a leisured society – a possibility raised in two Social Credit pamphlets of 1934, A. R. Orage's *The Fear of Leisure* and Storm Jameson's *The Soul of Man in the Age of Leisure*.

Social Credit represents a confluence of left- and right-wing utopian thinking (Pound linked both Kropotkin and Mussolini to Douglas). It can also be seen as a response to economic modernity, seeking to remove im-balances between production and consumption, figuring the marketplace in terms of harmonious relations rather than surplus and shortage. Like so many reform movements, it is ultimately concerned with unblocking energies and releasing flows. The most visible blocking agent was, for many, the Jewish financier, conceived as the figure for parasitic and unnatural accu-mulation – a recurrent figure in the period, linked to official attacks on bankers like the Macmillan Report. A vein of anti-Semitism, muted or viru-lent, runs through the work of Eliot, Pound, Lewis, David Jones and others.

Social Credit had followers throughout the world; literary supporters included Orage, who made the *New Age* a Social Credit organ, Lewis, Pound, Goram Munson and the New Zealand writer A. R. D. Fairburn; many others including Eliot were strongly influenced by its ideas. For Pound, who read Douglas in 1919, it seems to have represented a desire for symbolic equivalence, for goods and money to be in productive relation. The binding of value represented by the fixed-rate investment and the Gold Standard becomes the curse of Usura, as opposed to the fecundating energies of 'Nature's increase': backing the credit of the Monte dei Paschi, the only bank Pound praised, was Siena's land, 'the growing grass that can nourish the living sheep' (1973: 270). Social Credit also represented for Pound a realization of the demand that the past's relation to the future be allowed for in the notion of 'interest': Douglas saw this as development costs or hidden overheads, not included in the banker's calculations but part of the 'cultural heritage'. Pound stresses the need to build on the past and not repeat it uselessly: *Guide to Kulchur* and other primers are designed to provide a fast route to what matters. Douglas Mao comments that 'a distributionist impulse broadly conceived subtends the *Cantos*, that enormous attempt to put to use the productions of the past while at the same time continuing the work of new making' (1998: 177). As Mao points out, Pound's determination to put the past to work building the future differs from its use in Eliot: 'distribution' means the exchange between producer and consumer is more important than any final meaning.

Douglas was also strongly supported by John Hargrave, leader of the most eccentric of British reform movements, the Kindred of the Kibbo Kift, founded in 1920 as a splinter group of the Scouting movement, with its focus on national revival. The Kindred employed an eclectic mix of vitalist spiritualism, wood-craft and body culture. While they have links to the anti-modernity of Ruskin and Morris, they employed vibrant modernist designs in their regalia, derived from Native American symbolism, and imagined a technologically-supported leisure culture, linking reform to economic modernity (Hargrave worked in advertising). The Kibbo Kift had many supporters in the arts: Lawrence was attracted to the movement (David Bradshaw has suggested that Mellors in *Lady Chatterley's Lover* is a Kibbo Kifter); and Pound praised Hargrave's novel *Summer Time Ends* (1935). Indeed, as Cathy Ross points out, Pound and Hargrave shared a number of aesthetic concerns: a stress on the hieroglyph; a biological conception of the avant-garde as a 'small cell of highly disciplined "culture Carriers" who would effect change by, in Hargrave's words, "penetrating" or "fertilizing" the chaotic flux of the many' (2003: 90).

Fascist thought as it is received in Britain is closely linked to the varieties of syndicalist thinking described above, in part via the influence of the French grouping known as the *Action française* on Hulme, Eliot and others. Hulme attacked the liberal doctrine, knitted into reform discourse, that 'man, the individual, is an infinite reservoir of possibilities' (1987: 116). Fascism offered some of the same qualities celebrated by Sorel. One link between Pound's earlier individualism and his later fascism is the fantasy of man whose actions count, who can break through accumulated resistance (bureaucratic; ideological). In his essay 'Machine Art' (1927–30) he stressed that it is in the moving parts of a modern machine, 'where the energy is most concentrated', that the pressure uniting form and function is apparent – the machine as a whole is less interesting (1996: 57). In politics this corresponds to a worship of the mover – Malatesta, builder of the temple;

Mussolini, drainer of marshes. Pound saw Mussolini (counterfactually) as a stimulator of local energies, binding the many. He also seems to have believed that Mussolini had an intuitive understanding of the project of the *Cantos*. To be sure, Pound's politics include darker elements, anti-Semitism and paranoia. The *Cantos*, especially with the explicitly fascist Italian cantos (72–3) included, are 'a poem including history'; a descent into the hell of the twentieth century.

Historically, fascist movements begin on the left: in Britain with the New Party (later the British Union of Fascists) founded by the dissident Labour minister Oswald Mosley in the crisis year of 1931; the year which saw the collapse of the Gold Standard. Mosley's ideas were initially close to Douglas's: stimulating the economy via expanded credit; eliminating unemployment; bypassing bankers. In *The Greater Britain* (1932) Mosley described fascism as 'The Modern Movement', centred on 'vital and determined youth' (Deane 1998: 35); its slogan 'VOLT' (Vigour, Order, Loyalty, Triumph) gestured towards technological modernity. Many in the labour movement were attracted to this vision, including Bloomsburyites: Harold Nicholson edited the fascist paper *Action*; Vita Sackville-West and John Strachey were involved. Woolf's work in the thirties is written in dialogue with such forces, exploring the oceanic feelings exploited by fascism in *The Waves* and suggesting a version of unstructured community at variance with fascist models (Berman 2001: 139–56).

As fascism developed in the 1930s, its lineaments became more apparent and fellow-travellers melted away. W. B. Yeats, who had established some connections with the Irish fascists, moved to distance himself – at least in terms of formal links. Yeats's involvement comes after the disillusioned end of his term as Senator, and reflects the preoccupation with historical and national violence that runs through his works from 'Meditations in Time of Civil War'; it manifests itself in the collective form of 'Three Marching Songs', as well as in the eugenics discussed earlier. Even Wyndham Lewis, one of the two modernist writers most often associated with Fascism, modified his stance. Only Pound, broadcasting from Italy and pouring out anti-Semitic diatribe against the Rothschild banks, remained fixed in his views.

RADICAL TRADITIONS

The politicization of writing in the 1930s, with the rise of fascism and mass unemployment, is central to accounts of that decade which separate it from 1920s modernism. In fact, there is more continuity than this suggests, especially in America. American modernism develops in close relation to a distinctly Midwestern tradition of socialist thinking, taking Whitman as its foundational figure, typified by Thorsten Veblen and John Dewey rather than Marx, its political hero Eugene Debs. This tradition speaks of hidden 'interests' (corporate capitalism) and shares with Pragmatism, the philosophical movement associated with William James and Dewey, a stress on education and the development of the potential of the individual. In the pre-war period the revival of Theodore Dreiser's work (beginning with the re-issue of *Sister Carrie* in 1907) was one expression of this tradition; another was the work of H. L. Mencken on the American language, positing Twain as the demotic pioneer.

In the period before the war, American socialism was at its strongest. The Patterson Strike Pageant of 1913, organized by journalist John Reed, Mable Dodge and others, represented one high point of radical art, its roots in syndicalist thinking. Following the defeat of striking mill-workers at Paterson, New Jersey, over 1,000 workers re-enacted the events at Madison Square Garden before an audience of 15,000, singing radical songs and roaring their approval in a spectacular, interactive event staged against a giant back-lit representation of the mill (Watson 1991: 140–8). If political defeat was thus turned into aesthetic victory, in the post-war context that seemed a harder trick to manage, and many radical texts of this period are chronicles of defeat. Two famous cases galvanized left-wing circles in America in the inter-war period: the trial of Sacco and Vanzetti; and the Scottsboro case. The former emerged from the post-war 'red scare' with the arrest for murder, on flimsy grounds, of the anarchists Nicola Sacco and Bartolomeo Vanzetti. After a six-year defence campaign they were executed in 1927. The huge Sacco and Vanzetti literature includes Millay's 'Justice Denied in Massachusetts', a fierce poetic sequence by Lola Ridge, a book by Dos Passos and his fictionalization of the defence at the climax of *U.S.A.* – the point in the novel where the subjective mode of the 'camera eye' finally intersects with the historical narrative, enabling a bitter jeremiad at a hijacked polity.

The Scottsboro case involved nine young black men arrested in Alabama in 1931 for supposedly raping two white women; they too were sentenced to death. After a series of retrials four were released and five received prison terms in 1937. Scottsboro helped radicalize the issue of race in America: it was the subject of a play by Langston Hughes, *Scottsboro Limited* (1932); Cullen's poem 'Scottsboro, Too, is Worth its Song', which accuses white poets of silence; Kay Boyle's poem 'A Communication to Nancy Cunard' (Cunard wrote extensively on the case) and many other writings. Boyle's poem is notable for a fragmentary style including prose and lyric, courtroom dialogue and a 'Blues', in an attempt to reproduce the fractured and often meagre voices of the public sphere.

In the UK, the thirties seems to have been a huge outpouring of pamphlets and collections on fascism, socialism, pacifism, feminism, the condition of England, and the civil war in Spain. The Auden circle has dominated accounts of this period, to the detriment of a broader picture: among other networks, Janet Montefiore points to a group of left-wing women writers in London – Storm Jameson, Rebecca West, Naomi Mitchison, Vera Brittain, Rosamund Lehmann, Stevie Smith. Alison Light points to a matching group of Conservative women, struggling to accommodate their vision of

England with historical change. A sense of crisis dominates writings of the period: of the bourgeoisie; of historical experience. The tropes of the thirties include an apocalyptic darkening of the skies and the abandonment of games for action; in the *Totentanz* of such poems as Louis MacNeice's 'Bagpipe Music' (1937). The latter is suggested by the 'lovers of cricket . . . lovers of nature, hikers, O touring cyclists' (Rex Warner); by 'plough up the playing-fields' (Day-Lewis); or 'The favourite down / At the blind ditch . . .' (MacNeice). One of the most characteristic stylistic gestures of thirties poetry, the abandonment of the article, gestures towards a world of nouns grown abstract and typical, sharing mass identities. The insistent address concluding the American Muriel Rukeyser's 'The Book of the Dead' (1938) similarly conjures up a world of types, crisis and decision with its non-specific address: 'You standing over gorges, surveyors and planners, / you workers and hope of countries / . . . and you young, you who finishing the poem / wish new perfection and begin to make' (1992: 39).

At the same time, literature debates the extent to which it can effect social change. The ambivalence of Christina Stead's 'Writers Take Sides', reporting of the International Congress of Writers held in Paris in June 1935, is representative: writers 'take lessons from workmen and use their pen as a scalpel for lifting up the living tissues, cutting through the morbid tissues, of the social anatomy'. But a few sentences later she adds: 'Artists are sensitized plated, bathed and kept out of the glare of the day, to be, when exposed, indicators and interpreters' (Kolocotroni 1998: 532). Active and passive; in the fray or registering change from afar – writers were called on to become involved, but at least after the 1934 declaration of the doctrine of Socialist Realism, they were aware of the dangers involved in notions of instrumentality. Laura Riding concluded, at the end of *The World and Ourselves* (1938), her circular letter on literature and politics with a collection of responses, that writers act as 'centres of communication, of mental contact' rather than as agents (1938: 418).

FORM AND REFORM

We can conclude with some additional comments on the intersection of the discourse of reform and modernism's desire to 'make it new', reform and re-form. As Michael Levenson puts it, 'The polemical vehemence of the avant-garde is only understandable when linked to a vision of the larger social whole, a vision of the whole as moribund, decadent and stifling to creative endeavour' (1984: 138). In the popular imagination the connection between political radicalism and artistic rebellion was strong: a point made by the Jane Heap cartoon which appeared in the famous 'blank' issue of the *Little Review*, depicting her co-editor (and lover) Margaret Anderson 'converting the sheriff to anarchism and vers libre'. Anderson supported Emma Goldman, anarchism, pacifism, and the labour movement in the period 1914–16, and the *Little Review* consciously aimed to be a forum for debate in its 'Comment' section. The blank pages of the September 1916 issue were meant to indicate a lack of publishable work: as with Bob Brown's later *Gems: A Censored Anthology* (1931), which suggestively blanked out sections of Palgrave's revered *Golden Treasury*, absence suggests a pregnant negation.

Indeed one way we can see modernism as a reform discourse is in its negativity; its concern with destruction. 'To break the pentameter, that was the first heave', Pound wrote in Canto 81. Daniel Tiffany argues that Imagism must be seen not as a clear programme – after all, injunctions as to precision and economy in writing were hardly that radical – but as a *critical* moment in the Hegelian sense; its aim was not to create anything in particular (the rather anodyne work of the Imagist anthologies) but, like Dada, to destroy a way of thinking (1995: 38–9). Harold Monro noted in the Imagist issue of *The Egoist* that its tenets largely consist of attacks on amateur poetry, superfluous words, rhetoric, iambs, making a positive aesthetics difficult: 'so much good material had to be thrown into the waste-paper basket of *Cliché*, that they remained now almost unprovided with a language or a style' (1915: 78). The ideas of economy and hygiene not only make poetry the elimination of superfluous materials, but a voiding of potential pollutants (the deathliness of 'emotional slither'). Language itself, in its mediation of the image, could ultimately be seen as such a pollutant, since 'The image is the word beyond formulated language' (Pound 1916: 102). As Pound wrote in 1938, 'It is not a revolution of the word but a castigation of the word' (1973: 162).

Levenson suggests that the split within Imagism in 1914 represents a division between the reformist, individualist wing of modernism (which located artistic freedom at the centre of its aesthetics) and an emerging formalism developed further in Pound's liaison with Eliot after 1917 (1982: 150–1). As we have seen, the picture is more complicated than that, with the continuation of reformist thinking *as* formalism. *Blast* adopted the strident rhetoric of both Futurism and Suffragism, polarizing audiences; it was, among other things, a response to a peculiarly British sense of national decline. Destruction is also central to what Stan Smith labels the 'rhetorics of renewal' in Yeats, Pound and Eliot: a threatened civilization; a crisis in which modernity has opened the possibility of a violent discontinuity – ideas about history, readership, cultural institutions and the dangers of democratic politics enmeshing in a potent mix. Even authors not attracted to such programmes, Michael Tratner argues, focus on moments of violence in imagining discontinuity and modernity: his examples include the soldier's attack on Stephen Dedalus in *Ulysses* and the death of Mrs Ramsay in a subordinate clause in *To the Lighthouse* (1995: 41).

The discourses of hygiene and efficiency discussed above are also directly incorporated into modernism – in Constructivism and Bauhaus for example.

Consider the Futurist F. T. Marinetti's definition of 'wireless imagination', involving the dissolving of a stagnant language into the flows of a new style:

The wireless imagination and words in freedom will lead us into the very essence of matter. In discovering new analogies between distant and apparently opposite things, we will evaluate them even more intimately. Instead of *humanizing* animals, vegetables and minerals (as we have done for so long) we can *animalize, vegetalize, mineralise, electrify, or liquefy* style by making it live with the very life of matter . . . Thus we have: **Condensed metaphors. – Telegraphic images. – Sums of vibrations. – Knots of thoughts. – Fans of movement opening and closing. – Abbreviations of analogies.**

(2002: 88)

As with Marinetti's Tactilism (*tattilismo*), one aim is the transfer of one sense into the modalities of another (touch becomes like the glance, a communication of self); but the more important aim is the elimination of a humanism which, for Marinetti, impeded the flow of language. That blockage could most effectively be destroyed by the flows of destructive energy which he associated with war, the 'world's only hygiene'.

A similar biologism and concern with flow, informed by the sexological tradition discussed above, is apparent in Pound's thinking after 1920. His preface to Remy de Gourmont's *The Natural Philosophy of Love* (1921), which he translated, confirmed his earlier thinking about 'germinal' consciousness, and ascribed to the masculine, the penis and 'seminal' thinking the role of creating the new: 'man really the phallus or spermatozoid charging, head-on, the female chaos; integration of the male in the male organ. Even oneself has felt it, driving any new idea into the great passive vulva of London, a sensation analogous to the male feeling in copulation.' Masculinity contrasts, in this tradition, with the more 'primitive' and conservative feminine body and consciousness:

Thought is a chemical process, the most interesting of all transfusions in liquid solution. The mind is an up-spurt of sperm, no, let me alter that; trying to watch the process: the sperm, the form-creator, the substance which compels the ovule to evolve in a given pattern, one microscopic, miniscule particle, entering the 'castle' of the ovule.

(1958: 204, 206)

This is an extrapolated and socialized form of the evolutionary and biological thinking of Otto Weininger and others. Yeats seems to be having a sly dig at Pound when he refers to his 'unexplained ejaculations' (1936: xxv), and it is unclear how seriously Pound took himself: one of his examples of the phallic 'stretch' of imagination is St Teresa. Nevertheless in the *Cantos* he repeatedly celebrates a phallic uprightness which also informs his economic thinking, since 'Nature's increase' underlies true production:

By 1934 Frazer is sufficiently digested for us to know that opposing systems of European morality go back to the opposing temperaments of those who thought copulation was good for the crops, and the opposing faction who thought it was bad for the crops (the scarcity economists of pre-history).

(1954: 85)

This location of the reformist politics of plenty in the context of sexual forthrightness neatly ties together some of the traditions we have been examining. Even the last modernist movement, Surrealism, can be seen as an expression of the reformist impulse, with its insistence that the psyche be made whole, that the world of desire be brought into relation to the real via what Walter Benjamin called a 'revolutionary negation'.

We have pursued 'reform' through a number of contexts, some of which are quite distant from the radical formulae of the avant-garde. Notions of the progressive could take on a decidedly liberal and establishment tone. A good example is *The Realist: A Journal of Scientific Humanism*, a short-lived monthly magazine published in 1929–30 in London, under the editorship of Archibald Church and Gerald Heard. The keynote is 'progress': 'Progress of the Novel' the opening article by Bennett; 'A Philosophy of Progress' (Collingwood), 'The Future of the Earth'. It included work on modernism (articles on 'Vertov and the Newest Film Spirit of Russia') as well as contributions from anthropologists (Malinowski), psychologists (Freud), scientists (Haldane, Zuckerman), economists, philosophers (Joad) and writers (Wells, Bennett, West, Huxley). The modern is packaged in the limp covers of an old-fashioned 'quality' journal, its sharp edges rubbed clean. A similar distancing from the aggressive energies of modernism are present in many retrospective accounts – as in Wyndham Lewis's comments in his autobiography on newspaper attacks on Vorticism: 'I might have been at the head of a social revolution, instead of merely being the prophet of a new fashion in art. Really all this organized disturbance was Art behaving as if it were politics' (1937: 35). But the relations between the reform of art, politics and the self are, as we have seen, not so easily disentangled.

5 The Self and the Senses

Here is an artificial conversation, reconstituted from two different sources:

I should say – to continue this jelly-fish metaphor – that long feelers reached down and through the body, that these stood in the same relation to the nervous system as the over-mind to the brain or intellect.

There is, then, a set of super-feelings. These feelings extend out and about us; as the long floating tentacles of the jelly-fish reach out and about him.

(Scott 1990: 94)

'Yes,' said Jinny, 'our senses have widened. Membranes, webs of nerve that lay white and limp, have filled and spread themselves and float round us like filaments, making the air tangible and catching in them far-away sounds unheard before.'

(Woolf 1992c: 101)

The texts are H. D.'s 'Notes on Thought and Vision', written in 1919; and Virginia Woolf's *The Waves* (1931). Both suggest that a heightened sensitivity to sensation is central to modern experience. There are a number of reasons why this is significant. One is aesthetic: philosophical tradition from Plato to Kant largely sees art in terms of universals – eliminating 'my' particular body and stressing what 'all men' feel. A reaction against this idealism is evident as early as Baudelaire's essay 'The Painter of Modern Life' (1860), in which he declares that while the 'eternal and invariable' is one half of aesthetic experience, its 'soul', the other is its 'body', that is 'contemporaneity, fashion, morality, passion' (Kolocotroni 1998: 103) – categories normally relegated to the trivial or pornographic. Modernism was to explore the pornographic with enthusiasm, but equally important is the inhabiting of the body typified by the epigraph of Wallace Stevens's poem 'Evening without Angels' (1934): 'the great interests of man: air and light, the joy of having a body, the voluptuousness of looking' (1997: 111). For Stevens this is part of a poetics which is vested in the everyday, nicely suggested by two phrases copied into his notebooks: 'Good common flesh, blood and mind are beside us here and now'; and 'the illumination of the usual' (1989: 25, 103).

The second reason for the centrality of sensation to modernism is that the senses themselves are reconceived. Writers on artistic modernism have emphasized its attack on representation and focus on abstraction, paralleling the literary stress on perspectivism and 'point of view'. Recent work on the history of the senses has linked these shifts more firmly to nineteenth-century developments in psychology, psychophysics (the study of the body's sensory apparatus) and in technology (devices which extend or interact with the senses, or store sensory material: the telegraph, telephone, phonograph, photograph, cinema). This chapter moves from sensation considered generally to modernist vision and (briefly) sound, exploring the suggestion that, as Sara Danius puts it, the senses are 'already embedded in processes of modernization' (2002: 7).

'SHOCK', MODERNITY AND THE ECONOMY OF SENSATION

In eighteenth-century natural philosophy, the body is a relatively transparent mechanism, passing impulses to a reflecting mind. In the nineteenth century this process takes on a new opacity: sensation is a function of a complex physiology involving sensory organs, nervous system, and a processing brain. The person becomes a mechanism for the processing of information. As a result, many fundamental categories – space, time – become physiological rather than ideal, analysable in terms of the machinery of the body (the processes of life itself) rather than abstract categories. Perception for Bergson involves 'a *variable* relation between the living being and the more-or-less distant influence of the objects which interest it' (1988: 33) – which is to say that perception is active, individual and contingent.

Time, discussed earlier, is a particularly rich example. The experimental psychologists who followed Wilhelm Wundt were preoccupied with measuring reaction times (the 'lost time' the body needs to process information); the smallest unit of perceivable time; the amount of time that can be contained in a 'moment' (Wundt had suggested 5 seconds). When William James in *Principles of Psychology* asks 'To what cerebral process is the sense of time due?', he answers that time is a product of the fact that sensations linger in the perceptual apparatus, like after-images: 'to state it in neural terms, *there is at every moment a cumulation of brain-processes overlapping each other, of which the fainter ones are the dying phases of processes which but shortly previous were active in a maximal degree. The* AMOUNT OF THE OVERLAPPING *determines the feeling of the* DURATION OCCUPIED' (1950: 635). Duration is produced by the 'overlapping of brain-processes of different phases'. As in Bergson the sense of time is not inbuilt, a Kantian a priori; rather it is an effect of the mind's functioning, affected by such factors as drugs, situation, or fatigue. Indeed, this description arguably makes time nothing but a kind of fatigue, the drag or noise in the perceptual apparatus. To say this is to enter the world of Joyce's *Ulysses*, in which the reception of time – as in the 'tired' and flabby prose and flat question-and-answer structure of 'Ithaca'; or the dreamlike temporal dilations and contractions in 'Circe' – reflects bodily states.

There is another consequence of this stress on embodiment. It proposes an economy of sensation founded on the defence of the self. The threat posed by specifically *modern* forms of sensation was described by the American physician George M. Beard, the popularizer of the diagnosis of neurasthenia or 'nervous exhaustion'. In *American Nervousness, Its Causes and Consequences* (1881) and elsewhere Beard saw neurasthenia as the disease of modernity, produced by new demands on a self whose energies are limited. 'From the standpoint only of economy of nerve-force', he writes, 'all our civilization is a mistake.' Among the factors creating this pressure were technology (the power of the steam engine, the speed of the train, the instantaneous communication of the telegraph, the noise of the city); the popular press with its excitements; the need for punctuality imposed by the timetable and wristwatch; and the excitement of debate and intellectual change, including 'the education of women'.

One of the most remarkable aspects of Beard's theories is that everywhere cause and consequence coalesce: technology is de-enervating; but in a reflexive metaphor in which the body is compared to a battery with 'so many additional lamps interposed in the circuit . . . supplied at the expense of the nervous system, the dynamic power of which has not correspondingly increased' (1881: 100). The body is seen in economic terms as overtaxed or over-spending; but in an argument in which economic expansion, debt and risk are part of the strains of modernity. Evolutionary thinking drives Beard's argument – technological evolution outstrips the human scale; but 'the dazzling swiftness' of the spread of evolutionary ideas is also cited as a challenge to the self. In their recursiveness, Beard's theories seem less an analysis of psychic structures than a direct expression of the anxieties of modernity; a repackaging of *unease* as *disease*.

In particular, Beard implies an analysis of modernity in terms of the 'shock' effect. This is often described in terms of 'trauma', though that word – Greek for 'wound' – is potentially misleading, suggesting a breach in the self produced by a particular event. What Beard enables for later writers including Freud is an *economic* conception of shock in which notions of everyday load, tolerance and stress are as important as trauma. This too has a long history – people began to notice a speeded-up world in the late eighteenth-century (Schnapp 1999) – and in the 1860s the train was widely seen as subjecting the body to dangerous speeds and jolting; the debate about 'railway spine', a hysterical response to railway accidents, fed into the later psychology of shell shock (Armstrong 2000).

Beard's analysis of modernity was influential. Max Nordau's *Degeneration* (1883) includes extended descriptions of the culture of neurasthenia, and imagines a future in which the 'capacity for attention and contemplation has diminished so greatly that instruction at school is at most two hours a day' (Kolocotroni 1998: 23). In 'The Metropolis and Mental Life' (1903) Simmel described the 'protective organ' and 'blasé attitude' needed by the city-dweller to protect himself against a flood of transient stimuli. Simmel makes explicit the logic of Beard's account when he describes the money economy, intellectualism and pocket watch as part of 'the conditions of the metropolis [which] are at once cause and effect' of what he observes (1997: 177) – another version of the paradox of culturalism. Freud's deployment of the term 'protective shield' (*Reizschutz*) in *Beyond the Pleasure Principle* had a similar aim, positing a psychic mechanism operating in real time (rather than the timeless world of the unconscious) which can 'sample' and de-amplify sensation. Walter Benjamin responded to Freud in his 1939 essay 'On Some Motifs in Baudelaire', in which he explores the flow of the walker through the city streets, encountering the 'shocks' of modern experience. And in 'Poetry and Abstract Thought' (1939), Paul Valéry described the poem itself as 'a kind of machine for producing the poetic state of mind by means of words', a state of mind measured in terms of the 'shock' received from stored energies: 'discoveries, connections, glimmers of expression that have been accumulated during months of research' (1977: 163).

The theoretical preoccupation with defence against stimuli has a number of parallels in modernist literature, for example in the literature of refusal in Kafka and Beckett. The term agoraphobia was coined by the German psychologist Carl Otto Westphal in 1871. Its origins lie in the Enlightenment sense that the self is defined in terms of the crowd (the public sphere, the marketplace), making, as Rousseau put it, each individual an actor on the public stage. Literary protests against this imperative appear as early as 1850s America, where Melville's 'Bartleby the Scrivener: A Tale of Wall Street' registers a refusal of the public sphere and a subversive domestication of the space of the office. Bartleby, the copyist who will not copy and who lives in his workplace, seems both agoraphobic and anorexic (Brown 1990). His immobility and formulaic 'I prefer not to' implies a refusal of preferment, career and progress, as well as a refusal of the circulation of information, signalled by the 'Dead Letter Office' which was his previous employment. Hypersensitivity is part of the psychopathology of modernism: the world-avoidance of Proust; Kafka's late stories about a trapeze artist who refuses to return to earth, and a 'hunger artist'. In the modern period anxiety and apprehension become vital subjects for art: in Schoenberg's song-cycle *Erwartung* (1909), in the hesitations of Prufrock, or the social and sexual uncertainties of Katherine Mansfield's characters.

A defence of the self is, it has been suggested, central to the aesthetics of 'high' modernism; a cultural correlative of widespread fears of masculine weakness and seminal depletion. Peter Nicholls has argued that the modernism of the 'Men of 1914' is impelled by the need to defend the self against collapse into the other (a collapse associated with the decadence of the 1890s), creating a stance of ironic mastery in which the other might be mastered as the object of art. For Wyndham Lewis, what *Tarr* calls 'jellyfish attributes' are the enemy of art, leading to a melting of self into others, rather than a concrete realization of the self in art. Lewis proposes art as a one-way song; as a flow outwards from a self modelled on the 'protective shield'. Whether describing the hot smoking interior of psychoanalysis, the 'intestines'; or the collapse of representation into perception which he saw as intrinsic to psychologism, Lewis insists that self and objective world must be separated.

The result is an art in which the only possible model for reading is a disinterested (and often mocking) contemplation in which the observing self must, paradoxically, be written out of the picture, even as its autonomy is asserted – because to include it would be to risk attending to its perceptual processes. As Douglas Mao points out, this fear of the collapse of the self has a political as well as a psychosexual dimension, since Lewis saw the world of technological modernity as abetted by the modernist critique of the imperial self, creating a confusion of man and technology (1998: 101) – indeed, in *Paleface*, rendering the European self a 'disintegrated' machine staggering under the weight of ' "complex" after "complex" '. Lewis's attack on Behaviourist psychology in *Time and Western Man* links it, rather paradoxically, to the philosophy of education which descends from Rousseau's *Émile* to Maria Montessori (1927: 319): both attempt a 'human training' imposed from without. In resisting 'training' (a central concern for James, Dewey and other pragmatists), Lewis exposes the technological underpinnings of modernity, but at the cost of an impoverished version of the self.

A more welcoming response to modernity can be seen in precisely those 'jellyfish attributes' Lewis attacks: H. D. and Woolf on the 'jelly-fish' brain – present also in Rebecca West's insistence, in *The Strange Necessity*, that art is created by projection into others and the creation of a 'collective and partially external super-cortex' (1987: 177). Such formulae reach towards the notion of a prosthetic self – the passage from Woolf suggests both radio and the telephone – and forms of sensation distributed between persons rather than 'owned' (as in the spiritualism described in chapter 6). The new century also saw a more positive judgement than Beard's on what William James called 'the energies of men': techniques like those reviewed in the previous chapter sought to increase energy and flow; to sexualize and stimulate. The Futurist F. T. Marinetti believed technology would enable a rewiring of the self, as in 'Words in Freedom' (1913):

Futurism is grounded in the complete renewal of human sensibility brought about by the great discoveries of science. Those people who today make use of the telegraph, the telephone, the phonograph, the train, the bicycle, the motorcycle, the automobile, the ocean liner, the dirigible, the aeroplane, the cinema, the great newspaper . . . do not realize that these various means of communication, transportation and information have a decisive influence on their psyches.

(Apollonio 1973: 96)

The implication is twofold. Firstly, a rethinking of the artwork as a series of impulses and shocks, assaulting the nerves; or as a device for the connection of impulses (collapsing distance by what Marinetti labels 'analogy'); or as a force-field in which different elements are held in tension – all these simultaneously, since the aim of Futurism is to multiply contexts. Secondly, a reciprocal rewriting in which a new body adequate to these shocks and flows is imagined. 'Man multiplied by the machine', the subject of Marinetti's manifestoes, is more than the extension of the human; it involves the 'creation of a non-human type' which does not reduce experience to an agreed standard, but is itself transformed by modernity.

ATTENTION, DISTRACTION AND THE STREAM OF CONSCIOUSNESS

If we turn from defence against stimuli to their processing, we need a paired set of terms important to turn-of-the-century psychology: attention and distraction. If attention refers to the mind's ability to sort its way through the clutter of experience, distraction signals the point at which it scatters. As Jonathan Crary shows, attention emerges as an issue because of a perceived sensory overload, and because of the close alignment between attention and mechanisms of social and visual control (industrial psychology, cinema). In this situation, forms of distracted experience have the potentiality to become the focus for modernist aesthetics. If the problem of mass culture is perceived, in the words which F. R. Leavis borrows in *Mass Civilization and Minority Culture* (1930), to be 'a vast and increasing inattention' (Deane 1998: 18), then attention becomes contested ground. We can be 'Distracted from distraction by distraction', as Eliot puts it in 'Burnt Norton' (1974: 192).

In modernist texts the fluctuating line of attention, and the looping, distracted walks of memory, impel a new kind of narration attached to the notion of 'stream of consciousness' – the term which May Sinclair borrowed from William James to describe Dorothy Richardson's writing (Scott 1990: 444). This is Woolf in 'More Dostoevsky' (1917):

From the crowd of objects pressing upon our attention we select now this one, now that one, weaving them inconsequently into our thought; the associations of a word perhaps make another loop in the line, from which we spring back again to a different section of our main thought, and the whole process seems both inevitable and perfectly lucid. But if we try to construct our mental processes later, we find the links between one thought and another are submerged.

(1987: 85)

Ford Madox Ford is more explicit in linking the flight of the mind to the exigencies of retrospective narration:

Life does not say to you: In 1914 my next door neighbour, Mr Slack, erected a greenhouse and painted it with Cox's green aluminium paint. . . . If you think about the matter you will remember, in various unordered pictures, how one day Mr. Slack appeared in his garden and contemplated the wall of his house. You will then try to remember the year of that occurrence and you will fix it as August 1914 because having had the foresight to bear the municipal stock of the city of Liège you were able to afford a first-class season ticket for the first time in your life. You will remember Mr. Slack – then much thinner because it was before he found out where to buy that cheap Burgundy of which he has since drunk an inordinate quantity.

(1924: 181)

This is the digressive narration of Ford's novels, in which truths appear in glimpses and memories questioned by 'some trick of mnemonics' (1984: 23). The weight of a single recurrent word in Ford – 'apparently' and its cognate 'appeared' – reflects a narration anchored in the contingency of point of view.

Woolf and Ford focus on memory and narration. It is possible to see language itself as implicated in the drift of attention, since, as Friedrich Kittler suggests, language was an important focus for nineteenth-century psychophysical study: its production, pathologies; its flow through persons considered as input–output devices, writing- and talking-machines akin to the typewriter, rather than as 'deep' sources in the romantic manner. Bram Stoker's *Dracula* (1897) is a primary exhibit, with its typewriter, phonograph used for dictation, collation of materials, telegraphic and telepathic trans-missions (Kittler 1990). A modernist version of psychophysical study is Dora Marsden's 'Lingual Psychology', serialized in *The Egoist* from July 1916. The September 1917 article, 'A Definition of Attention', places attention at the centre of a theory of knowledge, and insists on its linguistic basis. To attend is to initiate a subconscious process of word-formation in which words are returned to their phenomenological roots as core elements of perception and action ('words play the role of *pioneer* not merely in relation to activ-ity proper, but also in the sphere of sensory activity'). All human activity involves symbolization, and conversely words 'stand proxy' for action. The result is that writing involves a vital flux of impulses – something the ha-bituation implicit in language allows us to forget. Marsden describes a tran-scription of embodied thought:

> If . . . it were sought to reveal all the deep secrets of the human heart, what one would require would be some delicate recording instrument capable of registering all those movements forming ceaselessly in the throat and head *as words*: words – often as not – unspoken and so incipient that they do not achieve specific and recognizable form as words, but attain only to the general setting of the muscles preparatory to the forming of specific words. Of this abortive kind of words must be our *subconscious* thoughts properly so called. The chronicle such an instrument would set forth would indeed render us knowable as we are: in all our vanities, our smothered impulses, our loves, hates, hopes, and fears.
>
> (1917: 114)

This is a better definition of 'stream of consciousness' than Sinclair's six months later, because it does not assume that mind can easily be repre-sented as language: this is a language of incipience. Indeed, it is only a con-ceptualization of writing as a *technology of registration* that is adequate to this embodied thinking.

The automatic writing investigated by Gertrude Stein at the Harvard Laboratories at the turn of the century and later practised by the Sur-realists provides another example of a pure productivity. Automatic writing works at the borders of consciousness, raising questions about the source of its materials: its externality or internality to the psyche (deep truth, or just the sound of the media, as Kittler implies?). The Behaviourist B. F. Skinner was to describe Stein as an automaticist in the 1930s, but the accusation came earlier, from Wyndham Lewis: 'the repetition is also in the nature of a photograph of the unorganised world dreaming of the mind when it is not concentrated for some logical functional purpose' (1989a: 346). For Lewis, this is a period style which takes in both modernists (Huxley) and popular culture (Anita Loos). Stein herself theorized her writing as a pure productivity in which one could only know what one wrote as one wrote it (Armstrong 1998). *The Making of Americans* constantly attacks the idea that one can 'know' the 'bottom nature' of a person or their states of mind. Instead Stein suggests the study of human input and output in, for example, this welter of adverbs:

how complicatedly, how simply, how joyously, how boisterously, how despondingly, how fragmentarily, how delicately, how roughly, how excitedly, how energetically, how persistently, how repeatedly, how repeatingly, how drily, how startlingly, how funnily, how certainly, how hesitatingly, anything is coming out of that one, what is being in each one and how anything comes into that one and comes out of that one makes of each one one meaning something and feeling, telling, thinking, being certain and being living.

(1995: 782–3)

This kind of lateral flow – in which language dissolves into the axis of association – characterizes a range of material in the period: *The Waste Land*, which Eliot later commented was produced 'in a way approaching the condition of automatic writing' (1964: 144–5); or Molly Bloom's soliloquy in *Ulysses*. More generally, the productivity of language itself informs much modernist writing: to put it simply, form is not imposed from without; poems go on for as long as language is produced and are arranged according to the demands of meaning. Mina Loy's 'Songs to Joannes' (1917), for example, includes stanzas of varying length, sudden spaces, thoughts which trail off, rapid changes of pace, hesitations, lines of dashes. Stein's prose-poems in *Tender Buttons* seem more like a *distribution* of language – analysable in terms of frequency of word-type and groupings of cognate words – than a sequential message.

A highly self-conscious example of wandering discourse is William Carlos Williams's prologue to *Kora in Hell* (1918). Williams writes that most writing depends on easy associations in which 'the attention has been held too rigid on the one plane instead of following a more flexible, jagged resort. It is to loosen the attention, my attention since I occupy part of the field, that I write these improvisations' (1970: 348). In *Kora in Hell* Williams recommends the use of a mirror as 'an exercise for the mind . . . conducive to that elasticity of the attention which frees the mind for the enjoyment of its special prerogatives' (1970: 78). The redistribution of attention is figured in the prologue by the actual walks of Williams's mother, Elena, losing her way in Rome or telling stories in which a 'dark turn' signals her ability to see 'the thing itself without forethought or afterthought but with great intensity of perception' (1970: 8). The mother exists in the space of automaticity proper; freed from the tyranny of narrative. Arguably that space is *reserved* for the mother; the automatic work is anchored in Williams's experience of the female body. If in *A Novelette* language is 'made a whore' by the 'idea-vendors', it is Stein, the mother of modernism, who reclaims language through her 'aimlessness' (1970: 281).

If we return to Ford's theory of literary 'Impressionism', it too is heavily reliant on notions of distributed attention:

It is . . . perfectly possible that a piece of Impressionism should give a sense of two, or three, of as many as you will, places, persons, emotions, all going on simultaneously in the emotions of the writer. It is, I mean, perfectly possible for a sensitised person, be he poet or prose writer, to have the sense, when he is in one room, that he is in another, or when he is speaking to one person he may be so intensely haunted by the memory or desire for another person that he may be absent-minded or distraught. . . . we are almost always in one place with our minds somewhere quite other.

(Kolocotroni 1998: 325)

The lack of self-presence and haunting effects described here are a hidden element in modernist formalism, for example in Yeats's doctrine of the Mask. Yeats insists that the artist must avoid being her- or himself, must turn away from self-representation to some other; Ford writes more prosaically 'The artist must never write to satisfy himself . . . He must write always so as to satisfy that other fellow.' The audience must also be seen as in a state of wandering attention; must be won over by 'surprise', 'fatigue', by 'shock'; by a restless alternation of mood – effects not unlike those proposed by Bertold Brecht, whose plays use 'alienation' or 'interruption' (*Verfremdung*) to disrupt the cosy compact of dramatic realism.

It was in the work of the Weimar cultural theorists Sigfried Kracauer and Walter Benjamin that distraction – both the audience's distracted reception and forms of recuperative artistic distraction – received its most dialectical treatment. In Kracauer's essay 'Cult of Distraction' (1926), he describes the revues at the Berlin picture houses in terms of a refusal to gloss over social reality:

the fact that these shows lack any authentic and materially motivated coherence, except possibly the glue of sentimentality, which covers up this lack only in order to make it all the more visible; the fact that these shows convey precisely and openly to thousands of eyes and ears the *disorder* of society – this is precisely what would enable them to evoke and maintain the tension that must precede the inevitable and radical change.

(1995: 327)

In Benjamin's 'The Work of Art in the Age of Mechanical Reproduction', the cinema is an art-form predicated on distraction, but able at the same time to provide an experimental optics (the cut, close-up and so on) which would retrain the eye. However, it is to architecture that Benjamin finally turns for an example of art received in a state of distraction. Why? One answer is that the relationship one has with buildings is intimate and everyday; defined by touch and familiarity rather than aesthetic distance. To see what would be involved in such a quotidian art, we would have to look in detail at the spatial practices of modernist writings: flats, teashops, pubs, streets. But an adequate sense of what might be involved is provided by Carl Sandburg's 'The Skyscraper', the climax of *Chicago Poems* (1916). Throughout the volume, Sandburg alternates between crowd and individual. When the reader comes to 'The Skyscraper', the question is: will the skyscraper finally offer a symbolic integration of the city, like the Eiffel Tower in Delaunay's paintings? Or a symbolic vision of the weight of capitalism? The answer is that the skyscraper is a non-transcendental icon; it remains simply the sum of the labour that made it, its inputs and outputs: wires which 'climb with secrets, carry light and carry words'; its range of classes from cleaners and stenographers to lawyers and efficiency engineers. Human inputs are the 'soul' of the building, but that seems to mean everyday praxis: even sun and rain 'use' the building. Much of the description concerns itself with the tactility and inhabitation described by Benjamin: smiles, tears, rhythms of work, the hand of the mason, the lick of a mop. Sandburg includes the building's role in capitalism – money stacked in the safe; advertising signs – but that is part of a list of functions. And the final image is of someone looking *out*:

A young watchman leans at a window and sees the lights of barges butting their way across a harbour, nets of red and white lanterns in a railroad yard, and a span of glooms splashed with lines of white and blurs of crosses and clusters over the sleeping city.

(1994: 31)

This is to use it as a visual device, discomposed sight into a kind of impressionism – an observation which leads us on to the more specific question of vision.

MODERNIZING VISION: THE BLIND MAN

Conrad's preface to *The Nigger of the Narcissus* (1897) includes a famous declaration that 'My task which I am trying to achieve is, by the power of the written word to make you hear, to make you feel – it is, before all, to make you see' (Kolocotroni 1998: 133). Pound goes further, citing a correspondent in *Gaudier-Brzeska*: 'I see, you wish to give people new eyes, not make them see some new particular thing' (1916: 98). But what is involved in making someone *see*? Poetry, for the Imagist philosopher T. E. Hulme, 'always endeavours to arrest you, and to make you continuously see a physical thing, to prevent you from gliding through an abstract process' (1955: 10). Arresting, preventing smooth motion: this is the aesthetic of the train crash. For the Russian Futurists and the linguistic theorists associated with them, terms like *ostranenie* ('making strange'), *zatrudnenie* ('making difficult') and 'renewing perception' are linked: the aim of the artwork is to break linguistic and perceptual habits – to make the real a little harder to see, as Wallace Stevens put it.

We need to briefly consider the history of vision. As Crary argues, the development of physiological optics in the nineteenth century destroyed the idea of perception modelled on the camera obscura, a camera-like box in which the eternal object is projected on a screen. Vision in nineteenth-century psychology is specific – disarticulated from the other senses – and bounded by the capacities of the eye; the mind constructs a world on the basis of cues rather than a direct mapping of inner and outer. Explorations of the physiology of vision stressed the limitations of the human perceptual apparatus (it could see only a fraction of the spectrum; could not see objects presented for small intervals). Psychophysics explored persistence of vision; peripheral vision (better at detecting movement); and optical illusions.

At the same time, new technologies of vision – photography, cinema, X-rays – threatened to displace human perception in the registering of reality, offering a truer account, as in the time-lapse photography of E.-J. Marey and Eadweard Muybridge, which for the first time could analyse the gait of a galloping horse. In Bergson's *Matter and Memory* (1911) this split between human vision and technology appears as a problem inherent in representation, seen in terms of the opposition of materialism and idealism: either perception is simply a mathematical trace, like Marey's graphs of motion; or so complex and subjective it defies transcription. This leads to a double legacy: on the one hand 'all the multiple affirmations of the sovereignty and autonomy of vision derived from this newly empowered body' (Crary 1993: 150), from the idea that individual perception (and its artistic rendition) has an absolute value; on the other hand the institutionalization of devices for creating illusion in the cinema.

Modernist texts struggle to reconcile these possibilities. One response to the particularization of vision is a radical empiricism. For Ernst Mach, one of the most influential writers on science at the turn of the century, it makes little sense to talk of the 'real' apart from a perceiving consciousness. 'Mach's philosophy', Theodore Porter observes, 'permitted neither subject not objects but only, and always, an interaction' (Ross 1994: 138). This leads to a stress on the *work* of perception – the mind constantly creating a world. Mach included in his *The Analysis of Sensations* a self-portrait which was remarkable for breaking with an episteme in which the mirror provides the perceptual model for writings on the self: it depicted a huge moustache and narrowing body; where the head should be was a blank. This is ourselves seen past our noses, like Bloom's vision of his body in *Ulysses*, genitals surfacing in the bath.

The implication of Mach's empiricism is that only the human gaze brings a world into focus. For Bertrand Russell in *The Theory of Knowledge* (written

1913), even peripheral phenomena are only intelligible as potentially part of the world of mind – Ann Banfield relates Russell's theory of *sensibilia*, units of perception existing independently of a perceiving mind, to Virginia Woolf's world of 'things barely made out', cries floating in from elsewhere, sights at the edges of vision, familiar objects abandoned or locked away (2000: 130–4). If the 'Time Passes' section of *To The Lighthouse* offers, as Banfield puts it, a world 'seen without a self', that is a realism founded on the perceiving apparatus – with the novel itself another example. 'Time Passes' is Bergsonian in the sense that time cannot be imagined *without* consciousness, even if that consciousness is located nowhere in the narration. Fiction in this view is not anchored to an objective world of real objects, but rather in a flux of possible points of view. In Woolf's novels objects emerge from this flux, like the green glass pebble of her story 'Solid Objects' – 'It pleased him; it puzzled him; it was so hard, so concentrated, so definite an object compared with the vague sea and the hazy shore' – gaining a significance only from 'the stuff of thought' in which they are anchored. 'Burnt Norton' again supplies a gloss: 'the roses / Had the look of flowers that are looked at' (Eliot 1974: 190).

A particular figure embodies the materiality of looking: the Blind Man. Walking after lunch in *Ulysses*, Leopold Bloom helps a 'blind stripling' across the road, before meditating on blindness: 'Weight. Would he feel it if something was removed. Feel a gap. Queer idea of Dublin he must have, tapping his way round by the stones' (1993: 173). He suggests the ability to construct a world from clues, and inhabit it like a dreamer – like Joyce himself, writing letters home to conform details of Dublin. Compare the amnesiac Chris Baldry in West's *The Return of the Soldier* (1918), who can move around his house in the dark but crashes into things put in place since his marriage – a metaphor for his inability to negotiate history. The world of the blind or somnambulist is held in place by the power of mind, its intersection with reality marked by violent shocks.

The episode in *Ulysses* touches on the philosophical *topos* know as the 'Molyneux problem' – the question of whether a blind man suddenly given sight would recognize anything on the basis of a prior understanding of forms garnered from touch. In Enlightenment versions of the problem, while space is not an a priori category, it is believed that the senses can be readily mapped onto each other, and that touch can supply a model for vision (as in Descartes's *La dioptrique* and Diderot's *Letter on the Blind*). Nineteenth-century study of the senses isolated and particularized them, and raised doubts about the reliability of vision. Where the Molyneux problem returns in modernism it makes the blind man's vision the metaphor of a visual primitivism, and even for the attack on vision which Martin Jay has identified as a strand of twentieth-century thought – literalized in the famous eye-slashing sequence in Buñuel's Surrealist film *Un chien andalou* (1928).

Perhaps for this reason blindness can signal the modern itself, as in the New York Dada publication *The Blind Man*, its second issue focused on

Duchamp's 'Fountain', the relabelled urinal which epitomizes modernist re-vision. In *Modern Painters*, Ruskin argued that the painter must paint what he sees, without the intervention of extraneous knowledge or perceptual habits. As he put it elsewhere, the artist should aim for 'a sort of childish perception of these flat stains of colour, merely as such, without consciousness of what they signify, – as a blind man would see them if suddenly gifted with sight' (cited Danius 2002: 116). In his *Letters on Cézanne*, Rilke depicts the post-Impressionists as realizing this vision:

> no one before him ever demonstrated so clearly the extent to which painting is something that takes place among the colours, and how one has to leave them alone completely . . . Whoever meddles, arranges, injects his human deliberation, his wit, his advocacy, his intellectual agility in any way, is already disturbing and clouding their activity.
>
> (1985: 75)

Instead of the object with all its social and habitual organization, we have dabs of colour; media. Blindness is also important in Stein's exploration of the senses in *Tender Buttons*. If Stein's *The Making of Americans* is an attempt to imagine time without prior organization into narrative, *Tender Buttons* reconsiders words and description in its first poem, 'A CARAFE, THAT IS A BLIND GLASS'. The 'blind glass' signals a perception feeling its way. *Tender Buttons* moves through a series of primary colours, differences imposed on a spectrum akin to Ruskin's 'naked pigment'. Stein's experimental mode reaches back to her work at the Harvard Laboratories: research, rapid stimuli, response; all terms contained in 'A BOX', alongside references to biology (blood, breeding, kindred; misogyny which assigns female sexuality a passive, non-penetrative role): 'Out of kindness comes redness and out of rudeness comes rapid same question, out of an eye comes research, out of selection comes painful cattle' (1971: 163). Stein demands a field of attention which cannot be stabilized, in which 'selection' cannot work. She liked to think of herself as a Cubist, and it is worth remembering that Cubism, in T. J. Clark's account, figures not the renewal of perception via technique or an abstract dwelling on technique itself, but instead an account of representation at a point where representation has become impossible.

At times the blind man simply flickers through modernist texts as an index of visual disruption. In Woolf's essay 'Street Haunting', whose subject is the 'sportive' eye, blind brothers suddenly 'cleave asunder the passers-by' and halt the narrative. Woolf constantly dwells on the physiology of vision. As Laura Marcus points out, one image for this is the insect's eye (1997: 19–20). The story *Kew Gardens* – which appeared in editions illustrated by Vanessa Bell, themselves post-Impressionist experiments – is focalized through a snail's 'vision', looking allied to touch:

> Yellow and black, pink and snow white, shapes of all these colours, men, women, and children were spotted for a second upon the horizon, and then, seeing the breadth of yellow that lay upon the grass, they wavered and sought shade beneath

the trees, dissolving like drops of water in the yellow and green atmosphere, staining it faintly with red and blue.

(1973: 41)

If this seems to gesture towards the world of art, it also suggests science: the red and blue stains of litmus paper; a sense of vision as a test of invisible qualities.

Modernism also includes, Joyce's blindness apart, some classic accounts of sight loss including Huxley's *The Art of Seeing* and Wyndham Lewis's article in *The Listener* announcing his retirement as art critic, 'The Sea-Mists of the Winter' (1951). Lewis describes how he sees friends 'fragmentarily, obliquely and spasmodically' in his peripheral vision:

as one turns one's head hither and thither, glimpses constantly recur, delivering to one's fading eye-sight a piece of old so-and-so's waistcoat or bald head, or dear Janet's protruding nose. These token odds and ends of personality are really just as good as seeing them whole, and their voices have an added significance.

(1989b: 343)

That Lewis should be resigning as art critic as he describes his vision as a kind of modernism is an example of the interplay between fragmented and integrated sensation which is central to the modern. One only has to remember his own description of dancers in *Tarr* 'Each new pair of dancers seemed coming straight for him: their voices were loud, a hole was cut out of the general noise, as it were opening a passage into it' (1968: 143). All sensation is de-naturalized and rendered prosthetic: Lewis uses a dictaphone, and talking is 'rather like telephone conversation'. The radical contingency of vision drives it back into the individual – this is *my* vision – even as it becomes mechanical.

VISUAL TECHNOLOGIES: PHOTOGRAPHY AND CINEMA

Modernism increasingly thinks of the sensory world as unique and individual. At the same time, the modern period sees the development of technologies designed to extend and store the material of human sensation and communication – to transmit messages (telegraph, telephone, radio, television); to record sound (phonograph) and sight (photography, cinema). These developments are dialectically related: it is the development of technologies of perception and storage which reveal the contingencies of individual perception and memory; those technologies are in turn absorbed into modernism. In the remainder of this chapter, I will explore some of the implications of seeing modernism as *media*.

Modernist photography – the Vorticist photography of Alvin Langdon Coburn and Man Ray's 'rayographs' for example – typically seeks to foreground the technology of perception. Aerial stereoscopic photography, designed to make objects leap out in exaggerated relief, has been related to

Cubism, not simply in their flat planes (a comparison made in the period) but in an analytic and synthetic approach to vision. The pioneer of modernist and commercial photography in America, Edward Steichen, became chief of the photographic section of the American Air Service in the war. His stress on the need to interpret and re-interpret the image, including stereoscopic views, seems to have motivated a more abstract position in which the formal qualities of the image are paramount. The potentiality of such techniques as slow-motion to reveal a grotesque reality appears in Wells's story 'The New Accelerator' (1901), in which the radically speeded-up narrator moves so fast relative to others that he can see an eye frozen grotesquely in mid-wink (in a parable of the dangers of fast living, friction with the air makes his clothes smoulder). Muybridge's work with motion can be seen in this way, as a new visual synthesis: unlike Marey's pre-cinematic photo-gun, which took pictures at set intervals, Muybridge's photographs are produced by trip-wires, producing a sequence directly linked to the person's or animal's speed: they register the way a body *inhabits* space and time. The early twentieth century even sees the origins of the 'scanned' image: a technique which depicts a body as no one ever sees it, in a synthetic 360-degree view.

Such techniques reconfigure looking, but we cannot see them as detached from human vision. The point often made about photography and film is that they remove from the novel the necessity of representation, and this, the argument runs, stimulates the modernist investment in what remains specific to literature: language. That claim is only partially true. As Nancy Armstrong argues, the modernist declaration of realism's obsolescence, typified by Virginia Woolf's 'Mr. Bennett and Mrs. Brown', in fact conceals a continuity founded on a shared, 'post-photographic' understanding of the real in which the image is absorbed into the text. Or as Sara Danius puts it, one response to 'the marginalization of epistemic mandates of the human senses in an age where technological devices increasingly claim priority' is the 'internalization of technological modes for reproducing the real' (2002: 23). Danius sees this effect in Joyce's stress on seeing and hearing for their own sake, liberated from the needs of representation; his radicalism lies in registering all sensation as atomized quanta, denaturalized and beyond the possibility of integration. Joyce thus refuses to comment on modernity as rupture, simply articulating its sensory modes. His incorporation of advertising, telephony and the streetcar into his construction of perception represents a naturalization of technological modernity.

The isolation of different senses in discrete media does have particular effects, including dissonances between public and private modes. In John Dos Passos's *U.S.A.* this is represented by the four modes of narration: third-person narration, 'Newsreels', journalistic biographies, and the 'Camera Eye'. It incorporates media most directly in the 'Newsreels', which in their disconnectedness and typography suggest the dispersal of the newspaper page (they preclude easy ordering and integration, forcing the eye to wander). The difficulty of attention in the modern 'streamed' media is suggested in Newsreel XI, interspersing arriving news of the *Titanic* with popular songs, speeches, a society wedding. The 'Camera Eye' sections – the subjective, autobiographical mode, initially set in childhood – suggest photography only in the sense of fragments of the available archive, storage, Bergson's *memoire involuntaire*; the photograph becomes a flashing up of disconnected moments.

The photograph, in Bergson's account, reifies and objectifies the flow of time. But as Elena Galtieri argues, this releases representation from historicity, producing a new form of temporality which is abstract, a–chronological, and whose rhythms can be technologically modulated (Murphet 2003: 168). For the Surrealists (and in Walter Benjamin's notion of the 'optical unconscious') photography is important because it bypasses the perceptual apparatus. It is thus able to deliver a shock: to open up the unseen, to persist and haunt. In his 'Little History of Photography' (1931) Benjamin insists that the photograph, in its contingency and inclusiveness, stimulates the 'politically educated eye':

No matter how artful the photographer, no matter how carefully posed his subject, the beholder feels an irresistible urge to search such a picture for the tiny spark of contingency, of the here and now, with which reality (so to speak) has seared the subject, to find the inconspicuous spot where in the immediacy of that long-forgotten moment the future nests so eloquently that we, looking back, may rediscover it.

(1999: 510)

The literary correlative of this urge is perhaps not easy to see; arguably it rests on a sense of potential dislocation rather than order (linked to Benjamin's notion of allegory) – detail which the text cannot integrate; montage and the incorporation of the 'document' into the text. An example is Muriel Rukeyser's 1938 sequence on the victims of West Virginia silica mining 'The Book of the Dead', which strips in committee reports, statements, stock listings; and throughout uses the camera to signal an enlargement of sight amidst the 'photograph of power' which is America. This is from the concluding poem:

> Defense is sight; widen the lens and see
> standing over the land myths of identity,
> new signals, processes:

> Alloys begin : certain dominant metals.
> Deliberate combines add new qualities,
> sums of new uses.

> . . . . .

> Carry abroad the urgent need, the scene,
> to photograph and to extend the voice
> to speak this meaning.

> (1992: 40)

The stress on integrating voice and vision points towards the medium which impacts most directly on modernism: cinema. Cinema offered conflicting possibilities: both the commodification of experience and leisure; and an experimental vision, an immediacy which the artist might emulate. The latter is most readily associated with the Soviet cinema, both in its practice and manifestoes; and with Surrealist writings on film. This is not the place for a survey of modernist engagement with film, a huge topic which would run from Futurism and Joyce's attempt to set up the Volta cinema in Dublin in 1909–10 to the rush of writers to Hollywood after the arrival of sound. Neither do I wish to discuss the incorporation of 'filmic' techniques (the tracking shot etc.) into literature. Rather what is at stake in placing literature alongside film is a series of analogies suggesting ways of rethinking textuality. I will consider particular aspects of cinema: notions of cinematic writing; animation; and the cinematic body.

First, writing. As a number of critics have suggested, cinema offered many modernists a new, universal language of images. As Eisenstein commented in *Close Up* in 1929, cinema was 'working out *its own language, its own speech, its own vocabulary, its own imagery*' (1929: 11) – a language he described as hieroglyphic. The notion of the film hieroglyph expresses the dream of a direct, unmediated language, freed from the play of linguistic *différence*. It is often traced to the American poet Vachel Lindsay's *The Art of the Moving Picture* (1915); but arguably it is already present in the notes on Chinese poetry made by Ernest Fenollosa before 1906, used by Pound to build his imagist aesthetics: with 'something like the vividness of a moving picture', the succession of idiograms conveys 'cross-sections cut through actions, snap-shots' (cited Kenner 1971: 289). Later Eugene Jolas's *transition* aimed to produce what Michael North calls a 'logocinema', typified by the electric sign and the radiant speech of the wireless (North 2002). Bob Brown, the American poet associated with *transition*, noted that photographic composition radically alters the possibility of the page, and in 1930 imagined 'Readies' which could be viewed as coloured typefaces speeding before the eye. In the work of Duchamp, Moholy-Nagy and others, the word itself begins to strain towards the status of moving image.

The second topic I want to discuss is cinema as animation. One of Bergson's main points of attack was what he called the 'cinematographic' model of time, by which he meant the work of his colleague at the Collège de France, E.-J. Marey, whose filmic analyses eliminated, for Bergson, the actual flow of time. But the cinema itself is a mode of representation eminently describable in more positive terms derived from Bergson, since it locks the reader into time-experience; indeed into a mode of being. This is a point made by Robert Nichols – war poet, broadcaster and novelist who worked in Hollywood – in a 1929 essay, 'The Movies as Medium':

For on the pseudo-actualistic screen we can see the very tissue which is the body of Bergson's Creative Evolution in *being*. Existence in time, according to Bergson, is life. In real change there are no states at all; everything is a finite, moving present. That living, moving present is exactly what the actualistic screen can give us, for a man looking at that screen lives, so to speak, in only that present which the screen offers him from moment to moment. Such a man does not seem to himself to *move in time* (he thinks of neither past nor future), because the rate of flow on the screen is parallel to and identical in pace with the flow of his own existence. This equilibrium has never hitherto been possible in visual art . . . The implications of this for a truly philosophical art are enormous.

(1929: 160)

The 'implications' include a hypnotic fixity of the kind that many commentators on film noted; but more importantly presentation rather than representation – since the distance involved in representation is collapsed into a 'parallel' existence. Nichols focuses on 'visual flow'; the principle that 'the nearer the artist comes to using the medium as the "movie" cartoon uses it today, the more correct will the use of the medium be, in that he will have incarnated what he deems characteristic in the story in what is characteristic of the camera's visual flow' (1929: 149). This is to say that the heart of cinema is *animation* rather than representation – the creation of a form of life, a flow of being separate from reality.

These comments on animation are illustrated by the work of the 'direct' film-maker Len Lye in this period, making films for the innovative GPO (the British post office) film unit. Lye's films, drawn by hand or stencilled onto film, sometimes used documentary stock, have an unforgettable vibrational intensity: lines, colours, shapes and even words dance across the screen in what he saw as a form of life. Animation is also implicit in Virginia Woolf's short 1926 essay 'The Cinema':

at a performance of Dr Caligari the other day, a shadow shaped like a tadpole suddenly appeared at one corner of the screen. It swelled to an immense size, quivered, bulged, and sank back again into nonentity. For a moment it seemed to embody some monstrous, diseased imagination of the lunatic's brain. For a moment it seemed as if thought could be conveyed by shape more effectively than by words.

If an accident could create this effect, Woolf comments, 'the cinema has within its grasp innumerable symbols for emotions that have so far failed to find expression. Terror has, besides its ordinary forms, the shape of a tadpole; it burgeons, bulges, quivers, disappears' (1993a: 56). This is to say that what film creates – even as accident – is more significant than what it records. Woolf describes film as 'life as it is when we have no part in it'. As Laura Marcus points out, the 'Time Passes' section of *To the Lighthouse* can be seen as an experiment in the animation of the object world (Donald 1998: 154). The stress on the play of surfaces and the eye which 'like a butterfly . . . seeks colour and basks in warmth' in Woolf's 1930 essay 'Street Haunting', with its relentless flow of perceptions burying the past, similarly demands a cinematic framing: this is a kind of looking predicated on mobility and flow. In a parallel way, Keith Williams has recently suggested that

Joyce reflects early cinema's fascination with animism and 'autokinesis' – such as with endowing objects with life by stop-motion. In the 'Circe' episode, with its talking soap, boot, and fly-button, and fantastic metamorphoses, Williams sees a history of the move from vaudeville and music-hall to early film, with specific references to Méliès and others (Murphet 2003: 96–124). Chaplin's *Modern Times*, for all that it ostensibly critiques the alignment of bodies and machines (as in the feeding-machine sequence), bears witness to an open secret: the fact that the cinema is an animation machine, creating technologically-informed laughter.

My third topic is the cinematic body. For many commentators, film offered a prosthetic extension and investigation of looking: visual tricks, backwards motion, close up, slow-motion, stop-frame animation, and so on. At the same time, after an experimental phase up to around 1915, film was increasingly yoked to realism via the continuity rules associated with D. W. Griffith, its excesses curbed, and the star system established as a means of stabilizing and exploiting cinematic desire. In 'Acinema', Jean-François Lyotard describes cinema as a technology which takes as its aim the management of libidinal energy:

Just as the libido must renounce its perverse outflow to propagate the species through a normal genital sexuality allowing the constitution of a 'sexual body' having that sole end, so the film produced by an artist working in capitalist industry . . . springs from the effort to eliminate aberrant movements, useless expenditures, differences of pure consumption. This film is composed like a unified and propagating body, a fecund and assembled whole transmitting instead of losing what it carries.

(1989: 172)

This cinematic body is what Nathanael West gives to Faye Greener in *The Day of the Locust* (1940): both generic (Faye is a Buzby Berkeley blond) and impenetrable. Faye is described as egg-like in her self-sufficiency, recalling the 'body-without-organs' of Deleuze and Guattari: both a desiring machine which cannot be configured within the norms of heterosexuality (homosexuality, pederasty and bestiality circulate in the text) and a detached splinter of Hollywood's mode of desire, which you pay to look at.

If silent film can be linked *both* to the Taylorized study of bodies-in-motion conducted by Frank and Lilian Gilbreth and to the unconscious, then sound film seems to suggest a 'middle way': a social world. In eliminating the unconscious dimension, sound was seen by many, including the modernists who wrote for the film journal *Close Up*, as a debasement of the experimental 'language' of silent film (Armstrong 1998: 226–34; North 2002). From the point of view of the industry, this was a further step towards the total economy described by Lyotard. It is interesting that one of the prime movers in the development of sound was Waddill Catchings, the lawyer for Goldman Sachs who raised the money for Warners' gamble on the new technology. Catchings was an advocate of a consumption-led economy. *The Road to Plenty* (1928), which he co-authored, lays out a Keynesian programme in dialogues on a train involving a manufacturer, a social-ist, a lawyer, and an economist. The key figure is 'the businessman', outlin-ing what he calls an 'Automatic Production–Consumption Theory' which will overcome the problem of economic cycles: consumption can be primed public works projects which place money in the hands of consumers when-ever recession threatens (1928: 173). Catchings wishes for a 'living wage', and even a 'cultural wage' – that is a wage which guarantees an excess, a component of spending which is pleasure rather than necessity. It is film itself which most successfully realized this desire.

SOUND

Modernity is usually described in terms of visual regimes. But sound is an important component of thinking about modernism. Because sound and voice are embodied and social, many famous moments of modernist outrage have been sonic: Jarry's *Ubu Roi* striding on stage to shout 'merdre'; the word 'shifts' in Synge's *Playboy of the Western World* causing a riot in Dublin; the Futurist sound machines (*intonarumori*) at the Coliseum in London; the uproar at Stravinsky's *Rite of Spring*; Vachel Lindsay's arrival on the Chicago poetry scene performing 'Congo' at a dinner in honour of W. B. Yeats in 1914, with its bawled chorus 'Boomlay, boomlay, boomlay, BOOM'.

Secondly, if modernist aesthetics stress embodiment and contact, sound has a special status. In Victorian philosophy and psychology, hearing was seen as less susceptible to error and illusion. Schopenhauer linked hearing to truth, and (in contrast to earlier thinkers) privileged music over other arts, since it involved a direct transcription of Being – life itself – rather than its representation. Rhythm was, Havelock Ellis insisted, a fundamental property of 'neuro-muscular tissue', music written into the body and its experience. Hearing immerses us in a world which is more immediate and less controllable than that of vision.

At the same time, sound is dissipative: it radiates outwards, echoes, escapes; unlike the image it is bound to the flow of time. The dream of making good these losses is articulated by the Professor in Djuna Barnes's last published story, 'The Perfect Murder' (1942):

after all, his Mistress was *Sound*, that great band of sound that had escaped the human throat for over two thousand years. Could it be re-captured (as Marconi thought it might) what would come to the ear? No theories for or against; no words of praise or of blame, only a vast terrible lamentation which would echo like the 'Baum!' of the Malabar Caves. For after all what does man say when it comes right down to it? 'I love, I fear, I hunger, I die.'

(1996: 439)

The possibility of recovering voice is, of course, offered by the phonograph – a device often described, in its early history, as bringing the dead to life (the automatic player piano offers real-time storage even earlier: the Angelus

in 1897 was advertised as featuring the *actual keying* – the ghostly presence
– of performers like Rachmaninov). Does phonography effect a shift in the
representation of sound, akin to that created by new visual media? Douglas
Kahn suggests it does:

Phonography foregrounded the parameters of *a sound* and *all sound*, presented the
possibility of incorporating all sound into cultural forms, shifted cultural practices
away from a privileging of utterance towards a greater inclusion of audition, placed
the voice of presence into the contaminated realm of writing, and linked textuality and literacy with sound through inscriptive practices.

(1999: 70)

The trace of the gramophone needle registers rather than filters (unlike the
ear), reconfiguring the relationship between 'noise' and meaning – noise
considered both in its commonplace sense and in the technical sense of that
which interferes with a message. It is perhaps easiest to see this in music,
where the discrete tones of the western scale are replaced, in Futurist practice, by Russolo's sirens and *intonarumori*; and where extra-musical noises
(cars, aeroplanes, street-cries) are incorporated. Russolo stressed the richness
of noise versus the abstraction and selectiveness of music; as Kahn comments, 'Music and sound thus could not be separated . . . because noise was
deeply imbedded in musical materiality' (Kahn 1999: 81). The space between
notes (the siren's glissandi) could be said to correspond to the *temps perdu*
of involuntary memory; the flow of experience as noise. Ezra Pound
defended George Antheil's music on a similar basis: it includes low frequencies that 'are merely noises that have not been considered as sonority'
(1996: 74), destroying the genteel ideals Pound associates with 'female
neurasthenic headaches': 'It is not for me a question of taking an impression of machine noise and reproducing it in the concert hall or of making
any more noise, but composing, governing the noise that we've got' (1996:
76). This might seem like a justification for the *Cantos* – 'composing' the
history we've got, including the engine-room rumble, the machines of
production.

   'All sound' is implicit in the sonic world of the modern novel. In *Ulysses*,
off-stage sounds constantly drift into the text, registering an acoustic environment. This is Bloom preparing to go to the shop, beginning with the
cat's 'Mrkgnao!': 'He listened to her licking lap . . . On quietly creaky boots
he went up the staircase . . . He said softly in the bare hall: – I am going
round the corner. Be back in a minute. And when he had heard his voice
say it he added: – you don't want anything for breakfast? A sleepy soft grunt
answered: – Mn. No. She did not want anything. He heard then a warm
heavy sigh, softer, as she turned over and the loose brass quoits of the bed-
stead jingled' (1993: 54). This density makes *Ulysses* a phonographic text.

   Kahn's comments on phonographic *writing* echo those of Theodor
Adorno. For all that Adorno saw technological reproduction as decontex-
tualizing and commodifying performance, it does, he admitted in 'The Form

of the Phonograph Record', save something: 'The dead art rescues the ephemeral and perishing art as the only art alive'– perishing because in Adorno's dialectical view technological modernity is ending the tradition of classical music: 'If the productive force of music has expired in the phonograph records, if the latter have not produced a form through their technology, they instead transform the most recent sound of old feelings into an archaic text of knowledge to come' (2002: 279–80). He adds that 'the phonograph record's most profound justification' is that it 'reestablishes by the very means of reification an age-old, submerged and yet warranted relationship: that between music and *writing*' (2002: 279).

The musical 'writing' described by Adorno is realized in the digital era. But within modernism we can see forms of sonic inscription: the collage in the works of the American composer Charles Ives in the period 1910–20, in which snatches of popular song compete with Debussy; in 'From Hanover Square North, at the end of a Tragic Day, the Voices of the People Again Arose' this cacophony is linked to the cityscape. Or consider the inscription of voice in Carl Sandburg's *Chicago Poems* (1916). Throughout the volume Sandburg enacts a struggle to represent the city – types, crowds – in which the gaze and recorded speech are the dominant motifs. In 'Passers-By' he recalls the faces which 'flash' from the crowd, amid voices which 'blend / To form the city's afternoon roar'. This sonic mass is individuated in terms of descriptions of throats, mouths and lips 'written over with strivings', concluding with an image which renders the crowd a soundstream registered by the poet:

> Yes,
> Written on
> Your mouths
> And your throats
> I read them
> When you passed by.
> (1994: 6)

Finally, it is worth noting Adorno's comments on the archiving of a dying tradition in relation to modernism's construction of 'folk' utterance. A good example is Sterling Brown's 'Ma Rainey' (1932), a poem which seems to describe a tight compact of shared experience involving singer, audience and the poet: 'O Ma Rainey, / Sing yo' song; / Now you's back / Whah you belong, / Git way inside us, / Keep us strong . . .' (1996: 62–3). But the poem makes clear that Ma's location is mobile; conditioned, implicitly, by her status as *recording artist*, with audiences assembled by mass transport:

> Folks from anyplace
> Miles aroun',
> From Cape Giradeau,
> Poplar Bluff,
> Flocks in to hear

> Ma do her stuff,
> Comes flivverin' in,
> Or ridin' mules,
> Or packed in trains

The category of the 'folk' is itself a product of the interface of modernity and an imagined past, mediated by the desire to record as much as possible of a vanishing world. Brown's poem offers a collage of voices and, at one point, what reads like a *vox pop* interview; it is a media experience.

FAULKNER AND RECORDING TECHNOLOGIES

I want to end with a general example; one whose work is not often discussed in this relation, William Faulkner. The way in which technological modernity relates to the literary text is often determined by local contexts: technology means different things in Dorset, Manchester, or New York. In the case of the American South, uneven development represented by the exclusion of technology was foundational to slavery and its aftermath. In *Absalom, Absalom!* (1936) Faulkner explores the relationship between the labour value of the body central to slavery and demands of technological modernity inherent in the New Deal (Godden 1997). In *The Sound and the Fury* (1929) it is the thin tread of the telegraph wire and the tape of the stock ticker which brings market reports south, a vital link to the wider world. And in *Light in August* (1932), a few years before the Lomaxes and WPA-funded researchers were to fan out across the South seeking 'folk' material, Faulkner compares fading memory to a gramophone record, 'familiar only because of the worn threading which blurred the voices' (1960: 137). The voice of Doc Hines and the 'dead voice' of his wife cease 'as if the machine had run down in midrecord' (1960: 279–80), suggesting their status as the echoes of a traumatic past which has marooned them in time like the stopped clock in Faulkner's story 'Barn Burning'. In a text fascinated by ghostly phantoms and even mediumship, the detached voice is one figure for its central character, Joe Christmas, whose origin is unknowable.

Faulkner's *As I Lay Dying* (1930) offers an expanded comment on media. The novella's fifteen characters revolve around the dying and dead Addie Bundren, her rotting corpse returned to her family grave in Jefferson. Her vision of the world is articulated in the soliloquy placed in her dead mouth at the centre of the novella, one of the most astonishing pieces of writing in the modernist canon. For Addie, the linguistic order is dependent on masculine control and is evacuated by the unspeakable space which is female sexuality. She thinks of her husband Anse's name:

Why are you Anse. I would think about his name until after a while I could see the word as a shape, a vessel, and I would watch him liquefy and flow into it like cold molasses flowing out of the darkness into the vessel, until the jar stood full and motionless: a significant shape profoundly without life like an empty door frame; and then I would find I had forgotten the name of the jar. I would think: The shape of my body where I used to be a virgin is in the shape of a   and I couldn't think *Anse*, couldn't remember *Anse*.

(1996: 161)

The implication is that the patriarchal language is deathly, empty, 'just sounds' in the mouths of the dead. Moreover the structure of the family itself partakes of the same emptiness, the arbitrary connection of signifier and signified:

And then he [Anse] died. He did not know he was dead. I would lie by him in the dark, hearing the dark land talking of God's love and His beauty and His sin; hearing the dark voicelessness in which the words are the deeds, and the other words that are not deeds, that are just the gaps in people's lacks, coming down like the cries of the geese out of the wild darkness in the old terrible nights, fumbling at the deeds like orphans to whom are pointed out in a crowd two faces and told, That is your father, your mother.

The 'deeds' here include both adultery and the pleasure she locates in her children: that which cannot be represented in the patriarchal economy of the household. The simultaneous inescapability and randomness of family romance – that we are thrown into our families without choice – is figured as a linguistic predicament.

At the end of the novel, Addie is replaced by a voiceless new wife ('"Meet Mrs Bundren"', he says') who comes with a 'graphophone' [*sic*] – an instrument of pleasure and reproduction, the path to a new consumerism: 'everytime a new record would come from the mail order and us sitting in the house in the winter, listening to it'. Music is rendered as a graphic trace, a language which Addie's soliloquy reveals as empty and mechanical. *As I Lay Dying* also includes an outsider within the family, Darl, whose sections of the narration are given a privileged status. What is attached to him often represents (and on one occasion is labelled as) a kind of telepathy: he can see things when he is not present, he has a tele-vision. In this, and in his war experience in France, he is close to the author. Since the coming of the new wife and the 'graphophone' are explicitly equated with his departure for the asylum, the text offers an account of modernity as the evacuation of experience.

This suggests that the 'open' archiving of experience, the copious accumulations produced by technological modernity, transferred by analogy to the novel, was not uncontested. Thomas Hardy – whose own novels are untidy enough – worried that the novel was 'gradually losing artistic form . . . and becoming a spasmodic inventory of items' (Hardy 1984: 309). Frank Swinnerton writes of Richardson's *Pilgrimage* as simply an accumulation of mess:

. . . there are limits to the curiosity of man, and for me 'Pilgrimage' passes beyond them. One is overwhelmed by the multitude of little things which Miriam notices in the course of her journey through life. They do not compose into a picture, but are like the collections of a lifetime, a boxful of scraps of old silk and stuff such as hoarding women gather and leave behind at death.

(1938: 403)

The gendered polemic is palpable, but equally interesting is the association of the corpse and an unedited naturalism (an association also deployed by Lewis in his attack on Stein's 'doll-like deadness'). We can follow Swinnerton a little further on this subject. His discussion of Richardson and others in a chapter headed 'Post-Freud' climaxes in a discussion of Joyce. Linking him to 'the men, journalists, *entrepreneurs*, and the like, who take a professionally knowing view of everything that goes on in the world', he again accuses the author of a deathly accumulation:

They know the *argot* of every language, the drinks and bywords of every nation, the 'shop' of every profession, the sewage of every mind. They are without reverence, hard as stone, proud of their knowingness and exhibitionary of it, but at heart wearied to death because they are without illusions. They automatically and professionally notice and remember forever headlines and solecisms in newspapers, the clichés of barmaids, slips made by common, genteel and ridiculous persons, smells, lingerie, betrayals of vulgarity, scandals about well-known persons, and the *faux pas* of ingénues.

(1938: 433)

'Automatically and professionally' is the keynote here. The novelist is depicted as a storage-device: 'mimicry and impersonation' are, he adds, Joyce's strengths. Richardson similarly makes 'no attempt . . . to extract significance from her experience; and so the work is as little comprehensive [*sic*] as a tape-machine'. On that note of protest – which can be read as an investigation of modernity's engagement with new media – we can end.

6 The Vibrating World: Science, Spiritualism, Technology

Literary representation in the era of realism and naturalism closely allied itself with the forensic habits and objectivism of science, including the human sciences (sociology, psychology, criminology). But at the turn of the century both the world which science depicts and the way in which science conceived the knowledge it generated were changing rapidly. The cultural implications of scientific and technological change are the subject of this chapter. But one must first offer a caveat: scientific developments, as philosophers of science like Bruno Latour have argued, cannot be seen as independent of culture. Rather, they are an expression of the culture which produces them, enabled by its forms of thought and supported by the institutions which give meaning to its methodologies, representations and conclusions. Einstein *is* a modernist in his background (*fin de siècle* Vienna), in his models (trains moving across time zones), and in the way he was represented (the genius-iconoclast). We should not read literary texts in terms of a unidirectional absorption of scientific ideas; science and literature lie in the same cultural field. For this reason spiritualism, a culturally specific form of science, is considered here.

ENERGY

Late nineteenth-century science is dominated by one term: energy. In the work of James Clerk Maxwell and others electricity, magnetism and electromagnetic waves are unified within a physics in which energy and work are central. The study of thermodynamics associated with William Thomson (Lord Kelvin) and Hermann von Helmholtz elaborated the laws of the conservation of energy and of entropy which, together, implied a universe in which energy existed in organized localities or nodes, but only against a background of the dispersal or 'heat-death' explored in texts like Wells's *The Time Machine* (1895) and Conrad's *The Secret Agent* (1907). D. H. Lawrence struggles against this world in his writing, fascinated both by entropy and the struggle for definition.

Modern physics challenged materialist thinking in which the universe is seen in terms of the mechanical action of solid bodies. Instead it is reconceived as a flux of force-fields and particles in motion through them. The

1890s, in particular, saw physics enter a revolutionary phase, with the discovery of radiation, X-rays, and the first real understanding of atomic structure. In the work of Rutherford, matter itself became insubstantial, electrons whirling through empty space – something one might slip through like Wells's time-traveller. In order to conceptualize electromagnetic waves as passing through a medium rather than empty space, the sea of particles known as the 'ether' was be postulated; but the Michelson-Morely experiment (1888) cast doubts even on the ether's existence.

The history of the abandonment of the ether suggests a declining need for a material substratum. The discovery of radioactivity was a further challenge to the materialist world-view: matter was reduced to energy in space, itself implicated in thermodynamic decay; acquiring in the 'half-life' a temporal as well as a spatial dimension. Einstein proposed a general equivalence of matter and energy, and exploded the assumptions of Euclidian geometry, demonstrating that relatively positioned frames of reference determine all measurements of space and time – which is to say there is no point of reference 'outside' the frame against which motion can be measured. In Einstein's physics space wraps itself around objects, and time seems to slow as velocity increases. Frames of reference could be multiplied, as in the multidimensional (non-Euclidian) geometries developed by Reimann and others: an important point of reference for Cubism. Quantum physics – inaugurated by Max Planck's discovery of discontinuous transitions in radiation in 1900, but having its major phase in the 1920s – struck a further blow against the idea of a 'hard' and mechanical universe, proposing that atoms must be understood statistically, and that the energies involved in particle collisions and other phenomena should be seen in terms of units (quanta) rather than a continuum. The quantum universe is dominated by noise, uncertainty, a cloudy clamour distant from the 'real' as we see it.

The result was a universe which could only be imagined. Hypotheses about matter at the limits of the observable had a tentative air: what was the status of a 'model' like James Clerk Maxwell's visualization of the ether as tiny whirling cogs or vortices? Indeed an important current of thinking supported the view that the world could not be isolated from our accounts of it, and proposed that scientific models were heuristic, useful rather than descriptive, and that fundamental notions like causation are linked to human perceptual habits. Ernst Mach argued that scientific 'laws' could be considered economical ways of describing observations. This anti-realist or 'Descriptionist' position was expounded by Karl Pearson in his *Grammar of Science* (1892), in which science becomes at best a series of rational protocols to overcome the contingency of human perception. The implication was that science's formalisms describe reality within a relationship of analogy rather than direct correspondence (Ezra Pound was to derive similar ideas from Fenollosa's writing on the ideogram). As Gillian Beer notes, the demonstrations of popularizers like John Tyndall – who would create a blue sky in a lecture-hall – reinforced the sense that science was a representation. Quantum theory was to reinforce the idea that different models were applicable to the same phenomena: as Louis de Broglie confirmed in the early 1920s, if light could behave either as particles or as waves, depending on the experiment, and required *both* terms for its description, then its 'nature' could not be conclusively linked to either model. The fact that in everyday life Newtonian mechanics worked perfectly well, with Einstein's effects only being observable in extreme situations – near the speed of light; light flowing past the sun – reinforced the sense that received accounts of time and space were at best adequate fictions.

A world-view in which mechanical, relativistic, perspectival and para-doxical models compete is part of the crisis of modernism. Bergson, for example, saw physics as justifying his assertion that 'homogeneous space is not logically anterior, but posterior to material things' – it is 'like an infi-nitely fine network which we stretch beneath material continuity to render ourselves master of it, to decompose it according to the plan of our activ-ities and needs' (1998: 231). The dissolving of materiality into the categories of energy, field and radiation, creates the world explored in Thomas Mann's *The Magic Mountain*, with its X-rayed bodies and uneven temporality. Or take a more figurative example, the description of the final moments between Adela and Fielding in Forster's *A Passage to India* (1924), its keynote the contrasts of scale and insolidity of modern knowledge:

Both man and woman were at the height of their powers – sensible, honest, even subtle. They spoke the same language, and held the same opinions, and the variety of age and sex did not divide them. Yet they were dissatisfied. When they agreed, 'I want to go on living a bit', or, 'I don't believe in God', the words were followed by a curious backwash as though the universe had displaced itself to fill up a tiny void, or as though they had seen their own gestures from an immense height – dwarfs talking, shaking hands and assuring each other that they stood on the same footing of insight.

(1983: 239)

Forster's sense of human understanding as carved out of space, tiny and con-tingent, was widely shared; his delicate inversion of the *topos* of moderns as 'dwarfs standing on the shoulders of giants' (used by Newton) suggests a radical uncertainty.

In looking at literature in the new scientific culture, three interpenet-rating categories can be deployed: texts which register shock; texts which incorporate the new science into their depiction of the world; and texts which deploy science at the level of poetics. Shock is most famously reg-istered in the American historian Henry Adams's essay 'The Dynamo and the Virgin' (1900). Reflecting on the Paris exposition, Adams points out that the giant dynamo, X-rays, liquid oxygen and radioactivity exceed the old scale of human measure (feet, horse-power):

In these seven years man had translated himself into a new universe which had no common scale of measurement with the old. He had entered a supersensual world, in which he could measure nothing except by chance collisions of movements imperceptible to his senses, perhaps even imperceptible to his instruments, but perceptible to each other, and so to some known ray at the end of the scale. [The Physicist] Langley seemed prepared for anything, even for an indeterminable number of universes interfused – physics stark mad in metaphysics.

(1973: 381–2)

Adams insists on procedural consequences for the humanities: the historian can no longer write the old narratives of cause and effect. Instead he must use his own intellect as an instrument, following 'the track of the energy' and registering the 'fields of force' attached to historical symbols like the Virgin. It is on this basis that, in the chapter entitled 'A Dynamic Theory of History', he plots history as intellectual autobiography. The simultaneous objectivism (a stance modelled on science) and subjectivism (the self as instrument) of this position, as well as the emphasis on the work as following a force-field, makes this a model for modernist texts. Compare Pound: 'Valid scientific thought consists in following as closely as possible the actual and entangled lines of force as they pulse through things' (1969: 12).

Shock is also registered in this refusal from D. H. Lawrence's *The Lost Girl* (1920):

'You don't understand! I want to be *myself*. And I'm *not* myself. I'm just torn to pieces by *Forces*. It's horrible –'
'Well, it's not my fault. I didn't make the universe,' said Alvina. 'If you have to be torn to pieces by forces, well, you have. Other forces will put you together again.'
'I don't want them to. I want to be myself. I don't want to be nailed together like a chair, with a hammer.'

(1920: 309)

The speaker, Effie, describes life as 'a mass of forces', and this massing against and within the human fascinates Lawrence, positing an otherness at the core of the self. In a famous letter of 1914 he asserts that 'that which is physic – non-human, in humanity, is more interesting to me than the old-fashioned human element' (Kolocotroni 1998: 407). Lawrence had been reading F. T. Marinetti, the founder of Futurism, and adds that 'what is interesting in the laugh of the woman is the same as the binding of the molecules of steel or their action in heat: it is the inhuman will, call it physiology, or like Marinetti – physiology of matter, that fascinates me.' This leads directly to these comments on the self:

You mustn't look in my novel for the old stable *ego* of the character. There is another *ego*, according to whose action the individual is unrecognizable, and passes through, as it were, allotrophic states which it needs a deeper sense than any we've been used to exercise, to discover are states of the same single radically unchanged element. (Like as diamond and coal are the same pure single element of carbon . . .)

The allotrophic state is borrowed from science: the term distinguishes between substance (the carbon atom) and structure (the arrangement of molecules which differentiates coal, graphite and diamond). But scholars have pointed out that the metaphor has a more specific source: F. W. Myers's *Human Personality and its Survival of Bodily Death* (1903), a classic of psychic research. Lawrence shares with Myers a sense that the real self is hidden, mysterious and shifting. John Rodker commented in 1926 that 'Certain writers, among them very consciously Mr Lawrence, do seem to reach out to the prey and store the answering vibrations as radium emanations are stored' (1926: 76) – though he singled out 'the Russians as the supreme registering instruments – masters of the art of capturing remote vibrations' (1926: 90). He was, perhaps, responding to Gudrun and Gerald in *Women in Love*: 'He was wonderful like a piece of radium to her. She felt she could consume herself and know *all*, by means of this fatal, living metal' (1960: 446). Rodker's own paired poems 'Hymn to Heat' and 'Hymn to Cold' similarly play among the atoms, registering sexuality and death as a physics:

> Mother
> Transcend us   renew us
> and atom from atom will creep –
> viscous –
> and like a snake uncoiling,
> slow – then fast and faster
> desire well up in us.
>
> (1996: 73)

Like Lawrence's Effie, neo-classical modernism sought to stabilize the flux of existence. As Daniel Albright suggests, some – most vehemently Lewis and Pound – espoused a 'hard' modernism, rejecting the relativistic, de-materialized universe of Einstein in favour of a return to Leibniz's 'monad', an indissoluble unit of being which was also a unit of consciousness (1997: 14–15). The image can be read in this way: as an attempt to stabilize the fundamental unit of poetics; as both a unit of perception (capable of instantaneous transmission) and a unit of being (grounding the reality of the poem). Lewis repeatedly attacks the Bergsonian stress on 'life', 'dynamism' and 'progress', as well as the philosopher Whitehead's world of motion and subjectivity, stressing permanence, concreteness and 'deadness' as necessary to the artist.

But Pound and Lewis were in this respect working against the grain of modern physics, in which substance is constantly dissolved into energy; and in Pound's work there are powerful counter-currents (the vortex, for example). Decay itself could be a form of liberation. In *Paterson* Williams uses radioactivity as a counter in a complex debate about the status of money, labour and value which runs something like this: money 'sequestered' in usury is a base metal, a mere accumulation akin, in bodily terms, to cancer; but radioactivity is fecundity (personified in the pregnant Marie Curie), an internal difference which splits the atom of being and leads to increase, healing and 'credit', the creation of value:

Uranium : basic thought – leadward
Fractured : radium : credit
(1983: 185)

There is also a political valency to radium, since Williams can write of who
oppose change 'the Gamma rays / will eat their bastard bones'.

Many modernists sensed that new discoveries demanded new ways of
thinking about the text. One of the most pervasive organizational metaphors
in modernism, running from Mallarmé's arrangement of words in space in
Un coup de dés to the aesthetics of Jackson Pollock, is that of the *field* –
conceived as the dynamic space of the page or as the space of action.
Albright argues that the modernist poem emanates from a 'deep field' in
which 'pre-textual elements' like the symbol and image are charged entities. *The Waste Land* 'aspires to a state of transubstantiation in which the
pre-text is physically present in the text; a state of radioactivity in which
the rays emitted by symbols, images, ideograms could register directly on
the reader's sense-organs' (1997: 7). The Russian painter Mikhail Larionov's
'Rayonism' similarly founded itself on 'the theory of radiation' and sought
to capture 'the new shapes created between tangible forms by their own
radiation' (cited Weston 1996: 143). Or consider Williams's *Spring and All*
(1923), which depicts a bombardment on the word which loosens it from
its array: 'Sometimes I speak of imagination as a force, an electricity or a
medium, a place. It is immaterial which: for whether it is the condition of
a place or a dynamization its effect is the same: to free the world of fact
from the impositions of 'art' . . . and to liberate the man to act in whatever
direction his disposition leads' (1970: 150).

Williams believed that Einstein's physics implied a new conception of
poetic form. What he later called 'composition by field' depicted poetry as
a discursive space with its own internal relations. Charles Olson followed
Williams in seeing non-Euclidian space (studied via Whitehead's *Process and
Reality*, 1929) as justifying his procedures, suggesting that the real may be
a matter of *form*: a dynamic arrangement of pathways; method is 'the science
of the path', he writes in *Letters for Origin* (1989: 106). His 1957 essay 'Equal,
That Is, to the Real Itself' spells out the implication of this view in terms
of a 'Riemannian' metrical field in which textual space bends around reality
(1997: 125). For the American poet Muriel Rukeyser the work of the theoretical physicist Willard Gibbs, often described as the founder of thermodynamics, inaugurates a 'language of process . . . of the kind of life that is
not a point-to-point movement, but a real flow in which everything is seen
as deeply related to everything else'. In *The Life of Poetry* (1949) she asserts
that the poet, scientist and mathematician seek 'a system of relations' in
which the exchange of energies is central.

Albright attempts to taxonomize these various analogies by proposing
both a 'wave model' in which the poem, novel or even literary corpus is
continuously emitted, and in which action and the verb are privileged over

the noun, and 'a particle model of literature', in which discrete units like the image are held in place by fields of force (1997: 19–20). The former is visible as early as the 'Conclusion' to Pater's *The Renaissance* (dated 1868, the year after Kelvin's vortex model), which memorably describes consciousness as an unstable confluence of forces:

Our physical life is a perpetual motion of them – the passage of the blood, the waste and repairing of the lenses of the eye, the modification of the tissues of the brain under every ray of light or sound – processes which science reduces to simpler and more elementary forces. Like the elements of which we are composed, the action of these forces extends beyond us: it rusts iron and ripens corn. Far out on every side of us those elements are broadcast, driven by many currents. . . . That clear, perpetual outline of face and limb is but an image of ours, under which we group them – a design in a web, the actual threads of which pass out beyond it. This at least of flame-like our life has, that it is but the concurrence, renewed from moment to moment, of forces parting sooner or later on their ways.

(1997: 186–7)

Hence 'that continual vanishing away, that strange, perpetual weaving and unweaving of ourselves' which is consciousness. This suggests the fluidity of Woolf's *The Waves* (1931), which has been related to her understanding of Tyndall and Einstein.

Modernism thus works within a radically altered scientific field; a world, as popularizers like Gerald Heard told their audiences, which seems to have dissolved into elegant paradox. In his essay 'Cinders', the Imagist theorist T. E. Hulme evokes James Clerk Maxwell in portraying humans as 'sorting machines', creating pockets of order in a 'cosmos [which] is only *organized* in parts; the rest is cinders' (1987: 220, 228). Those pockets of order included the laws of science themselves, as well as social fictions. It is against this background – Hulme's cinder-heap, Eliot's *Waste Land*, Wallace Stevens's 'The Man on the Dump' – that we need to see the tentative ordering of so many modernist texts. As Stevens put it in 'July Mountain', 'We live in a constellation / Of patches and of pitches, / Not in a single world . . .', adding that we are 'Thinkers without final thoughts / In an always incipient cosmos' (1997: 476). Weather is a particularly engaging metaphor for that which resists order, signalling, as Daniel Tiffany has argued, a world of shifting contingency conceptually linked to the new physics. Stevens's late poem 'Reality is an Activity of the Most August Imagination' describes a nighttime drive in Connecticut:

> There was a crush of strength in a grinding going round,
> Under the front of the westward evening star,
>
> The vigor of glory, a glittering in the veins,
> As things emerged and moved and were dissolved . . .
> (1997: 471)

This scene of transformation is described as 'approaching form' and 'suddenly denying itself away'; poetry as physics. Matter for Stevens glitters, dissolves; it is an event, a theatre; light 'encrusts' the body ('Evening without Angels'). In his essay 'Imagination as Value' he insists that only the imagination can stabilize this world, producing those temporary accommodations which we call the 'real'.

Finally, scientific sources for the emphasis on flux in modernist texts are not limited to physics. Darwinian biology also proposed a world of constant change, reflected in the writings of Marianne Moore (the printed patterns which she linked to genetics). Herbert Spencer had suggested that evolution always progressed towards states of complexity – states which Henri Bergson would read as a series of momentarily reintegrated totalities rather than 'final' outcomes. Both Bergson and the American pragmatist philosophers William James and John Dewey espoused a vitalism in which process and change are central – echoing Emerson's declaration in 'Self-Reliance' that 'Power ceases in the instance of repose; it resides in the moment of transition from a past to a new state; in the shooting of the gulf; in the darting of an aim' (1983: 271). Form is a momentary stay against chaos, a containing structure; never final and fixed.

SPIRITUALISM

We have seen Henry Adams describing matter as increasingly 'occult' and supersensual. This is to move towards another topic important to modernism: psychical research, the study of phenomena like mesmerism, telepathy, the subconscious self. It may seem odd to treat spiritualism in a chapter devoted to science and technology. But scientific thinking between 1870 and 1920 exists in close relation to psychic research: scientific writers had deep interests in borderline phenomena; and spiritualists interpreted the findings of science as confirming their own ideas about spiritual substance, telepathy, and action at a distance. In *Isis Unveiled*, Madame Blavatsky commented that 'The corner-stone of MAGIC is an intimate practical knowledge of magnetism and electricity, their qualities, correlations, and potencies' (1877: ii.588). One of her Theosophical followers, the painter Kandinsky, pointed to 'The disintegration of the soulless, materialistic life of the nineteenth century, i.e. the destruction of the very basis of matter, its fragmentation into parts and then the dissolution of those parts' as one of the foundations of the modern (Kolocotroni 1998: 275). Spiritualism describes a universe pulsating with hidden forces, in which it is possible to slide effortlessly from personal emanations to X-rays. It also has links with the reformist traditions discussed in chapter 4, including mesmerism, abolitionism and feminism. An emblematic figure is Zadel Turner Barnes. Abolitionist and temperance campaigner, writer and spiritualist, she moved from Boston to London in 1880 as a correspondent for *McCall's*, befriending Lady Wilde, Eleanor Marx and Charles Reade; among the spirits she invoked were Franz Liszt and Jack London. Her grand-daughter Djuna Barnes's work deploys some of the tropes of spiritualism – the dialogue with the dead; the obscure rituals of *Nightwood* – with an irony typical of modernist responses to such enthusiasms.

Spiritualism has its origins in a number of cultural factors: a backlash against attacks on received religion; the Victorian cult of mourning; anthropological interest in the origins of religion; science itself. The Fox Farm seances in upstate New York in 1850 initiated a wave of mediumship using table-tapping, automatic writing, the Ouija board, 'materialization', spirit-photography and other techniques. Many spiritualists believed that they were communicating with a spirit world, perhaps with other planets. But at the same time, the phenomena fitted Darwinian accounts of the mind in which it was portrayed as having atavistic survivals and unexplored potentials, and spiritualism attracted those interested in powers of mind. The Society for Psychical Research (SPR), founded by Henry Sidgwick, Frederic Myers, Edmund Gurney, William Barrett and others in 1882, set out to systematically investigate telepathy (a new coinage) and related phenomena. Its founders were respectable scientists, journalists and politicians; it had links with Bergson and Freud; and William James sponsored an American association.

The connections between modernism and spiritualism are complex and pervasive, involving both writers who were active spiritualists and many more influenced by spiritualist practice (Surette 1993; Tiffany 2000; Thurschwell 2001; Sword 2002; Luckhurst 2002). A shortlist of the former includes Yeats, H. D., Radcliffe Hall, May Sinclair as well as Georgians like Conan Doyle and Kipling; the latter Henry James, Eliot, Pound, Joyce, Woolf and Lawrence. Modernist interest in spiritualism runs the spectrum from belief to distanced reflection. The modernist for whom the subject was most important was undoubtedly W. B. Yeats. His engagement was sustained from early esoteric study to the automatic writing sessions which his wife George began a few days into their marriage in 1917. Initially an attempt to distract an uncertain husband, the automatic script expanded to the thousands of pages systematized in *A Vision* in 1925 (George Yeats, herself an adept, must be seen as the co-author). The resulting 'wisdom' flows through Yeats's late work as a cyclic philosophy of history, and a theory of creativity and artistic stance focused on ideas of sexual mystery and the 'completed' self. There are even formal traces in his texts: Arnold Goldman suggests that in the late work 'entrances and exits resemble somewhat those in the stenographic records of seances', and he sees a mediumistic tone in poems like 'The Second Coming' (1975: 186).

At the other end of the spectrum, spiritualism is a matter of traces and tones. For Mary Butts, writing on 'Ghosties and Ghoulies' in *The Bookman* in 1933, there is a continuity between William James's writings on the occult, May Sinclair's *Uncanny Tales*, Jessie Weston's *From Ritual to Romance*, and 'the bright and dark thread running through the world scene of Mr Forster' (1998: 363) – and, presumably, her own Celtic mysticism in *Ashe of Rings* (1925), with its struggle between poisoned and pure souls and hints of magic. The supernatural may simply flicker by, as in the apparition of a husband just dead in the trenches in Sinclair's *The Tree of Heaven* (1917), or Virginia Woolf's comment on the 'pursuit' of character in 'Mr. Bennett and Mrs. Brown': 'Few catch the phantom; most have to be content with a scrap of her dress or a wisp of her hair' (1992d: 319). I will highlight three inter-related issues: the issue of the subject in investigations of mediumship and multiple personality; the interpretive practices and theory of language involved in spiritualism; and the question of history.

First, the subject. The notions of action at a distance and communication in spiritualism are, as Pamela Thurschwell points out, ways of thinking about intimacy which enter the accounts of desire and identification offered by Freud and Ferenczi. Psychoanalysis shares a forgotten history with spiritualism, preoccupied with questions of dangerous proximity, the invasion of the self by others (including the dead); the possibility of telepathy encoded in the notion of 'transference' (2001: 118). In Myers's *Human Personality and its Survival of Bodily Death*, telepathy and mediumship are attributed to the 'subliminal self' – an influential pre-Freudian version of the unconscious which, unlike Freud's, is permeable and undynamic (in the sense that it is not produced by repression). Myers's work was closely related to the turn-of-the-century interest in multiple personality in Pierre Janet and others. Accounts of multiples like Morton Prince's *The Dissociation of a Personality* (1908) posit a psyche which could, like a computer, be partitioned into separate entities, with different selves able to work in the background or suddenly manifest themselves.

In this and in its fascination with telepathy, psychic research opens up a new space in which intersubjectivity and perspectivism are dominant. As Roger Luckhurst comments, 'Telepathy is the product of ambivalent modernity: spooky experiences of distance and relation, of traumatic severances and equally disturbing intimacies' (2002: 276). Niklas Luhmann insists, in what almost amounts to a tautology, that people do not communicate, only communication systems communicate – which is to say that all communication or knowledge of others is mediated by language or other signals. Telepathy offers to collapse persons into the communication system, enabling a direct linkage of selves. Woolf's work offers many examples of such effects: the unexpected flows of empathy between Septimus and Mrs Dalloway; the hidden relation between Mrs Ramsay and Lily Briscoe in *To the Lighthouse*; the overlapping minds of *The Waves*.

Perhaps unsurprisingly, then, the conceptualization of same-sex desire is also linked to telepathy – to dangerous proximity – in Freud, Henry James, H. D. and Bryher. Radcliffe Hall, the lesbian author of *The Well of Loneliness*, and Una Troubridge published extensive records of their communication with Hall's dead lover. Richard Bucke's influential *Cosmic Consciousness* (1901) singled out Whitman and his English disciple Edward Carpenter as writers who had communicated the possibility of a higher life: there is a gay subculture implicit here, in which mesmeric exchange enables the flow of desire. Conversely, consider the blockages suggested by another exchange from *A Passage to India*:

'How could she [Mrs Moore] have known what we don't?'
'Telepathy, possibly.'
The pert, meagre word fell to the ground. Telepathy? What an explanation! Better withdraw it, and Adela did so. She was at the end of her spiritual tether, and so was he [Mr Fielding]. Were there worlds beyond which they could never touch, or did all that is possible enter their consciousness? They could not tell.

(1983: 238)

As this suggests, intimacy can cause uneasiness, and even paranoia. Yeats suspected that Pound's mind was being 'rifled' by spirits. Eliot's work registers an ambivalence about female mediumship. *The Waste Land* owes much to occult sources, but they are distanced. The origins of the poem's Tarot sequence are usually said to be a dinner at the Ladies Poetry Circle at the Lyceum Club in November 1920, where Eliot was taught the tarot; it may however have been inspired by an earlier encounter with Mina Loy's 'At the Door of the House', in the 1912 *Others* anthology which Eliot reviewed (Kouidnis 1980: 34). Loy's affectionate satire on the tarot suggests a complicity with the female medium unlikely in Eliot. Spiritualism in this sense is part of the poem's struggle with femininity; with the rescuing of meaning from debased forms and disturbing intimacies.

Perhaps the most important area in which spiritualism can be related to modernism is language. Spiritualism gives rise to forms of automatic writing produced by the hand, planchette or other device. The *Proceedings of the Society for Psychical Research* published lengthy 'stenographic records of seances', often with a peculiarly literary character, combining fragmentary citation of classics, poetry, other languages, code-words, gender-switching, different voices and interruptions. Extensive footnotes tracked sources and cross-referenced topics, myths and texts alluded to in different sessions. This is from Helen de G. Verrall's 'A Further Study of the Mac Scripts', published in the *Proceedings* in 1914:

> I am he that endureth
> (*Drawing of a gate*)
> The beginning is here; the end is not yet.
> The beginning of years
> Whoso knocketh
> They are not long the weeping and the laughter
> Love and desire and hate.
> I think they have no portion in us after
> We pass the gate.

Verrall, a classics lecturer, dutifully footnotes the Psalms, the Gospels, Swinburne, and Dowson, and places this script in a sequence (Verrall 1914: 261). Such texts from the era of the SPR's 'cross-correspondences' (in which the ghost of Myers communicated through different mediums, whom he suggested should be collated) suggest a nascent theory of intertextuality – a circulation of texts in which the 'author' must be regarded as composite, transcending the individual.

For this reason, descriptions of mediumistic writing necessarily emphasize the fragmentary and decentred. In his 'Preliminary Examination of the Script of E. R.', Yeats writes:

In the middle of one subject another will be interpolated; solemn sentences, in the midst of matter of fact statement, sometimes a meaningless sentence where all the rest is plain, such as 'There are no lambs' and the allusion to radium on page –. The mood shifts, the surface seems to melt away and then another surface and another – a perpetual change of consciousness – allegory or vague religious sentences . . . interrupting some practical advice [or information] often so definite and simple that we seem talking merely to some particularly business-like and well-informed acquaintance.

(1975: 161; brackets in original)

Given these effects, authority in the mediumistic text is only partial, particularly since the control, in Yeats's sceptical version, 'may be cunning, but not profound, for it is only a dissociated fragment of a living mind'. With its multiplication of largely feminine voices, citations and allusions, its different languages, *The Waste Land* is an obvious point of comparison. Eliot himself later described the text as automatic, but he was careful to stress that its source was in his own mind rather than from 'outside'.

To be sure, there are significant differences between the texts of modernism and spiritualism. As Luckhurst points out, spiritualist texts are often conservative and repetitive. One could also suggest that they imply a totality of meaning 'behind the veil', in contrast to the programmatic fragmentation of many modernist texts. – for spiritualists the obscurity of the dead was a product of their hyper-advanced state: it was as if they were trying to explain calculus to a six-year-old. However this was contested: in the psychological theory of mediumship, the theory of the 'dissociated fragment of mind' which Yeats alludes to, there is no necessity for a hidden depth to the utterance. In many ways the issue of meaning in the automatic message parallels that in modernism: is there a totality behind the fragments? Are they 'noise' or message? Arguably the crucial issue is simply the interpretive protocols involved: the work of the SPR provides models for reading fragmented, multivocal and 'open' texts like *The Waste Land*.

In its extraction of meaning from the fragments of culture, spiritualism can be seen as a response to Kelvin, Maxwell and the world of statistically-considered particles and the Second Law of Thermodynamics. Which is to say that the loss behind it is that of an ordered universe, a fall into noise from which a meaning must be extracted – even if the cost of that extraction is a paranoid relation to the 'message'. Language itself is implicated in that noise: language is broken, mediated by the medium who transmits rather than originates; all historical registers and styles are potentially available. Spritualism produced an outpouring of glossolalia, speaking in imaginary languages; the speech of the Other (Yaguello 1991: 88). It included complex artificial languages like those produced by the medium Hélène Smith and recorded in the psychologist Théodore Flournoy's *From India to the Planet Mars: A Case of Multiple Personality with Imaginary Languages* (1900), which he asked his linguist colleague Saussure to examine. One can see a methodological response to spiritualism in Joyce's poly-lingual epic *Finnegans Wake*; as Helen Sword points out (2002: 67–9), the *Wake* incorporates references to spiritualism including a sarcastic riposte to medium Hester Dowden's *Psychic Messages from Oscar Wilde*, in which she had used Wilde to attack Joyce (the story is a complicated set of cross-references: Dowden's father, Edward Dowden, a Dublin professor, had been caricatured in *Ulysses*).

As I said at the outset, spiritualism has a close relation to developments in science and technology: to photography, which could 'store' the image – leading to spirit photography, which purported to literally photograph the dead; and to radio, often linked to telepathy. Ernst Bloch argued in 1929 that 'the more advanced and unfrivolous technology is, the more mysteriously it mingles with the realm of taboo, with mists and vapours, unearthly velocity, golem–robots, and bolts of lightning. And so it comes into contact with things that were formerly conceived as belonging to the *magical sphere*' (1998: 310). When Marinetti writes of 'the day when man will be able to externalize his will and make it into a huge invisible arm', his model is the spiritualist seance; the 'invisible arm' is an occult technology (1972: 99). Two pioneers of radio, Nikolai Tesla and Sir Oliver Lodge, were fascinated by psychic phenomena: Lodge's book on his son killed in the war, *Raymond, or Life After Death*, was a best-seller. The journalist and psychic researcher W. T. Stead also saw Marconi's experiments with radio transmission as a scientific basis of telepathy. (There is an irony here: Stead, with notable lack of prevision, was last seen in the smoking room of the *Titanic* – a sinking often attributed to the misuse of radio. However it *was* widely reported that victims contacted mediums before the news broke.) Radio forms a ready metaphor, with the hand as transmission device: Yeats's control comments that 'those actual words were spoken and caught by a highly sensitive hand as waves of sound take shape – think of wireless' (1975: 156). Or compare George Yeats, writing to her husband:

Spirits were present at a seance only as impersonations created by a medium out of material in a world record just as wireless photography or television are created: that communicating spirits are mere dramatizations of that record; that all spirits in fact are not, as far as psychic communications are concerned, spirits at all, are only memory.

(cited Jochum 1993: 332)

This technologizes mediumship, making it an extension of the body's powers. The recourse to a television, rather than radio confirms Bloch's point that prosthetic thinking is linked to technological innovation. Radio as telepathy has a long afterlife: Upton Sinclair popularized 'Mental Radio' in a 1930 book; Ralph Ellison reaches us on 'unassigned frequencies' at the end of *Invisible Man*; and David Gascoyne's dreamlike 'radiophonic poem' in different voices *Night Thoughts* was broadcast by the BBC in 1955.

The third topic I proposed in relation to spiritualism is the possibility of contact with the past. Many notions of anamnesis and writing have roots in ideas of haunting: Yeats's 'phantasmagoria'; Pound's 'Phantastikon', Lawrence's 'Fantasia of the Unconscious', and Eliot's insistence in 1919 that in great poetry 'dead voices speak through the living voice' in a form of 'reincarnation' (1996: 400). The dead, Yeats wrote, may read the works of the living as well as appearing in their texts; a potent metaphor for the interchange between past and present described in Eliot's 'Tradition and the Individual Talent'. One influential text, as James Longenbach shows, was *An Adventure* (1911), co-authored by Elizabeth Morison and Frances Lamont (the pseudonyms of Anne Moberly and Eleanor Jourdain, Principal and Vice-Principal of St Hugh's College, Oxford). It is an account of a walk in the gardens of Versailles on 10 August 1901, in which the two women appeared to step back to the court of Louis XVI; or rather, as they later postulated on the basis of historical research, into an 'act of memory' in the mind of the doomed Marie Antoinette, attached to the day, 5 October 1789, on which she was forced to flee. Pound and Yeats read the book at Stone Cottage, and it contributed to their semi-occult, emotionally-charged modes of historical recovery: Yeats's notion of the 'Dreaming Back', expounded in *A Vision*, and the encounters with ghosts in late plays like *The Dreaming of the Bones* and *Purgatory*; Pound's visionary encounters with 'ghosts patched with history' in the early drafts of the *Cantos*. One historical mode of modernism is thus the return of the ghost – but a particular kind of ghost, amenable to ventriloquism and crowding up against others in a dynamic space.

The idea that one *might* step back is explored in Henry James's *The Sense of the Past* – his final, unfinished novel, in which his hero, the historian Ralph Pendrel, relives the year 1820 via a psychic connection with an ancestor and his London house. In his essay 'Is There a Life After Death?' James writes that a belief in the survival of death might have 'the effect of making us desire it as a renewal of the interest, the appreciation, the passion, the large and consecrated consciousness, in a word, of which we have so splendid a sample in this world' (1999: 115). These words suggest a central subject of his novels, and posit the possibility of an afterlife as an extension of – as written into – his aesthetics. Lawrence's short story 'A Fragment of Stained Glass' is another example. The narrator dines with the vicar of Beauvale, who reads a medieval account of the Devil fighting with a saint at the abbey, leaving a hole in the stained glass. He then 'puts a shade over the lamp so the room was almost in darkness', asks 'Am I more than a voice?', and proceeds to ventriloquize a first-person tale of a serf who burns down his manor and flees through the night, finally attempting to get in through the abbey window. This, it is implied, is not simply a fantasy, but rather a response to the fragment, an evocation of its life-energies. Similar strategies inform the work of H. D., whose *The Gift* enters the distant past via her grandmother's empathy with early Moravian settlers and Native Americans, setting in motion a flurry of ghosts (Sword 2002: 124). In such texts, historicism becomes an encounter with ghosts.

Mediumship disappeared from the agenda of the Congress of Experimental Psychology after 1909. The work of the SPR continued, but especially after the upsurge in popular mediumship after the war – Conan Doyle was one of the many bereaved who became obsessed with contacting a dead son – spiritualism became more readily seen as suspect, sentimental. Yet it persists as a secret within modernism, an important way of registering human exchanges in a world rendered strange, super-sensual, technologically-connected.

TECHNOLOGY

The discussion of radio above places in question the values traditionally associated with technology and science. The equation between technology and modernity is, by the end of the nineteenth century, established as a truism which operates in a number of distinct areas: in the linking of technology, progress and evolutionary thinking; in the discourse of efficiency; in forms of prosthetic thinking which imagines the extension of human capacities; and in the reconfiguration of time and space by technology. At the same time, technology is also posited as a set of problems relating to its demands and structural implications. At the bodily level technology is seen as overload or as dwarfing the human, as in Adams's dynamo or in the photography of Charles Sheeler. At the level of production technology it is seen as standardizing the commodity and displacing or regulating the human maker. And at the level of social metaphor technology functions as an image of alienation, instrumentalization, and estrangement from the natural order.

Taylorism, the 'science of work' developed by F. W. Taylor, exemplifies the body–machine equation: tools and motions are standardized, tasks broken down into component movements; unnecessary actions identified in 'time and motion' studies; fatigue managed. Despite the fact that large-scale assembly-line production remained a limited sector of manufacturing, Fordism and Taylorism provided powerful metaphors for subordination: as Fritz Lang's film *Metropolis* suggested, we are trapped in 'the machine'. One could turn to any number of works for a critique of the machine age, from the comic (Chaplin's film *Modern Times*) to the tragic (O'Neill's play *The Hairy Ape*). Sophie Treadwell's play *Machinal*, a success on Broadway in 1928, provides a particularly savage version. Describing a secretary simply named the 'Young Woman' who marries her boss, has a child, a lover, and kills her husband, it depicts urban life as culturally impoverished and the self as evacuated by a cacophony of mechanical language. The heroine is 'artistic' and 'inefficient', but the only song she can muster is 'Hey diddle diddle'. Marriage is the only route out of the office in which women are trans-mission-devices: telephonists, stenographers and typists. But maternity – a bodily making often paired with technological productivity in this period – offers no solace; the play depicts a factory-like maternity ward with indus-trial noise and birth reduced to numbered production. Even her violent attempts at rebellion are circumscribed by their status as versions of tabloid fantasies. The justice system and the electric chair are a final version of the iron cage. If Nietzsche had declared that leaving, walking out of the door like Ibsen's Nora in *The Doll's House*, is the first job of the liberated spirit, Treadwell's heroine anticipates later rebels like Winston Smith in *1984* in having no place to go.

At the same time – or rather, possibly because of its uncanny status as the 'dead' objectification of human drives – technology could be mysteri-ous and atavistic. In Kipling's 'The Lord of the Dynamo' this is literalized and projected onto the other: a black machine-tender offers a human sac-rifice to his giant dynamo. Why is technology so often linked to primi-tivism? For John Cournos, Germany produces the war because it is most bound to the machine, and therefore most liable to revolt into savage vio-lence. For Wyndham Lewis, in similar fashion, machine-worship is linked to primitivism because it represents the enslavement of the bourgeois self to the mythology of modernity; to identify with the machine is to desire the simplicity of the reflex arc rather than real thinking. Indeed it is because it is linked to automaticity that discourse on the machine turns to addic-tion: 'But yet there is beauty narcotic and deciduous / In this vast organ-ism grown out of us', as Louis MacNeice writes in 'An Eclogue for Christmas' (1979: 35). Dreiser's *Sister Carrie*, Forster's couch-potato Vashti in 'The Machine Stops' – both are addicted to technological flows.

To be sure, for some modernists technological progress offered a synec-doche for modernity in general, the arts included. The Futurists, in partic-ular, saw technology as informing an art which was progressive, efficient in communication. Marinetti argued for a language modelled on mathematics and the charged particle; his 'wireless imagination'; the 'intelligence electri-fied by flood of Naivety' of *Blast* (Lewis 1997: 38). Socialist art in the USSR was also happy to see technology as itself pleasurable: as the editors of *Blok* wrote in 1924, 'Constructivism does not imitate the machine but finds its parallel in the simplicity and logic of the machine' (Bann 1974: 106). Music – from Stravinsky's *Rite of Spring* to Antheil's *Ballet Mécanique* – evoked the harsh new world of technology and mechanized war, celebrated by Futurism as 'the world's only hygiene'. Modernist texts constantly register technology as prosthesis; modern desire is quickened to the pulse of electricity, flowing freely and demanding discharge. We can link this to the consumer economy. Businessman Edward Filene, in his *Successful Living in this Machine Age* (1931) contested the idea that mass-production 'mechanizes and standardizes human life', insisting that on the contrary it offers choice, leisure, and a mobility which liberates the individual from class, localism, even nationalism. He was right to the extent that attacks on Taylorism, Fordism and mass-manipulation, like Dos Passos's *The 42nd Parallel* (1930), Huxley's *Brave New World* (1932) and Upton Sinclair's *The Flivver King* (1937) misrepresent techniques which sought to align the human body with technology while remaining aware of the *limits* of that alignment, opening up the spaces of leisure and desire which in some senses become the place of modernist activity. Which is to say that even in attempting to map the limits of technology, to work creatively with waste, fatigue and resistance, modernism shares a paradigm with Taylorism.

THE CASE OF EZRA POUND

The modernist who most consistently deploys and indeed synthesizes the terms I have been discussing is Ezra Pound. The programme of modernization which he devised is suffused with techno-scientific professionalism. Science offers a range of terms: a vitalism in which the electromagnetic, mechanical, biological and traces of the occult intermingle; a stress on technique, precision, hygiene and 'cure' allied to notions of the writer as scientist, engineer, economist or surgeon – all pursued with a vehemence which belies their metaphoricity. Above all Pound found in science an authority in which a relation to the 'real' grounds the work. The doctrine of the image in 1912 and of the vortex in 1914, are suffused with scientific thinking: the poem is a machine; poetry is 'energized' prose; the serious artist is a chemist, 'the poet is a sort of steam-gauge, voltameter, a set of pipes for thermometric and barometric divination' (1973: 115). Critics are surgeons who should cut through dead material and maintain 'hygiene' or apply 'vaccine'.

Pound uses these terms relatively loosely, and only a general taxonomy is possible. Negatively, they centre on reformist notions of waste-elimination and efficiency: the poet as engineer, with a stress on points of pressure (load and work). Pound's imagist writings stress objectivity, precision and professionalism. The image is defined by its hardness and clarity; by the elimination of the 'superfluous word' (especially the dependent word, the adjective); by 'the precise rendering of the impulse'; and by a stress on discovery modelled on science. To contemporaries, Imagism already looked like Taylorism. This is Rebecca West's introduction to Pound's poems in *The New Freewoman*: 'there has arisen a little band who desire the poet to be as disciplined and efficient at his job as the stevedore. Just as Taylor and Gilbreth want to introduce scientific management into industry so the *imagistes* want to discover the most puissant way of whirling the scattered star dust of words into a new star of passion' (cited Clarke 1996: 125).

More positively, Pound's writings depict poetry in terms of ideas of charge, energy flow and the field. Pound derived his idea of the dynamism of poetry from a variety of sources: Neoplatonism, the work of Helmholtz and others, and such books as Hudson Maxim's *The Science of Poetry and the Philosophy of Language*, which he reviewed in 1910 (Bell 1981: 28–31). Their use is always synthetic: terms are detached from their original contexts and 'plugged into' aesthetic thinking in ways which make Pound's writing itself a machinic assemblage. Pound could audaciously connect the 'radiant world . . . a world of moving energies' in the medieval poetry of Cavalcanti to the new physics:

> For the modern scientist energy has no borders, it is a shapeless 'mass' of force; even his capacity to differentiate it to a degree never dreamed by the ancients has not led him to think of its shape or even its loci. The rose that his magnet makes in the iron filings, does not lead him to think of the force in botanic terms, or wish to visualize that force as floral and extant (*ex stare*).
>
> (1954: 154)

This is to leap towards Pound's later thinking (he dated the Cavalcanti essay 1910–31), in which a biologism has been added to the mix. Science is an expression of the individual's understanding of these forces: 'I passed my last *exam*. In mathematics by sheer intuition. I saw where the line had to go, as clearly as I ever saw an image, or felt *caelestem intus vigorem*' (1916: 106). Like Adams's historian, Pound follows the flows of energy, seeking nodes and switches. In 1911 he wrote that period can be defined in relation to 'certain facts or points, or "luminous details", which governed knowledge as the switchboard the electric circuit' (1973: 24). The critic leads readers to those nodes: 'Excernment . . . The ordering of knowledge so that the next man (or generation) can most readily find the live part of it, and waste the least possible time among obsolete issues' (1954: 75). Reading his essays, one repeatedly comes across the same charged moments: the arrival of the Fenollosa manuscripts; finding a century-old textbook on metrics in a Sicilian hotel; an elderly Oxford don saying of a poem 'he "Couldn't be bothered to stop for every adjective"'.

Pound's emphasis on the correspondence of words and things is closely related to his thinking on science (as well as his economic concern for 'real' value). From Ernest Fenollosa, whose manuscript on the Chinese written character was handed to Pound by his widow in December 1913, as he was preparing the Imagist anthology, Pound garnered an insistence on the mind's direct relation to the image, a pre-grammatical singularity which responds to the weight of reality. Among other things science signals the excess of knowledge over language: 'the scientist, say the biologist, knows a great many things for which there is no proper and ready verbal manifestation. He falls back on photos and coloured slides' (1996: 106).

Admitting the difficulty of defining Imagism in his 'Vorticism' essay of 1914, Pound referred the reader to his own poetic evolution towards an 'intensive' art, concerned with relative intensities:

> The image is not an idea. It is a radiant node or cluster; it is what I can, and must perforce, call a VORTEX, from which, and through which, and into which, ideas are constantly rushing . . . And from this necessity came the name 'vorticism'.
>
> (1916: 106; 1980: 207)

Pound derived the term 'vortex' in part from Helmholtz's work on the vortex in hydrodynamics, developed by Kelvin for use in describing the twisting of the 'ether' to form atoms (Bell 1981: 163). The fact that he was still willing, in *Blast*, to call the vortex a 'turbine' and claim that 'It represents, in mechanics, the greatest efficiency' reinforces the sense of syncretism involved. The vortex is at once a source of energy and the trace of a charged mind, a record of its movement through time and its dynamization of the past. In Pound's famous example, 'In a Station of the Metro', it involves the understanding of an underlying equation:

> The apparition of these faces in the crowd:
> Petals on a wet, black bough.
>
> (1990: 251)

The supposedly instantaneous perception here disguises a complex temporal effect involving both the juxtaposition of images – placing them in the same field (one spaced, at Pound's insistence on first publication, with gaps signalling a rhythmic relation) – and the poem's origin, since it evolved from a destroyed thirty-line original and echoes an early poem on lost love. There are also literary resonances: the myth of Orpheus in the underworld; the faces of the metamorphosed dead alluded to in 'Coda', where Pound asks his songs: 'Why do you look so eagerly and curiously into people's faces, / Will you find your lost dead among them?' (1990: 106). The poem is a miniature vortex in itself. As Pound wrote in *Blast*, 'All experience rushes into this vortex. All the energized past, all the past that is living and worthy to live. ALL MOMENTUM, which is the past bearing upon us, RACE, RACE-MEMORY, instinct charging the PLACID, NON-ENERGIZED FUTURE' (Lewis 1997: 153). This combines the physics of the field and a Lamarckianism which sees the poet as engendering as well as engineering the future.

One might say that Vorticism, and its concept of the charged field, is needed to protect Imagism from becoming moribund; to keep the Image in dynamic movement through a linguistic field. In *Guide to Kulcher* Pound again expounds the rose in the steel dust image, and concludes 'Thus the *forma*, the concept rises from death' (1966: 152), figuring poetry as an energization of dead material. Pound wrote to Harriet Monroe in 1931: 'Having done your bit to provide a scrap of rudimentary ganglia amid the wholly bestial suet and pig fat, you can stop; but I as a responsible intellect do not propose (and have no right) to allow that bit of nerve tissue (or battery wire) to be wrecked . . .' (1951: 317).

The temporality of Vorticism can also be related to the moving image. In his 'Vorticism' essay Pound contrasts the vortex to the 'impressionism' of the cinema image; but in 'How to Write' (1930) he comments that the ideograph 'takes the static image . . . But if you try to put the static image into ideograph you at once feel the void. The ideograph wants the moving image, the concrete thing plus its action' (1996: 88). The ideogram, Pound learns from Fenollosa, is 'noun and verb in one'. In 1916 Alvin Coburn, with Pound's assistance, had invented the Vortograph, a device for taking superimposed stills suggestive of motion; a few years later it was applied to film. This is to move the ideogram towards cinema – a suggestion latent in cinema theory of the period, as we have seen.

Finally, while science is central to the image and vortex, they also have an occult component originating in Yeats's and Pound's reading in the Stone Cottage winters of 1913–16, and in their interest in *Noh*, highly stylized Japanese ghost drama, which for Pound offered both a proto-modern economy of expression and what he called the 'phantasmagoria' of the dead. One of the three tenets of Imagism as described in *Poetry* in March 1913 was 'a certain "Doctrine of the Image", which they had not committed to writing; they said it did not concern the public'. The secret, recent critics have suggested, is revealed in the short prose piece 'Ikon' which Pound published in an obscure journal in 1913 (Longenbach 1988: 31; Tiffany 1995: 140). Here he writes that the soul after death needs 'an abundance of sounds and patterns in that long dreaming'. The Yeatsian invocation of the furniture of a soul contrasts sharply with formalist definitions of the image. In 1918 Pound writes of 'imagism, or poetry wherein the feelings of painting and sculpture are predominant (certain men move in phantasmagoria; the images of their gods, whole countrysides, stretches of hill land and forest, travel with them)' (1973: 424); the same year he published 'Phanopœia', a poem in which this phantasmagoria is evoked. Earlier, the influence of Theosophy on abstract painters like Kandinsky was noted. In *Gaudier-Brzeska*, immediately after mentioning Kandinsky, Pound cryptically remarks that 'The Image is the poet's pigment. The painter should use his colour because he sees it or feels it . . . It is the same in writing poems, the author must use his *image* because he sees or feels it . . .' (1916: 99). The image is in this account an emanation: something seen and projected.

The *Cantos*, begun as early as 1915, can be read as a seance, beginning with the *nekuiaa* (the voyage to the Underworld of classical epic) and involving a return to charged historical moments (Malatesta's Rimini; America's founding) on the model of *An Adventure*. Pound's sense of visionary places – Provence, Venice, the Tempio Malatestiano in Rimini – sees them bound into what Peter Nicholls calls a 'network of memories and fantasies' in which the notion of 'return' is central (Davis 2000: 162). But the *Cantos* move from listening to broadcasting, and Pound went on to make wartime broadcasts for Fascist radio. The radio, as Daniel Tiffany has stressed, functions as an occult device for Pound; a form of mediumship offering influence at a distance. If we began with Adams following the lines of force which define history, we have ended with Pound attempting to use technology to bend those lines to his will – an enterprise which in its failure registers the limits of metaphor.

7 Modernism's Others: Race and Empire

One interpretation of the 'modern', present in the thought of Adorno and others, is that it is driven by the necessity to identify and subsume – to destroy or incorporate – various 'others', from the Jew to the Native to the madman. This chapter concerns itself with the presence of the 'other' (of various others) in modernism; those who have been bound into the West's self-definition since the beginnings of colonial expansion in the Renaissance. The period of modernism falls uneasily between the climax of imperial competition in the late nineteenth-century and post-1945 decolonization. In England, the novel of Empire represented by Kipling and Buchan is replaced by the uncertainty registered in the texts of Forster, Woolf and Orwell, and the bracing encounter of self and (external) other is replaced by a more troubling internal negotiation, in which the self might itself be or incorporate an other. In America, the certainties of race begin to fray and begin to be replaced by forms of racial interchange.

What does it mean to have the other at the centre of self-definition? We can begin with one of the most influential accounts of modern conscious-ness, mentioned in chapter 1: the description of the master–slave relation in *The Phenomenology of Spirit*, which gives birth to the fractured con-sciousness of modernity. Crudely put, Hegel's argument runs as follows: identity cannot be ideal, it must be expressed in the world through mutual recognition. But that can only be achieved, in the first instance, through struggle and the risk of life, which results in subordination – the defeated accepting slavery rather than death. In the dialectic which ensues, Hegel reserves a special place for the slave. The master cannot see himself (his self) reflected in those around him whom he reduces to the status of objects; he lives an illusion. The slave, on the other hand, is first shaken by the fear of death which founds slavery, and then forced to recognize that he has his being for another. He thus sees identity in a truer light: as achieved by struggle and work. The subsequent stage of the 'unhappy consciousness' rep-resents the internalization of this dialectic: an internal otherness (a split be-tween an ideal self and actuality) comes to constitute the subject.

This is a rather roundabout way of introducing a chapter dealing mainly with race and primitivism. But it is important to remember that the dialec-tic of recognition and misrecognition described by Hegel is central to modernity, both historically and in terms of its psychology. The great African-American intellectual W. E. Du Bois, studying in Berlin in the 1890s, derived his notion of 'double consciousness' from Hegel, implying that in their struggle for self-expression his people were the first moderns (that is, other to themselves) – an observation which places racial encounter at the heart of modernity.

THE GEOGRAPHY OF EMPIRE

'Primitivism' is a rather unsatisfactory term which can de-historicize and homogenize what is involved in cross-cultural encounters. The interests labelled the 'primitive', from the influence of *The Thousand and One Nights* to jazz, are bound up with specific histories: trade, spices, slavery; the scramble for Africa; the opening up of Japan. Moreover 'primitivism' as an accusative term often obscures what is at stake, whether the formal content (Picasso's use of African masks, often seen as the European artist seeking 'confirmation' of his thinking rather than 'real' influence) or the politics (for instance of Nancy Cunard's *Negro* anthology).

Begin with the geography of Empire. Modernism is to a large extent produced by immigrants: Americans and Irishmen in London and Paris; Joyce in Trieste; Duchamp in New York. But London is the scene of broader cultural encounter. What John Berger calls the 'vertical invader', the artist who comes from a provincial or working-class context is matched by the colonial invader: Anna Wickham, Olive Schreiner, Katherine Mansfield, Henry Handel Richardson, Len Lye ('the wildest man in town') and Christina Stead; Claude McKay, C. L. R. James and George Padmore. All brought an outsider's perspective to the metropolis, a sense of cultural relativity and social freedom: Schreiner and Wickham an unabashed feminism; the New Zealander Lye a fascination with Pacific and aboriginal art; Stead a radicalism born of Australian working-class movements.

In the presence of the black writers, a modernism of decolonization can be seen between the wars: London was a crucible of post-1945 independence movements. In part this represents the continuation of a long tradition of radical connection in the context of what Paul Gilroy calls the 'Black Atlantic', an internationalism represented by the Pan-African Congresses held in London and elsewhere in 1919, 1921 and 1923. The radical pamphleteer George Padmore was at the centre of a group of intellectuals in the 30s and 40s including Jomo Kenyatta (future Kenyan president, studying anthropology under Malinowski). Black Americans joined the mix: the Jamaican and Harlem poet and novelist Claude McKay worked for Sylvia Pankhurst's socialist paper the *Workers' Dreadnought* in London in 1920; Paul Robeson made films about the Welsh miners. The vogue for jazz brought over performers including clarinettist Sidney Bechet, who purchased his first alto sax in London, revolutionizing jazz. Indian nationalists like the novelist Mulk Raj Anand also mixed in Bloomsbury circles.

We can pick out two figures in this rich milieu: the radical Trinidadian critic C. L. R. James and Nancy Cunard. James is worth particular comment because of the way modernity, politics and race interlock in his work. He arrived in the UK in 1932 and quickly began to take part in politics and cultural life, working closely with Padmore and publishing a pamphlet on *The Case for West Indies Self-Government* (1933) with the Hogarth Press (Leonard Woolf was a committed anti-imperialist). His *Letters from London* describe a black and Indian Bloomsbury, a world of young students, writers, performers and artists; they convey a sense of a young man fully alive to modern culture, debating with Edith Sitwell on Faulkner, talking excitedly about Chekov and Pirandello, lecturing on the West Indies. He wrote a play on Toussaint L'Ouverture in which he appeared with Robeson, historical works and a novel, before departing for the USA in 1938. Throughout his life, James wrote on modern arts: on Eisenstein and Hollywood; on Whitman, Melville and literary criticism; on Baldwin's attack on *Native Son*; on Picasso and Pollock. His letters to his future wife, Constance Webb, in the 1940s (published as *Special Delivery*) offer vivid essays on modern culture, moving rapidly from T. S. Eliot to the actress Jennifer Jones; from Stravinsky and Joyce to Hegel and Dryden; describing conversations with Richard Wright or Robeson as Othello; discussing the poetry of Muriel Rukeyser or the revolutionary potential of music. For James, aesthetic and political crisis are linked, and decolonization is part of an analysis of aesthetic modernity. Hence his celebration of cricket as a dramatic spectacle, as Hegelian tragedy in which the individual confronts necessity, and as national style, seeing in the great West Indies player Garfield Sobers 'a living embodiment of centuries of a tortured history' (1992: 389).

The disowned heiress Nancy Cunard is more immediately identified with modernism, running the Hours Press and forging links with a range of modernist writers. George Padmore worked with Cunard on the huge *Negro* anthology which she published in 1934. The material in *Negro* represents the confluence of Pan–Africanism and modernism; one of the first attempts to forge an African diasporic identity. Beside future African leaders like Kenyatta, African-American intellectuals like Du Bois, Arna Bontemps, Langston Hughes and Zora Neale Hurston, and writers from the Caribbean and Brazil, the anthology included a range of modernists: Dreiser, Pound, Williams, Beckett (who translated the francophone material), composer George Antheil. *Negro* claims a black contribution for modernism, for example in Robert Goffin comparing jazz to Surrealism: 'What Breton and Aragon did for poetry in 1920, Chirico and Ernst for painting, had instinctively been accomplished as early as 1910 by humble negro musicians, unaided by the control of that critical intelligence that was to prove such an asset to the later initiators' (Cunard 2002: 239) – the condescension here is palpable, but nonetheless agency *is* attributed to these musicians. Cunard has been accused of sexual adventurism because of her association with the black musician Henry Crowder (a contributor to *Negro*) and the cultivated exoticism of her image, her arms decked with ivory bracelets. In fact, her commitment to racial causes was sustained and deep.

The centripetalism which brought these writers to London is matched by a centrifugal tendency which took English writers abroad. Paul Fussell describes a post-war flight south, the mud and cold of the trenches inspiring a 'new heliophily': Lawrence in Italy and Sardinia, Robert Graves in Mallorca, Norman Douglas in Italy. Writers availed themselves of an expanding market for travel writing in which cultural difference was commodified and rendered pleasurable. Ethel Mannin, the dashing exemplar of 1920s style, was typical of a restless generation: she published accounts of journeys to Connemara, Brittany, Germany, Italy, Morocco, the Lebanon, Jordan, Egypt, India, Burma, Japan and America. Lawrence's travelogues are particularly significant, an extension of the thinking about self, geography and culture in his writings on American literature and Thomas Hardy. Lawrence wrote accounts of Sardinia and Italy, the Alps, Ceylon, Australia, Mexico and America (Roberts 2004). Rebecca West's massive autobiography *Black Lamb and Grey Falcon: A Journey Through Yugoslavia in 1937* (1942) is one culmination of this literature: a complex layering of travel, memory, competing Balkan histories and cultural traditions; a conflation of three separate trips to the Balkans in which history is increasingly understood as catastrophe (Montefiore 1996).

The literature of travel includes a quest for renovation which has its origins in the late Victorian imperial romance. Conrad's *Heart of Darkness*, Forster's *A Passage to India*, and Lawrence's *Mornings in Mexico* and *Kangaroo*, move to the fringes of Empire in search of a revitalizing lesson – a pattern also present in the less explicit voyage to central Asia in *The Waste Land* (Trotter 1986). Often, as in Buchan or Kipling, the 'primitive' is embedded within a controlling frame; a cycle of voyage and return like that endured by Conrad's narrators, within which the repellent 'truths' of the savage world may be contained and mediated. American literature had in historian Frederick Jackson Turner's 'frontier hypothesis' a ready-made theory of such cultural encounters: the frontier offers, for Turner, a transforming encounter with a savage land and its inhabitants. American nationalism had, from the Revolution, been represented by what Philip Deloria calls 'playing Indian'; a tradition continued in the poetry of Vachel Lindsay and Amy Lowell. An example is Willa Cather's novel *The Professor's House* (1925), in which perceptions of race, the primitive, frontier vitality, domestication and modernity converge. The protagonist lives in a house near Chicago, dominated by a wife and daughters for whose materialism he has a scarcely concealed contempt; he escapes by spending a last summer in his old home, completing his history of the South-west. There he dreams of his former colleague, the blue-eyed Tom Outland, who was killed in the war and whose embedded narrative of adventures in New Mexico – his discovery of a lost village left by cliff-dwelling Indians – forms the core of the novel, offering as its central image the skull of a Native American 'grandmother' with whom Tom forms an imaginative link. (One might compare the fashion for Indian 'controls' in seances.) It is Tom's invention which produces the family's wealth, and since he has been supplanted as son-in-law by the commercially-minded and Jewish Louis Marcellus, this is a myth of 'native' inheritance corrupted by modernity.

In other texts, the drama of encounter produces ambivalence, a crisis mixing fascination and revulsion. Lawrence's work constantly presents such a drama, from the dark Italian peasantry of *The Lost Girl* (1920) to the violent Mexico of *The Plumed Serpent* (1926). The various cultures which he encountered on his world tour in the early twenties offered versions of a deeper truth – just as, at the end of his life, in the uncompleted *Apocalypse*, he claimed to discover the modes of pre-Socratic thought underlying the Revelation of St John. At the same time, Lawrence's narrators typically step back from an immersion in that which fascinates and horrifies them; the primitive is held at a distance even as resistance to its (masculine) power is largely attributed to women. Consider the description of Kate's response to Cipriano in *The Plumed Serpent*:

In his black, glinting eyes the power was limitless, and it was as if, from him, from his body of blood could rise up that pillar of cloud which swayed and swung, like a rearing serpent or a rising tree, till it swept the zenith, and all the earth below was dark and prone, and consummated. Those small hands, that little natural tuft of black goat's beard hanging light from his chin, the tilt of his brows and the slight slant of his eyes, the domed Indian head with its thick black hair, they were like symbols to her, of another mystery, the bygone mystery of the twilit, primitive world, where shapes that are small suddenly loom up huge, gigantic on the shadow, and a face like Cipriano's is the face at once of a god and a devil, the undying Pan face. The bygone mystery, that has indeed gone by, but has not passed away. Never shall pass away.

(1955: 307–8)

The cliché is in the evocation of phallic power; more troubling is the overturning of Lawrence's equation of sexual power with the sun, and the paradoxical opposites the passage struggles to unite: big–small, devil–god, invisible–visible, past–present, abstract sculpture–human reality. Primivitism in this mode is condemned to enact the play of differences.

E. M. Forster's *A Passage to India* offers a more intricate cultural negotiation, but is likewise dominated by what Aziz calls the 'cycle' of encounter, retraction and re-encounter, and an uncertainty conveyed by the recurrent metaphors of mistiness and blurring which the 'net' of imperial rule cannot encompass. At the end of the festival a minor collision of boats and a peal of thunder announces 'the climax, as far as India admits of one'; as the narrator comments, 'no man could say where was the emotional centre of it, any more than he could locate the heart of a cloud'. Where the novel does find an emotional centre is in the death of Mrs Moore (the mother who 'did not signify' for Ronnie), but in terms of a sacrificial logic in which the debt is suddenly on the side of the native. 'Mixing herself up with natives' in her tomb as cults spring up in her honour, death is the ultimate encounter with the other – and as inescapable 'gain' for western consciousness. A similar ambivalence and uncertainty runs through one of the greatest of modernist autobiographies, T. E. Lawrence's *The Seven Pillars of Wisdom* (1926) – ostensibly the account of Lawrence of Arabia's wartime exploits, but in fact an agonized mediation on the impossibility of becoming or writing the other.

MODERNIST PRIMITIVISM: VITALISM, MAGIC THINKING, ABSTRACTION

Thus far, we have considered the patterns of encounter created by Empire. We need to look more closely at the uses of the 'primitive' in modernist texts – a usage often seen as typified by Picasso's introduction of elements of the African mask into his 1907 painting *Les demoiselles d'Avignon*. Modernist primitivism can be considered under three headings: vitalism; magic thinking; and abstraction.

If civilization is identified with mechanisms of censorship and with the debilities associated with distance from the 'natural' order, then primitivism ostensibly offers a route back to the 'original' and whole self; a vitalist self at one with its sexuality and being, freed from modes of censorship imposed by civilization. To encounter the primitive is to time-travel, returning to earlier stages of human development of which 'vestiges' are buried within the psyche. Primitivism was readily linked to vitalism. Gombarov, the hero of *Babel* (1922), John Cournos's novel of London modernism, attends a 'Primitivists' gathering (thinly disguised versions of Pound, H. D. and others) at which there is talk of Bergson, a statue of 'a pregnant negress' and a picture of a phallic railway engine. 'Man was returning to primitive, to sexual symbols in art . . . All this flashed across Gombarov's brain in a single instant. A Bergsonian intuition, Rodd would have called it' (1922: 255).

The primitive is linked to another supposedly primary entity, the death drive. The ambivalent energies which Gaugin found in Tahiti; the dances borrowed from early Cretan art by Matisse; Picasso's appreciation of African and early Iberian art; Lawrence's and Eisenstein's exploration of blood and death in Mexico – in such cases the human itself is called into question as the de-individuating powers attributed to the primitive subside into quiescence; into the inertness of matter only temporarily energized by fetishism – a model for the modernist artwork in its return to the origins of representation in animism. Blaise Cendrars's poem 'The Great Fetishes' (published 1922) resolves its ten sculptures (ostensibly in the British Museum) into found objects: a woman with 'Two sharp lines around a mouth shaped like a funnel' and so on (1992: 98). The confluence of the primitive and the technological (as in Cournos's train) is a recurrent motif: both displace the human in favour of an object-world, a world without thinking.

To be sure Cendrars's ironic gaze, and the fact that he seems to have invented these statues, signals the knowing way in which the 'primitive' is often treated in modernism. Primitivism in its most direct form belongs to baroque texts like Edith Sitwell's 'Gold Coast Customs', with its 'cannibal /Sun' and shrunken heads, and Vachel Lindsay's 'The Congo'. Lindsay's poem is shaped as a mock-missionary anthropology (its subtitle 'A Study of the Negro Race') in which 'Mumbo-Jumbo' is banished by 'the apostles with their coats of mail' but still echoes from the Mountains of the Moon: 'Mumbo . . . Jumbo . . . will . . . hoo-doo . . . you' (the marginal perform- ance script says 'Dying down into a penetrating, terrified whisper'). As Rachel Blau DuPlessis points out, the cry of the witch-doctors – 'Hoo, Hoo, Hoo' – echoes through American modernism, with variants in Stevens's 'Bantams in Pine-Woods' and Eliot's 'Sweeney Agonistes'. Lindsay's poem testifies to a linguistic philosophy which attributes an immediacy to 'primitive' utterance: an 'authentic' language which can only be approached via a simultaneous invocation and exorcism.

A conscious interplay of the primitive and comical is also present in Eliot's scatological epic of Great King Bolo, a sequence begun as early as his Harvard years. It includes the 'Columbo and Bolo verses' which Eliot eventually gave to Pound, who sealed them in an envelope marked '*Chançons ithyphallique*'; stanzas appeared in letters to Aitken, Pound and Joyce from 1914; and it continues into the 1920s and beyond in letters to Bonamy Dobrée (Eliot 1996: xvi, 321). The poems describe Bolo and his court and a mock-anthropology including the great god Wux, with his four duck feet, two penises, four testicles and speedometer (Crawford 1992: 223). While they are not part of the official corpus, they are interesting in their formation: egregiously racist in the manner of *The Bab Ballads*, regular in scansion, and determinedly obscene – the dirty underside of cultivated taste. Eliot joked to Pound that he planned to recite them at a reading of 'big wigs' including 'OSWALD and EDITH Shitwell'; both seem to have regarded them as an aggressive assault on high-mindedness. But the fact the Eliot continued them after he became an establishment figure suggests that the contradictions they embody are internal: one point of identification seems to have been Bolo's queen, suggesting a fantasy of anal passivity also present in the Pound–Eliot 'Sage Homme' verses.

The second heading under which we can investigate primitivism is the 'magic thinking' described in Sir James Frazer's *The Golden Bough* and other anthropological writings. To see primitive thought as a mode of containing the world is potentially to see all belief systems as defined by internal coher- ence and motivated by a need to control reality. This is in turn related to an understanding of literature as an expression of magic thought. Sympa- thetic magic thinking as it is described by Frazer is poetic thinking: arranged along two axes, that of 'the association of ideas by similarity' (homeopathic magic) and 'the association of ideas by contiguity in space or time' (conta- gious magic) – that is metaphor and metonomy. While Frazer everywhere

stresses that magic thinking is fallacious (and champions progress), the conclusion to *The Golden Bough* suggests a convergence of primitives and
moderns:

We must remember that at bottom the generalizations of science or, in common
parlance, the laws of nature are merely hypotheses designed to explain that ever-
shifting phantasmagoria of thought which we dignify with the high-sounding names
of the world and the universe. In the last analysis magic, religion, and science are
nothing but theories of thought; and as science has supplanted its predecessors, so
it may hereafter be itself superseded by some more perfect hypothesis, perhaps by
some totally different way of looking at the phenomena. . . .

(1922: 712)

This conclusion places Frazer closer than is usually acknowledged to
thinkers who propose what one might label a poetics of culture.

Frazer's thinking was influential; and was taken up, most famously, into
the mythography of *The Waste Land* (Fraser 1990). Like *The Golden Bough*,
Eliot's poem is at once fragmentary and syncretic; at once learnedly classical and anthropological. The canonical readings of *The Waste Land* which
attempt to reconstruct from its splintered surface a 'deep' structure of ritual
respond directly to the poet's citation of Frazer and Weston on 'vegetation
ceremonies' and on the themes of drought, sterility, sacrifice and fecunda-
tion in the Grail story. Anthropology provides a mode of reading in which
fragments may be gathered and unified, producing a poem which resonates
with contradictory possibilities; positioning itself as a kind of 'primitive'
utterance even as it displays its hyper-civilized consciousness – internaliz-
ing the dialectics of cultural encounter. In a parallel fashion, Pound derived
from the German anthropologist Leo Frobenius the belief that the collo-
cation of a few carefully selected items of culture (or artefacts) can intimate
a whole civilization; and by implication that such a part-for-whole relation
might inform both what he called the method of the 'luminous detail' in
the *Cantos* and its overall structure.

Our third heading for the discussion of primitivism is abstraction; the
derivation from 'primitive' and ancient art of an anti-representational aesthetics. For T. E. Hulme, influenced by the account of abstraction in
Wilhelm Worringer's *Abstraction and Empathy* (1908), 'primitive' art is anti-
representational, interested in surfaces rather than the interior states intu-
ited via romantic empathy. Hulme invokes Byzantine as well as African
models, and linked this art to classicism. In his essays on 'The Art of the
Bushmen' and 'Negro Sculpture', the Bloomsbury critic Roger Fry
expressed similar ideas: with its directness of vision African art is free from
western assumptions about the human body and the laws of perspective;
the African sculptor is closer to his material, and can think in a fully plastic
way. The resulting forms are animated with a 'disconcerting vitality, the suggestion that they make of not being mere echoes of actual figures, but of
possessing an inner life of their own'. Paradoxically, what limits this art for
Fry is the absence of another form of perspective; of the 'conscious criti-

cal appreciation and comparison' (like that which Eliot describes in 'The Function of Criticism') which might convert a potent tradition into real development (1998: 72–3). Implicit in this mode of thinking is a dialogue of 'civilized' self-consciousness and timeless 'primitive' integrity which can never be resolved; which continually holds out the promise of a fresh raid on the supposedly static forms of non-western art.

Abstraction in this mode can be seen in Pound's early interest in Chinese poetry, a form of Orientalism founded on the idea of simplicity and economy. Chinese and Japanese forms like *haiku* appear in and influence the first Imagist anthology of 1914. During the final stages of organizing the anthology, Pound finally received Ernest Fenollosa's manuscripts on the Chinese written character from his widow, Mary, and Pound worked with Yeats on the *Noh* drama during the winters they spent together at Stone Cottage in Sussex. The outcome included Yeats's *At the Hawk's Well* and Pound's *Noh* translation – texts which form an important route to the more formally experimental work each of them undertook after 1918.

We can finish with a general comment on modernist use of the 'primitive'. Picasso's ambivalence towards the African art he encountered at the Old Trocadero in 1906 is curious: it is oppressive, deathly, threatening, stinking; he denies its formal influence. As Simon Gikandi argues, critics have marginalized African art in similar terms: it serves as an unlocking agent; a vague presence – it remains a fetish whose reality is in a sense irrelevant; a 'source' from which modernism must struggle to extricate its alienated forms. But this is disingenuous, a repetition of the Andalusian narrative of modernity as extraction from the world of the Moor. Both hidden and apparent at the centre of his art – in the central figures of *Les demoiselles d'Avignon* – African art remains a formal as well as a psychological presence. To place beside Picasso the *Negro* anthology, or Franz Fanon's sense of a world splintered by colonialism, is to move beyond 'primitivism' to actual histories.

THE HARLEM RENAISSANCE AND CULTURAL PLURALISM IN AMERICA

Questions of race, ethnicity and national identity within modernism have a particularly strong focus in relation to the upsurge of African-American culture in New York in the 1920s. In the discussion which follows, I will stress the way in which the Harlem Renaissance belongs to the debates on cultural revival and nativism discussed briefly in chapter 2, in which American identity is understood in terms of race.

What the theologian Reinhold Niebur called 'the problem of the "hyphen"' (1916: 13) was a compelling question in the context of World War I, especially for German-Americans. Questions of ethnicity became central to debates on national culture. Horace Kallen coined the term 'cultural pluralism' in 1913, defining America in terms of its many ethnicities and their local inheritances rather than 'universal' values. Kallen's rather romantic notions of race are reflected (and critiqued) in a range of writing, from Randolph Bourne's essay 'Transnational America' to the work of Harlem Renaissance leaders like Alain Locke, who was taught by Kallen at Harvard. In 1909, Herbert Croly published *The Promise of American Life*, arguing for a reconstruction of American culture to reflect the nation's diversity and energy. Croly co-founded *The New Republic* in 1914, a vehicle for a radical generation of critics including Walter Lippmann and Bourne. Many were also associated with another journal, *Seven Arts*, which ran for a year from November 1916. The manifesto, probably written by the literary editor Waldo Frank, spoke of 'the coming of that national self-consciousness which is the beginning of all greatness', and added: 'It is the aim of *The Seven Arts* to become a channel for the flow of these new tendencies: an expression of our American arts that shall be fundamentally an expression of our American life' (Wertheim 1976: 179). The *Seven Arts* critics developed a cultural nationalism modelled on European movements, expressed in Brooks's article 'Young America'; it ran articles by Padraic Colum on 'Young Ireland'; Dos Passos on 'Young Spain'; on young Japan and India. In the radical journals *The Masses*, *The Liberator* and *New Masses*, a distinctly American tradition of cultural nationalism and progressive politics, with the Whitman of *Democratic Vistas* as its point of origin, does battle with the Communist Party line on the one hand, and international modernism on the other, in formulating a national culture in which African-Americans would find an important place.

A second important component of pluralist thinking was the anthropology of Franz Boas. For Boas, all cultures need to read as internally coherent ways of arranging a world; he attacked racial thinking and racial hierarchy of the kind implicit in Frazer and in the Victorian anthropology of E. B. Tylor, for whom 'civilization' was linked to notions of biological development in which races which must pass through a series of defined stages. Boas believed all cultures were historically specific and defined by interactions with other cultures. American identity, through the efforts of such thinkers, became linked to race. The ideas of Boas and the new left, as George Hutchinson puts it, 'helped spawn – and create audiences for – new magazines and publishers that transformed the cultural landscape and opened spaces for the emergence of African-American literary modernism' (1995: 93). The black contribution to America was stressed by Du Bois, James Weldon Johnson, Alain Locke and others. The Irish Literary Renaissance was repeatedly invoked as a model: by Locke in his introduction to *The New Negro*, where he argued that Harlem was one of the 'nascent centres of folk-expression and self-determination' in which cultural achievement was a path to political recognition (Gates 1997: 964). Floyd Dell had argued that 'It is the business of the Negro poet to attune his ear to that peculiar grace, to study it just as Synge studied it in the speech of the fisherman and tinkers and peasants of the Aran Islands' (Hutchinson 1995: 259), anticipating the turn to 'folk' expression in Johnson's *God's Trombones* (1927) and work by Langston Hughes, Zora Neale Hurston and Sterling Brown. A more political linkage is implicit in Anne Spencer's poem on Terence McSweeney, the Lord Mayor of Cork who died after a hunger strike in 1921 (Honey 1989: 55).

But was this thinking riddled with assumptions about race which themselves perpetuate racial categories (as Walter Benn Michaels has recently argued in *Our America*)? Michaels suggests that American nativism is not primitivist in Lawrence's neutral sense, interested in a shared aboriginality; rather it sees culture as ineluctably connected to a racial 'truth' which is shaped by American society: 'Pluralism . . . essentialized racism' by fetishing racial difference, rather than seeing races as measured against a universal scale (1995: 64). Race becomes inescapable, the core of culture. Part of the problem that Michaels addresses is the (erroneous) description of inheritance in terms of 'blood': 'blood-blending'; the 'taint' in the blood associated with racial 'others'; and the parallel insistence on a polygenist conception of race (ideas of racial groupings as ancient and distinct, akin to sub-species). Jean Toomer commented that 'blood-blending' was a mistake: while continuing to speak of 'blood' he insisted that 'black' or 'white' blood merely signalled 'pigmentations'; blood did not maintain its integrity within the body (1993: 109). But black writers themselves succumb to metaphors of 'blood', as in Countee Cullen's 'Heritage' – a poem which, even as it debates an African heritage, nevertheless assigns it to the place of passion, the rhythm in the blood. Kallen, Du Bois and others speak of 'blood', but by 1920 it was increasingly displaced by notions of ethnic identity derived from Boas, and in the 1920s 'race' becomes a more ambiguous entity – often seen as performative rather than inscribed. Moreover racial *interchange* is one of the defining features of the Harlem Renaissance.

The Harlem Renaissance was produced by a confluence of factors: the great migration north to urban centres; political energies unleashed by returning black servicemen in the riot summer of 1919; and a greater sense of black solidarity in the face of organized racism (black Americans could no longer identify themselves as 'mulatto' on census forms after the war). The movement was characterized by fierce (though sometimes coded) internal debates, for example between the culturalism of Locke, Charles Johnson and *Opportunity* magazine, on the one hand, and the more political line of Du Bois, Jessie Faucet and *Crisis* on the other. There were arguments about class and about the role of 'folk' expression and the vernacular; about the status of Africa; and about forms of separatism. The affiliations and stances within the movement were also complicated by the fact that many of its leaders were gay.

The notion of a black cultural nationalism was one of the contradictory currents of Alain Locke's introduction to his anthology *The New Negro* (1925), the work, beginning as an issue of the magazine *Survey Graphic*, which defined the movement. The historiography of the Harlem Renaissance has founded itself on this nationalism, which for Locke was not separatist but rather expressive of an Americanism forced to consider itself in racial terms. For Locke, 'the revaluation by white and black alike of the Negro in terms of his artistic endowments and cultural contributions, past and prospective' offers a route to participation in American life (Gates 1997: 969). If Du Bois was to reply that artistic expression is often denied at the first hurdle – black artists could not get into art schools – and if Locke's position looks elitist, his answer was also present in Du Bois's work: racism and the political exclusion of the African-American produces a spirituality and a self-consciousness which is the greatest gift of American culture. The African-American, for both Du Bois and Locke, is prophetic, carrying a power generated from repression – a power Du Bois sees in Hegelian terms as emerging from the self-knowledge intrinsic to slavery.

Early studies of the Harlem Renaissance either located a nascent 'black aesthetic' in the period or criticized its writers for adopting 'bourgeois' models and accepting white patronage; the same white patrons have been accused of primitivist condescension. But recent historians have come to see the Harlem Renaissance as a scene of cultural interchange. This is not simply the tourism represented by Harlem nightlife; it includes liberal white interest in the 'racial' voice, involving sponsorship and interest from publishers like Knopf and A. & C. Boni, and from both radical journals like *The Liberator* and mainstream ones like *The Nation*. From Locke's point of view, any cross-over between black and white could be potentially progressive; Du Bois himself praised Eugene O'Neill for engaging with unidealized black characters in *The Emperor Jones* and *All God's Chillun Got Wings*.

The issue of cultural exchange finds a rather literal focus in the novel of 'passing'. 'Passing' is sometimes said to be a marginal topic: only whitish people can pass; most are middle class; it is a phenomenon of a deracinated urban population. But passing is important for reasons related to racial identity, as well as the peculiar asymmetry of race in America, which could deem a person with one black great-grandparent irreducibly black (definitions varied from state to state). This asymmetry generates both the 'white' African-American and subtextual gaps in relation to unacknowledged parents: the white father who appears as a pair of shoes in Johnson's novel; the missing Danish parent in Nella Larsen's *Quicksand*. If racial discourse declares that one *must* be a race, then adopting another – even if it represents the majority of one's genetic inheritance – is construed as a betrayal of identity. For Toomer the person who passes 'leaves the colored group and "loses" himself in the white world' (1996: 57); for others, including Johnson in *The Autobiography of an Ex-Colored Man* (1912) and Larsen in *Passing* (1929), it involves the loss of self, culture, even death. Or if culture is retained, it remains a deracinated trace, as in Johnson's protagonist's ragtime piano, which raises the unnerving possibility that he is a reverse passer, a white man exploring black culture.

Understandably, the reading of culture in terms of race was something some black writers rebelled against: George Schulyer insisted that there could be no 'Negro' art, and acidly deconstructed the tropes of passing narratives in *Black No More* (1932), which culminates in a scene in which the president of the Anglo-Saxon Association is lynched by blanched 'Negroes' (1998: 183). The meditation on dusk in African-American writing is one trope for the effacement of race: abstract in William Stanley Braithwaite's 1912 essay 'Twilight: An Impression' (Wilson 1999: 221–3); more concrete in the dissolving of colour into purples in *Cane*; a recurrent trope in the poetry of Angela Weld Grimké who wrote poems on dusk, dawn, twilight and 'Tenebris' (Honey 1989: 179–85). In Larsen's *Quicksand* the insistent binaries of race are, in similar fashion, momentarily dissolved into infinite gradations. In the Cabaret scene: 'A dozen shades slid by. There was sooty black, shiny black, taupe, mahogany, bronze, copper, gold, orange, yellow, peach, ivory, pinky white, pastry white' (1992: 90). But at the novel's end the biological imperative is reasserted with a savage vengeance, the heroine married to a Southern minister and becoming a 'racial mother', buried under a wave of babies.

Toomer's attitude to race is particularly complex. *Cane* is insistent on the equation of race and voice, as we saw in chapter 4. The individuated narrator emerges slowly from the collective voice of the opening story; moves through southern violence to the city; and there rediscovers the traces of race: roots, fellow-feeling, passing as self-betrayal. But Toomer himself had, as *Cane* was published, begun to move 'beyond' race, refusing to 'feature Negro' in his publicity, and declaring that his identity was irrevocably mixed; an identity he defined as 'a new race . . . at once interracial and unique' (1996: 58); a race he would call 'American'. This threatens to make *Cane* both an expression of racial identity and its deconstruction – a 'passing' narrative of someone in a 'Negro' phase – were it not for the obvious utopianism involved. Yet *Cane* can be described both as a fantasy of race in its poetic version of the South; and as an aestheticization of race in which defining scenes – lynching, passing – are explored as tropes, for example of the collapse of desire and violence, the blazon and the burnt body, in the poem 'Portrait in Georgia', with its hair 'coiled like a lyncher's rope' and the body of the beloved 'white as the ash/of black flesh after flame' (1988: 29). *Cane* simultaneously asserts the importance of race and dissolves it into the aesthetic, not least in its multi-generic complexity and range of point of view. Unlike Langston Hughes and others, Toomer believed that African-American folk culture was inevitably dying; his text preserves its fragments. Later Eugene Jolas saw, like Toomer, an 'inter-racial synthesis' in American culture, one symptom of which was a new language (Jolas 1936).

A final aspect of racial interchange which needs discussion is the link between communism and black America. Retrospective accounts like Ralph Ellison's *Invisible Man* (1952) – which implies that the unspecified 'party' merely saw Harlem as a source of radical energy – offer a revisionism conditioned by the Cold War, effacing an important history. Even Ellison's key aesthetic reference, Louis Armstrong's performance of 'Black and Blue', conceals a political trace: it was written by communist Andy Razaf (Billie Holiday's anti-lynching anthem 'Strange Fruit' has a similar background). Claude McKay's experience offers a trajectory which we might place alongside that of Ellison's hero: having published dialect poetry in Jamaica, he studied agriculture at the Tuskegee Institute before moving to Harlem. In England in 1920 he worked for *The Worker's Dreadnought*, and back in New York was briefly co-editor of *The Liberator*. In 1922 he travelled to the Third Communist International in Moscow and lectured in Russia, publishing *Negroes in America*; much of the rest of the decade he spent in France. Since it was only in 1924 that Alain Locke took up McKay's poetry, and in 1928 that his novel *Home to Harlem* appeared, his radicalism *predates* the 'Harlem Renaissance' – in sharp contrast to Ellison's hero, who is seduced after his arrival.

In fact, the alliance of black writers and communism in the 1930s was important for the continuation of black writing, and as Cary Nelson shows, represented a politics in which race was a vital component; and in which white authors also engaged with lynching, the Scottsboro case, and black heroism: *The Poetry of the Negro*, the collection edited by Arna Bontemps and Langston Hughes in 1949, includes forty-eight 'Tributary Poems by Non-Negroes'. Hughes's 'Air-Raid Over Harlem' and 'Advertisement for the Waldorf Astoria' (published in the *New Masses* in 1931 with pictures of diners and limousine imitating an up-market advertisement) directly anticipate the radical address of the Black Arts Movement. Hughes and twenty-one others travelled to Russia in 1932, planning to make a film called *Black and White*; and Hughes continued to support radical causes throughout the 1930s (for example translating the Spanish republican Frederico Garcia Lorca's poems for the *New Masses*).

The confluence of politics, race and notions of national identity reaches one terminus in the Federal Writers' Project (discussed briefly in chapter 3). Between 1935 and 1939 the FWP employed many black writers on projects reflecting its vision of America as a patchwork of regional and ethnic cultures: the collection of folklore and the narratives of surviving ex-slaves. Sterling Brown served as director of the 'Negro' section of the American Guide series; Richard Wright, Zora Neale Hurston, Ralph Ellison, Arna Bontemps, Robert Hayden, Margaret Walker, Frank Yerby and others worked for the project, later producing a range of later texts in which its aims are reflected: Brown's anthology *The Negro Caravan* (1941) and Walker's 'Bad Woman Folk Ballads' and 'Folk Sermon' are examples. Even in *Invisible Man* the legacy of a FWP project on New York 'beneath the streets' is apparent – a project censored because of Cold War fears that it would be used by subversives (Gitelman 1992). In this sense, Ellison's alienated, anonymous narrator conceals a suppressed collective voice.

Race is, as we have seen, of particular importance to American modernism. But notions of national identity and national character as 'tribal' can

also be seen in English, Irish, Scottish and Welsh modernisms. Racial thinking sometimes appears in more subtle forms – the emphasis on continuity
of occupation and on Anglo-Saxon roots in *Howard's End* – but also finds
a more explicit form in Yeats's late excavation of a 'true' Anglo-Irish line
and in Eliot's meditations on blood and Englishness in the *Four Quartets*.
Or one might consider the discourse of peoples – 'and kindreds / *et gentium,
cenhedloed, und Völker*' – of David Jones's *Anathemata* (1952); as the footnote
says, 'we are Germans, Latins, Celts and can apprehend only in a Latin,
Germanic and Celtic fashion' (1972: 241).

It should also be noted that a discourse of the 'counter-primitive' is
another component of modernism: for example in relation to jazz. Many
saw it as the natural expression of the era, both in its freedoms and pathologies. The white bandleader Stan Kenton wrote: 'I think the human race today
may be going through things it never experienced before, types of nervous
frustration and thwarted emotional development which traditional music is
entirely incapable of not only satisfying but expressing. That is why I believe
jazz is the new music that came along just in time' (Dyer 1998: 193–4). In
the 1920s, 'Jazz' could be used as a term for a variety of stylistic dislocations:
the art deco ceramics of Clarice Cliff; clothes, dance styles; or attacked in
such essays as Clive Bell's 'Plus de Jazz', which criticized the 'jazz' style of
Ulysses. John Howard Lawson's *Processional*, a radical play about a miner's
strike in the American South, could use jazz as an emblem of chaos; and
even the leading black organization, the NAACP, was high-mindedly suspicious of popular music. Theodor Adorno saw jazz in terms of a co-opted
'primitive' musical utterance whose freedoms became another bourgeois
accomplishment via the dance class and commercial music.

The counter-primitive appears at its starkest in Wyndham Lewis's *Paleface* (1929), a text which, notwithstanding its extravagant defence of western
('paleface') art in the face of the 'jazzification' of American culture, offers
one of the most sustained and in some ways sympathetic contemporary engagements with the Harlem Renaissance. Lewis's targets include the
'Colour phantasies' (1929: 21) of enthusiasts for black literature and the
guilty liberal sentimentalism which would focus on racial rather than more
broadly conceived political injustice; his own celebration of the *daimon* of
whiteness is advanced as a kind of ironic deconstruction of racial thinking
in favour of the abstract idea. The book also offers a remarkable analysis of
what he calls 'political primitivism', that is the violent regression implicit in
technological society (and war) which depicts itself as progress – an analysis in which the hidden link between the technological and the primitive
is again articulated.

THE ANIMAL

A final 'other' one might ponder briefly is the animal – a presence in human
life which declines rapidly in the period of modernism. Between 1905 and
1911, horses were replaced by electricity and gasoline powering trams and

buses in London: 7,000 vanished from the trolleys alone, and with them a world of steaming bodies and flowing waste. One might speculate that technological expansion places pressure on the equivalence of bodies and machines so important to the Industrial Revolution: horsepower seems inappropriate to a 20-ton press; it is difficult to see technology as 'standing in' for bodies. One of the earliest 'event' films is Thomas Edison's *Electrocuting an Elephant*, in which the conspicuous waste of flesh seems to signal a different economy, that of the spectacle itself.

What does the vanishing of animals from our lives mean? In 'The French Poodle' Wyndham Lewis suggested that it represents a collapse of distance, increasing human cruelty since what had previously been inflicted on the animal is now inflicted on man. The disappearance of the working bodies of animals might also be linked to the reappearance of the animal under the sign of the perverse, or the obsession with voicing animals – Georg Grotz's 'Revolution of the Beasts' in his play *Methusalem*, Thomas Mann's *Bashan and I*, Woolf's *Flush*, the talking dogs and parrots opening Lawrence's *Mornings in Mexico* and so on. Freud's Wolf Man and Rat Man cases are of a different order, but here too the animal and the human are placed together at the origins of psychic life. The mocking voice of the parrot echoes through a number of modernist texts – from the 'Allez-vous-en!' of Chopin's *The Awakening* – urging her protagonist to wander beyond limits – to the 'Perro! Oh, Perr-rro!' of the parrots mocking the dog in *Mornings in Mexico*. The cry of Lawrence's birds is linked by Lewis to a flight from mind, into the primitive, visceral and communal. As the human interior becomes animal, the exterior becomes in parallel fashion simply a machine-like surface: a marionette-body; a robotic blank from which the animal has been excluded – another version of primitivism.

The apotheosis of the modernist writing of the animal is surely Djuna Barnes's *Nightwood* (1936), which describes humans in terms of dogs, elephants, hyenas, birds, horses, deer, swans. If *Nightwood* has as one of its primary impulses a horror at the human, that horror has two axes, as suggested above. One is the doll: a self imagined nostalgically or perversely before gender, whether the impermeable puppet-body of the ambiguously named circus performer Frau Mann, the prince-princess of childhood, or the dolls exchanged by the novel's lesbian lovers. The other is 'the beast', understood as dirt, the decay of sexual division into desire and loss. These two come together in an extraordinary passage describing Robin Vote, the text's obscure object of desire:

The woman who presents herself to the spectator as a 'picture' forever arranged, is, for the contemplative mind, the chiefest danger. Sometimes one meets a woman who is beast turning human. Such a person's every movement will reduce to an image of a forgotten experience; a mirage of an eternal wedding cast on the racial memory; as insupportable a joy as would be the vision of an eland coming down an aisle of trees, chapleted with orange blossoms and bridal veil, a hoof raised in the economy of fear, stepping in the trepidation of flesh that will become myth; as the unicorn is neither man nor beast deprived, but human hunger pressing its breast to its prey.

(1963: 59–60)

This is not easy, but it seems to gesture towards a kind of primary fixation, an image of a plenitude which hovers on the borders of the human, which stabilizes a savagery which is nevertheless enacted in a kind of eucharist: this woman is 'eaten death returning'.

The novel's final chapter, 'The Possessed', ends in a 'decaying chapel' (in part parody of the climax of *The Waste Land*). Robin enacts a strange scene with her abandoned lover Nora's dog, 'going down' with him, striking her body against his, and finally weeping with him. This is like the mimetic impulse as described by the Surrealist Roger Caillois: insect camouflage represents an enthralment which displaces the self from the centre of the picture – the image blending into the background becomes a function of that background and the gaze of another. Robin, whose self and desire can never be stabilized, who is described in terms of somnambulism and ambulatory automatism, 'goes down' into the animal. The textual flows of *Nightwood* work in an analogous way, blending Nora and others into discourse.

We began with Hegel, and as we have seen modernism can be portrayed as an encounter of self and other in which difference is effaced and reasserted; or collapsed with problematic results. The subject in the 'slave' position often claims a particular insight. But many accounts portray modernism in terms of mastery rather than enslavement; an armouring of the self against a collapse into the other. Or to turn this around, paranoia becomes a way of life, and defence against others and the flows of feeling associated with them – women, crowds, Jews – becomes an imperative. But as we also saw in the discussion of telepathy in the last chapter, in a world conceived of in terms of flows of energy boundaries are always permeable. Rejection of the other and its incorporation work in tandem. If the self is constituted by a series of identifications which undercut its fantasies of autonomy, then the very denial of linkages exposes a narcissistic identification with some prior and supposedly 'integral' object. As Diana Fuss puts it, 'Identity is the psychical mechanism that produces self-recognition', but when she asks 'What happens when the subject refuses to incorporate and resists identifying with the Other?', her answer is that the subject becomes haunted (1955: 2, 36). As indeed the other haunts the texts of modernism.

I opened this study by pointing out that modernity involves, at least potentially, the representation of everything in human knowledge and experience as a form of culture. Perhaps we should recognize that to speak of animal as 'other' is to confront the cost of the assimilation of everything to the standard of the modern – a cost which postmodernism has at best simply confirmed. The aesthetics of modernism, variously founded as they are on visions of reform and experimental freedom, on notions of scientific exactitude, on embodiment, desire, connection and consumption, offer a culture in which the expansion of the human and the rejection of standards perceived as external to the human are keynotes; in which culture forms an all-enveloping totality. That stance has its dangers, in particular the fantasy that aesthetic renovation would produce new thought, new forms of political life, a better world. As the history of the twentieth century so often demonstrated, that can be a dangerous illusion, shot through with a restless utopianism in which the obdurate truths of reality – of what we call Nature, or what Slavoj Žižek likes to call the 'Big Other' – are denied. Modernism's inheritance includes both hope and a bitter disappointment, and perhaps the best image of the dangers of that hope is the end of Pound's *Cantos*, often (mistakenly, surely) read as a retraction – fragments in which the ageing Pound contemplates his 'errors and wrecks' but insists on the 'gold thread' of rightness in the pattern of his poetic and political thought, extracted from the 'shambles' of history. But it is, finally, to the 'squirrels and bluejays' which saved him in prison – the world outside; the 'pale flare over marshes' – to which Pound makes his most moving references in these lines; a recognition, perhaps, of the limits of literature's desire to assimilate or create a world.

References and Further Reading

Date of original publication of primary texts is given in square brackets.

PRIMARY SOURCES

Adams, Henry 1973. *The Education of Henry Adams*, ed. Ernest Samuels. Boston: Houghton Mifflin.

Adorno, Theodor 2002. *Essays on Music*, ed. Richard Leppert, trans. Susan H. Gillespie et al. Berkeley: University of California Press.

Aldington, Richard 1930. *A Dream in the Luxembourg*. London: Chatto and Windus.

Apollonio, Umbro, ed. 1973. *Futurist Manifestoes*. London: Thames & Hudson.

Arlen, Michael 1923. *The Green Hat*. London: Collins.

Auden, W. H. 1958 [1937]. *The Ascent of F.6 and On the Frontier*. London: Faber & Faber.

Bann, Stephen, ed. 1974. *The Tradition of Constructivism*. New York: Da Capo.

Barnes, Djuna 1963 [1936]. *Nightwood*. London: Faber & Faber.

Barnes, Djuna 1996. *Collected Stories*, ed. Phillip Herring. Los Angeles: Sun & Moon.

Beard, George M. 1881. *American Nervousness, Its Causes and Consequences*. New York: G. P. Putnam & Sons.

Beckett, Samuel 1983. *Disjecta: Miscellaneous Writings and a Dramatic Fragment*. London: John Calder.

Benjamin, Walter 1973a. *Illuminations*, ed. Hannah Arendt, trans. Harry Zohn. London: Fontana.

Benjamin, Walter 1973b. *Understanding Brecht*, trans. Anna Bostock, intro. Stanley Mitchell. London: NLB.

Benjamin, Walter 1999. *Selected Writings*. Vol. 2: *1927–1934*, trans. Rodney Livingstone et al., ed. Michael W. Jennings et al. Cambridge, MA: Belknap Press.

Bergson, Henri 1988 [1896]. *Matter and Memory*, trans. N. H. Paul and W. S. Palmer. New York: Zone.

Bergson, Henri 1998 [1907]. *Creative Evolution*. Trans. Arthur Mitchell. Mineola, NY: Dover.

Bergson, Henri 1919. *Time and Free Will*, trans. F. L. Pogson. New York: Macmillan.

Blakeston, Oswell 1928. *Through a Yellow Glass*. London and Territet: Pool.

Blavatsky, [Madame] Helena 1877. *Isis Unveiled*. 2 vols. New York: J. W. Bouton.

Bloch, Ernst 1998. *Literary Essays*, trans. Andrew Joron et al. Stanford: Stanford University Press.

Bourne, Randolph 1977 [1916]. 'Transnational America', in *The Radical Will: Selected Writings 1911–1918*, ed. Olaf Hansen. New York: Urizen. 248–64.

Bowen, Marjorie 1909. *Black Magic: A Tale of the Rise and Fall of Antichrist*. London: Alston Rivers.

Broch, Hermann 1983 [1945]. *The Death of Virgil*, trans. Jean Starr Untermeyer. Oxford: Oxford University Press.

Brooks, Cleanth 1939. *Modern Poetry and the Tradition*. Chapel Hill: University of North Carolina Press.

Brown, Bob 1931. *Gems: A Censored Anthology*. Cagnes-sur-Mer: Roving Eye Press.

Brown, Sterling A. 1996. *The Collected Poems of Sterling A. Brown*, ed. Michael S. Harper Evanston, IL: Triquarterly Books.

Butts, Mary 1991. *With and Without Buttons and Other Stories*. Manchester: Carcanet.

Butts, Mary 1998. *Ashe of Rings and Other Writings*. Kingston, NY: McPherson.

Caillois, Roger 1984 [1935]. 'Mimicry and Legendary Psychasthenia', *October*, 31: 59–74.

Carpenter, Edward 1889. *Civilization: Its Cause and Cure*. London: Swan Sonnenschein.

Catchings, Waddill and William Trufant Foster 1928. *The Road to Plenty*. Boston & New York: Houghton Mifflin.

Cather, Willa 1994 [1918]. *My Ántonia*, ed. Charles Mignon et al. Lincoln: University of Nebraska Press.

Cather, Willa 2002 [1925]. *The Professor's House*, ed. James Woodress et al. Lincoln: University of Nebraska Press.

Cendrars, Blaise 1992. *Complete Poems*, trans Ron Padgett, intro. Jay Bochner. Berkeley: University of California Press.

Clarke, Graham, ed. 1990. *T. S. Eliot: Critical Assessments*. 4 vols. London: Christopher Helm.

Cournos, John 1922. *Babel*. New York: Boni & Liveright.

Croly, Herbert 1965 [1909]. *The Promise of American Life*, ed. Arthur Schlesinger Jr. Cambridge, MA: Harvard University Press.

Cunard, Nancy, ed. 2002 [1934]. *Negro: An Anthology*, abridged by Hugh Ford. New York: Continuum.

Dilthey, Wilhelm 1985. *Poetry and Experience. Selected Works*, vol. 5, ed. Rudolf A. Makkreel and Frithjof Rodi. Princeton: Princeton University Press.

Donald, James, Anne Friedberg and Laura Marcus, eds. 1998. *Close Up 1927–1933: Cinema and Modernism*. London: Cassell.

Dos Passos, John 1937. *U.S.A.* New York: Random House.

Dreiser, Theodore 1954 [1915]. *The Genius*. Cleveland: World.

Du Bois, W. E. 1996. *The Oxford W. E. B. DuBois Reader*, ed. Eric J. Sundquist. Oxford: Oxford University Press.

Eisenstein, Sergei 1929. 'The New Language of Cinematography', *Close Up*, IV/5: 10–13.

Elias, Norbert 1998 [1935]. 'The Kitsch Style and the Age of Kitsch', in *The Norbert Elias Reader*, ed. Johan Goudsblom and Stephen Mennell. Oxford: Blackwell, 1998, 26–35.

Eliot, T. S. 1929. *For Lancelot Andrews*. New York: Doubleday.

Eliot, T. S. 1951. *Selected Essays*, 3rd edn. London: Faber & Faber.

Eliot, T. S. 1964 [1933]. *The Use of Poetry and the Use of Criticism*. London: Faber & Faber.

Eliot, T. S. 1971 [1922]. *The Waste Land: A Facsimile and Transcript of the Original Drafts*, ed. Valerie Eliot. London: Faber & Faber.

Eliot, T. S. 1974. *Collected Poems*, rev. edn. London: Faber & Faber.

Eliot, T. S. 1975. *Selected Prose of T. S. Eliot*, ed. Frank Kermode. London: Faber & Faber.

Eliot, T. S. 1996. *Inventions of the March Hare: Poems 1909–1917*, ed. Christopher Ricks. New York: Harcourt, Brace.

Ellis, Havelock 1926 [1905]. *Studies in the Psychology of Sex*. Vol. IV: *Sexual Selection in Man*. Philadelphia: F. A. Davis.

Ellison, Ralph 1965 [1952]. *Invisible Man*. London: Penguin.

Emerson, Ralph Waldo 1983. *Essays and Lectures*, ed. Joel Porte. New York: Library of America.

Faulkner, William 1960 [1932]. *Light in August*. London: Penguin.

Faulkner, William 1996 [1930]. *As I Lay Dying*. London: Vintage.

Faulkner, William 1995 [1929]. *The Sound and the Fury*. London: Vintage.

Fisher, Rudolph 1995 [1932]. *The Conjur Man Dies*. London: X Press.

Fitzgerald, F. Scott 1986 [1934]. *Tender is the Night: A Romance*, rev. edn. London: Penguin.

Fitzgerald, F. Scott 2000 [1925]. *The Great Gatsby*, ed. Tony Tanner. London: Penguin.

Flournoy, T. 1994 [1900]. *From India to Planet Mars*, ed. Sonu Shamdasani. Princeton: Princeton University Press.

Ford, Ford Madox 1924. *Joseph Conrad: A Personal Remembrance*. London: Duckworth.

Ford, Ford Madox 1984 [1929]. *No Enemy*. New York: Ecco.

Ford, Ford Madox 1987. *The Ford Madox Ford Reader*, ed. Sondra J. Stang, foreword Graham Greene. London: Paladin.

Ford, Ford Madox 1990 [1915]. *The Good Soldier*, ed. Thomas C. Moser. Oxford: Oxford University Press.

Forster, E. M. *Aspects of the Novel*. 1927. London: Edward Arnold.

Forster, E. M. 1975. [1910]. *Howard's End*, ed. Oliver Stallybrass. Harmondsworth: Penguin.

Forster, E. M. 1983 [1924]. *A Passage to India*, ed. Oliver Stallybrass. Harmondsworth: Penguin.

Forster, E. M. 1997. *The Machine Stops and Other Stories*, ed. Rod Mengham. London: Andre Deutsch.

Frazer, James George 1922. [2 vols., 1890] *The Golden Bough: A Study in Magic and Religion*, abridged edn. London: Macmillan.

Freud, Sigmund 1990 [1918]. *From the History of an Infantile Neurosis. Case Histories II*. Penguin Freud Library, vol. 9, ed. Angela Richards. London: Penguin.

Freud, Sigmund 1991 [1917]. *Mourning and Melancholia. On Metapsychology: The Theory of Psychoanalysis*. Penguin Freud Library, vol. 11, ed. Angela Richards. London: Penguin.

Freud, Sigmund 1993 [1919]. *'A Child is being Beaten'. On Psychopathology*. Penguin Freud Library, vol. 10, ed. Angela Richards. London: Penguin, 159–94.

Freud, Sigmund 1987. *A Phylogenic Fantasy*, ed. Ilse Grubrick-Simitis. Cambridge, MA: Belknap Press.

Fry, Roger 1998 [1920]. *Vision and Design*, ed. J. B. Bullen. New York: Dover.

Gardner, Brian 1976. *Up the Line to Death: The War Poets 1914–1918*, foreword Edmund Blunden. London: Methuen.

Gascoyne, David 1998. *Collected Poems 1988*. Oxford: Oxford University Press.

Gates, Henry Louis, Jnr. and Nellie Y. McKay, eds. 1997. *The Norton Anthology of African-American Literature*. New York: W. W. Norton.

Glynn, Elinor *Three Weeks*. 1907. 2nd edn. London: Duckworth.

Hardy, Thomas 1984. *The Life and Work of Thomas Hardy*, ed. Michael Millgate. London: Macmillan.

Honey, Maureen, ed. 1989. *Shadowed Dreams: Women's Poetry of the Harlem Renaissance*. New Brunswick: Rutgers University Press.

Hulme, T. E. 1987 [1924]. *Speculations: Essays on Humanism and the Philosophy of Art*, ed. Herbert Read. London: Routledge.

Hulme, T. E. 1955. *Further Speculations*, ed. Samuel Hynes. Minneapolis: University of Minnesota Press.

Huxley, Aldous 1962 [1939]. *After Many a Summer*. London: Chatto & Windus.

Huxley, Aldous 1985 [1943]. *The Art of Seeing.* London: Triad.

Ibsen, Henrik 1980. *Plays: One. Ghosts, The Wild Duck, The Master Builder*, trans. Michael Meyer. London: Eyre Methuen.

James, C. L. R. 1933. *The Case for West Indies Self-Government.* London: Hogarth Press.

James, C. L. R. 1992. *The C. L. R. James Reader*, ed. Anna Grimshaw. Oxford: Blackwell.

James, C. L. R. 1995. *Special Delivery: The Letters of C. L. R. James to Constance Webb 1939–1948*, ed. Anna Grimshaw. Oxford: Blackwell.

James, C. L. R. 2003 [1932]. *Letters from London*, ed. Nicholas Laughlin, intro. Kenneth Ramchand. Oxford: Signal Books.

James, Henry 1992. *The Turn of the Screw and Other Stories.* Oxford: Oxford University Press.

James, Henry 1999. *Henry James on Culture: Collected Essays on Politics and the American Social Scene*, ed. Pierre A. Walker. Lincoln: University of Nebraska Press.

James, William 1950 [1890]. *Principles of Psychology.* 2 vols. New York: Dover.

James, William 1988. *On Vital Reserves.* Westminster, MD: Christian Classics.

Jameson, Storm 1982 [1933]. *Men Against Women*, intro. Elaine Feinstein. London: Virago.

Jolas, Eugene 1936. 'Race and Language', *transition* 24: 111–12.

Johnson, James Weldon. 1990 [1912]. *The Autobiography of an Ex-Colored Man.* New York: Penguin.

Johnson, James Weldon. 1976 [1927]. *God's Trombones.* New York: Penguin.

Jones, David 1972 [1952]. *The Anathemata. Fragments of an Attempted Writing.* London: Faber & Faber.

Jones, David 2002. *Wedding Poems*, ed. Thomas Dilworth. London: Enitharmon.

Jones, Peter, ed. 1972. *Imagist Poetry.* Harmondsworth: Penguin.

Joyce, James 1993. *Ulysses*, ed. Jeri Johnson. Oxford: Oxford University Press.

Joyce, James 2000. *Occasional, Critical and Political Writings*, ed. Kevin Barry. Oxford: Oxford University Press.

Kolocotroni, Vassiliki, Jane Goldman and Olga Taxidou, eds. 1998. *Modernism: An Anthology of Sources and Documents*, Edinburgh: Edinburgh University Press.

Kracauer, Siegfried 1995. *The Mass Ornament: Weimar Essays*, trans. and ed. Thomas Y. Levin. Cambridge, MA: Harvard University Press.

Larsen, Nella 1992. *An Intimation of Things Different: The Collected Fiction of Nella Larsen*, ed. Charles R. Larson. New York: Anchor.

Lawrence, D. H. 1920. *The Lost Girl.* London: Martin Secker.

Lawrence, D. H. 1950 [1927]. *Mornings in Mexico.* London: Heinemann.

Lawrence, D. H. 1955 [1922]. *The Plumed Serpent.* London: Heinemann.

Lawrence, D. H. 1960 [1920]. *Women in Love.* Harmondsworth: Penguin.

Lawrence, D. H. 1972. *The Complete Poems of D. H. Lawrence.* 2 vols. ed. Vivian de Sola Pinto and Warren Roberts. London: Heinemann.

Lawrence, D. H. 1990. *England, My England and Other Stories*, ed. Bruce Steele. Cambridge: Cambridge University Press.

Lawton, Anna, ed. 1988. *Russian Futurism through its Manifestoes 1912–1928*, trans. Anna Lawton and Herbert Eagle. Ithaca: Cornell University Press.

Leavis, F. R. 1963 [1932]. *New Bearings in English Poetry: A Study of the Contemporary Situation.* Harmondsworth: Penguin.

Leavis, Q. D. 1965 [1932]. *Fiction and the Reading Public.* London: Chatto & Windus.

Le Bon, Gustave 1896. *The Crowd: A Study of the Popular Mind.* London: Ernest Benn.

Lee, Gerald Stanley 1913. *Crowds.* London: Curtis Brown.

Lewis, Wyndham 1927. *Time and Western Man*. London: Chatto & Windus.

Lewis, Wyndham 1929. *Paleface. The Philosophy of the 'Melting-Pot'*. London: Chatto & Windus.

Lewis, Wyndham 1937. *Blasting and Bombardiering*. London: Eyre & Spottiswoode.

Lewis, Wyndham 1963. *The Letters of Wyndham Lewis*, ed. W. K. Rose. New York: New Directions.

Lewis, Wyndham 1968 [1918]. *Tarr*. London: Calder & Boyars.

Lewis, Wyndham 1989a [1926]. *The Art of Being Ruled*, ed. Reed Way Dasenbrock. Santa Rosa, CA: Black Sparrow.

Lewis, Wyndham 1989b [1951]. 'The Sea-Mists of the Winter'. *The Essential Wyndham Lewis*, ed. Julian Symonds. London: Andre Deutsch. 340–4.

Lewis, Wyndham, ed. 1997 [1914]. *Blast 1*. Santa Rosa, CA: Black Sparrow.

Lewis, Wyndham ed. 2000 [1915]. *Blast 2*. Santa Rosa, CA: Black Sparrow.

Lindsay, Vachel 1922. *The Art of the Moving Picture*. 2nd rev. edn. New York: Macmillan.

Lindsay, Vachel 1992 [1914]. *The Congo and Other Poems*. New York: Dover.

Loy, Mina 1996. *The Lost Lunar Baedeker*, selected and ed. Roger L. Conover. New York: Farrar, Straus, Giroux.

MacGreevy, Thomas 1931a. *T. S. Eliot: A Study*. London: Chatto & Windus.

MacGreevy, Thomas 1931b. *Richard Aldington: An Englishman*. London: Chatto & Windus.

MacNeice, Louis 1979. *Collected Poems*. London: Faber & Faber.

Mach, Ernst 1959 [1906]. *The Analysis of Sensations*, trans. S. M. Williams, rev. Sidney Waterlow. New York: Dover.

Mallgrave, Harry Francis and Eleftherios Ikonomou, ed. and trans 1994. *Empathy, Form and Space: Problems in German Aesthetics, 1873–1893*. Santa Monica: Getty Center.

Mann, Thomas 1970. *The Letters of Thomas Mann 1889–1955*, trans. Richard and Clara Winston. 2 vols. London: Secker & Warburg.

Mann, Thomas 1960. *The Magic Mountain*, trans. H. T. Lowe-Porter. Harmondsworh: Penguin.

Mannin, Ethel 1925. *Sounding Brass*. London: Jarrolds.

Mansfield, Katherine 1962 [1920]. *Bliss and Other Stories*. Harmondsworth: Penguin.

Marinetti, F. T. 1972. *Selected Writings*, ed. R. W. Flint. London: Secker & Warburg.

Marinetti, F. T. 2002. *Selected Poems and Related Prose*, selected by Luce Marinetti, trans. Elizabeth R. Napier and Barbara R. Studholme. New Haven: Yale University Press.

Marsden, Dora 1913. 'Views and Comments', *New Freewoman* I/1 (June): 5.

Marsden, Dora 1917. 'A Definition of Attention', *The Egoist*, IV/8 (September): 114–15.

Marx, Karl and Frederick Engels 1975 [1848]. *Manifesto of the Communist Party*. Peking: Foreign Languages Press.

Marx, Karl and Frederick Engels 1979. *The Letters of Karl Marx*, selected, trans. and ed. Saul K. Padover. Englewood Cliffs, Prentice-Hall.

McDougall, William 1921. *National Welfare and National Decay*. London: Methuen.

Melville, Herman 1984 [1853]. 'Bartleby the Scrivener. A Tale of Wall Street', in *Pierre and Other Works*, ed. Harrison Hayford. New York: Library of America.

Mirrlees, Hope 1919. *Paris: A Poem*. London: Hogarth Press.

Monro, Harold 1915. 'The Imagists Discussed', *The Egoist*, Special Imagist Number, II/5: 77–80.

Moore, Marianne 1951. *Collected Poems*. New York: Macmillan.

Moore, Marianne 1987. *The Complete Prose of Marianne Moore*, ed. Patricia C. Willis. Harmondsworth: Penguin.

Musil, Robert 1995 [1978]. *The Man Without Qualities*, trans. Sophie Wilkins and Burton Pike. London: Picador.

Nichols, Robert 1929. 'The Movies as Medium', *The Realist*, 1/1: 144–64.

Niebur, Reinhold 1916. 'The Failure of German-Americans', *Atlantic Monthly*, 118, 13–18.

North, Joseph, ed. 1972. *New Masses: An Anthology of the Rebel Thirties*, intro. Maxwell Geismar. Berlin: Seven Seas.

Olsen, Charles 1989 [1969]. *Letters for Origin: 1950–1956*, ed. A. Glover, foreword J. Tytell. New York: Paragon House.

Olsen, Charles 1997. *Collected Prose*, ed. D. Allen and B. Friedlander, intro. R. Creeley. Berkeley: University of California Press.

Oppenheim, James 1918. 'The Young World', *The Dial*, LXIV (Feb.): 175–80.

Owen, Wilfred 1983. *The Complete Poems and Fragments*, ed. Jon Stallworthy. London: Chatto & Windus, Hogarth Press, Oxford University Press.

Pater, Walter 1980. *The Renaissance: Studies in Art and Poetry. The 1893 Text*, ed. Donald L. Hill. Berkeley: University of California Press.

Poe, Edgar Allan 1948. *The Letters of Edgar Allan Poe*. 2 vols., ed. John Ward Ostron. Cambridge, MA: Harvard University Press.

Poe, Edgar Allan 1984a. *Essays and Reviews*, ed. G. R. Thompson. New York: Library of America.

Poe, Edgar Allan 1984b. *Poetry and Tales*, ed. Patrick F. Quinn. New York: Library of America.

Pound, Ezra 1916. *Gaudier-Brzeska*. London: John Lane.

Pound, Ezra 1966 [1938]. *Guide to Kulchur*. London: Peter Owen.

Pound, Ezra 1951. *The Letters of Ezra Pound 1907–1941*, ed. D. D. Paige. London: Faber & Faber.

Pound, Ezra 1954. *Literary Essays of Ezra Pound*, ed. T. S. Eliot. London: Faber & Faber.

Pound, Ezra 1958. *Pavannes and Divagations*. New York: New Directions.

Pound, Ezra 1969 [1920]. *The Chinese Written Character as a Medium for Poetry*. San Francisco: City Light Books.

Pound, Ezra 1973. *Selected Prose 1909–1965*, ed. William Cookson. New York: New Directions.

Pound, Ezra 1975. *The Cantos*. London: Faber & Faber.

Pound, Ezra 1980. *Ezra Pound and the Visual Arts*, ed. Harriet Zinnes. New York: New Directions.

Pound, Ezra 1990 [1926]. *Personae: The Shorter Poems of Ezra Pound*, rev. edn., ed. Lea Baechler and A. Walton Litz. New York: New Directions.

Pound, Ezra 1996. *Machine Art and Other Writings: The Lost Thought of the Italian Years*, ed. Maria Luisa Ardizzone. Durham: Duke University Press.

Powell, Anne, ed. 1996. *The Fierce Light: The Battle of the Somme July–November 1916. Prose and Poetry*. Aberporth: Palladour Books.

Rait, Suzanne, and Trudy Tait, eds. 1997. *Women's Fiction and the Great War*. Oxford: Oxford University Press.

Riding [Jackson], Laura 1938. *The World and Ourselves* [*Epilogue* 4]. London: Chatto & Windus.

Riding [Jackson], Laura 1980 [1938]. *The Poems of Laura Riding*. Manchester: Carcanet.

Riding [Jackson], Laura, and Robert Graves 1927. *A Survey of Modernist Poetry*. London: Heinemann.

Rilke, Rainer Maria 1985 [1952]. *Letters on Cézanne*, ed. Clara Rilke, trans. Joel Agee. New York: Fromm.

Roberts, Michael 1933. *Critique of Poetry*, London: Jonathan Cape.

Rodker, John 1926. *The Future of Futurism*. London: Kegan Paul, Trench & Trubner.

Rodker, John 1996. *Poems & Adolphe 1920*, ed. Andrew Crozier. Manchester: Carcanet.

Rosenberg, Isaac 1984. *Collected Works*, ed. Ian Parsons. London: Chatto & Windus.

Rukeyser, Muriel 1949. *The Life of Poetry*. New York: A. A. Wyn.

Rukeyser, Muriel 1992. *Out of Silence: Selected Poems*. Evanston, IL: TriQuarterly Books.

Sandburg, Carl 1994 [1916]. *Chicago Poems*. Mineoloa, NY: Dover.

Sassoon, Siegfried 1947. *Collected Poems*. London: Faber & Faber.

Schwartz, Delmore 1949. 'The Literary Dictatorship of T. S. Eliot', *Partisan Review*, 16: 119–37.

Schulyer, George 1998 [1932]. *Black No More*. London: X Press.

Scott, Bonnie Kime, ed. 1990. *The Gender of Modernism: A Critical Anthology*. Bloomington: Indiana University Press.

Simmel, Georg 1997. *Simmel on Culture*, ed. David Frisby and Mike Featherstone. London: Sage.

Sinclair, May 1917. *The Tree of Heaven*. New York: Macmillan.

Sinclair, May 1980 [1922]. *Life and Death of Harriett Frean*, intro. Jean Radford. London: Virago.

Spender, Stephen 1951. *World Within World*. London: Hamish Hamilton.

Stead, Christina 1970 [1940]. *The Man Who Loved Children*, intro. Randall Jarrell. Harmondsworth: Penguin.

Stein, Gertrude 1938. *Everybody's Autobiography*. London: Heinemann.

Stein, Gertrude 1971. *Look at Me Now and Here I Am: Writings and Lectures 1909–45*, ed. Patricia Meyerowitz, intro. Elizabeth Sprigge. London: Penguin.

Stein, Gertrude 1995 [1925]. *The Making of Americans. Being a History of a Family's Progress*, foreword William H. Gass, intro. Steven Meyer. Normal, IL: Dalkey Archive Press.

Stevens, Wallace 1966. *Letters of Wallace Stevens*, ed. Holly Stevens. New York: Knopf.

Stevens, Wallace 1989. *Sur Plusieurs Beaux Sujects. Wallace Stevens' Commonplace Book*, ed. Milton J. Bates. Stanford: Stanford University Press.

Stevens, Wallace 1997. *Collected Poetry and Plays*, ed. Frank Kermode and Joan Richardson. New York: Library of America.

Swinnerton, Frank 1938. *The Georgian Literary Scene: A Panorama*, rev. 2nd edn. London: Hutchinson.

Tait, Trudi, ed. 1995. *The Great War: Women, Men and the Great War: An Anthology of Stories*. Manchester: Manchester University Press.

Toomer, Jean 1988 [1923]. *Cane*. New York: W. W. Norton.

Toomer, Jean 1993. *A Jean Toomer Reader: Selected Unpublished Writings*, ed. Frederik L. Rusch. New York: Oxford University Press.

Toomer, Jean 1996. *Selected Essays and Literary Criticism*, ed. Robert Jones. Knoxville: University of Tennessee Press.

Tranter, John and Philip Mead, eds. 1994. *The Bloodaxe Book of Modern Australian Poetry*. Newcastle: Bloodaxe Books.

Treadwell, Sophia 1993 [1928]. *Machinal*. London: Nick Hern.

Valéry, Paul 1977. *Paul Valéry: An Anthology*, ed. James R. Lawler. London: Routledge & Kegan Paul.

Verrall, Helen de G. 1915. 'A Further Study of the Mac Scripts', *Proceedings of the Society for Psychical Research*, 27: 250–78.

Walberg, Patrick, ed. 1965. *Surrealism*. London: Thames & Hudson.

Wells, H. G. 1901. *Anticipations of the Reaction of Mechanical and Scientific Progress upon Human Life and Thought*. London: Chapman & Hall.

West, Nathanael 1957. *Complete Works*. London: Secker & Warburg.

West, Rebecca 1980 [1918]. *The Return of the Soldier*, intro. Victoria Glendinning. London: Virago.

West, Rebecca 1982. *The Young Rebecca: Writings of Rebecca West 1911–17*, ed. Jane Marcus. Bloomington: Indiana University Press.

West, Rebecca 1987 [1928]. *The Strange Necessity*, intro. G. Evelyn Hutchinson. London: Virago.

West, Rebecca 1993 [1942]. *Black Lamb and Grey Falcon: A Journey Through Yugoslavia*. Edinburgh: Canongate.

Whitman, Walt 1982. *Complete Poetry and Collected Prose*, ed. Justin Kaplan. New York: Library of America.

Williams, William Carlos 1954. 'The Poem as a Field of Action' [1948], *Selected Essays*. New York: Random House. 280–91.

Williams, William Carlos 1967 [1958]. *I Wanted to Write a Poem*. London: Jonathan Cape.

Williams, William Carlos 1970. *Imaginations*, ed. Webster Schott. London: MacGibbon & Kee.

Williams, William Carlos 1974. *The Embodiment of Knowledge*, ed. Ron Loewinsohn. New York: New Directions.

Williams, William Carlos 1983. *Paterson*. Harmondsworth: Penguin.

Wilson, Sondra K., ed. 1999. *The Crisis Reader: Stories, Poems and Essays from the N.A.A.C.P.'s Crisis Magazine*. New York: Modern Library.

Woolf, Virginia 1967. *Collected Essays*. 4 vols. London: Hogarth Press.

Woolf, Virginia 1973 [1944]. *A Haunted House and Other Stories*. London: Penguin.

Woolf, Virginia 1976. *Moments of Being: Unpublished Autobiographical Writings*, ed. Jean Schulkind. London: Chatto & Windus.

Woolf, Virginia 1987. *The Essays of Virginia Woolf*. Vol. II: *1912–1918*, ed. Andrew McNellie. London: Hogarth Press.

Woolf, Virginia 1992a [1925]. *Mrs Dalloway*, ed. Stella McNichol, intro. Elaine Showalter. London: Penguin.

Woolf, Virginia 1992b [1927]. *To the Lighthouse*, ed. Stella McNichol, intro. Hermione Lee. London: Penguin.

Woolf, Virginia 1992c [1931]. *The Waves*, ed. Kate Flint. London: Penguin.

Woolf, Virginia 1992d. *A Woman's Essays: Selected Essays*. Vol. 1, ed. Rachel Bowlby. London: Penguin.

Woolf, Virginia 1993a. *The Crowded Dream of Modern Life: Selected Essays*. Vol. 2, ed. Rachel Bowlby. London: Penguin.

Woolf, Virginia 1993b. *A Room of One's Own, Three Guineas*, ed. Michèle Barrett. London: Penguin.

Yeats, William Butler, ed. 1936. *The Oxford Book of Modern Verse*. Oxford: Clarendon.

Yeats, William Butler, ed. 1939. *On the Boiler*. Dublin: Cuala Press.

Yeats, William Butler, ed. 1966. *The Variorum Edition of the Plays of W. B. Yeats*, ed. Russell K. Alspach. London: Macmillan.

Yeats, William Butler, ed. 1975. 'Preliminary Examination of the Script of E. R', in *Yeats and the Occult*, ed. George Mills Harper. Toronto: Macmillan. 130–71.

SECONDARY SOURCES

Albright, Daniel 1997. *Quantum Poetics: Yeats, Pound, Eliot and the Science of Modernism.* Cambridge: Cambridge University Press.

Anesko, Michael 1986. *'Friction with the Market': Henry James and the Profession of Authorship.* New York: Oxford University Press.

Ardis, Ann 2002. *Modernism and Cultural Conflict 1880–1922.* Cambridge: Cambridge University Press.

Armstrong, Nancy 1999. *Fiction in the Age of Photography: The Legacy of British Realism.* Cambridge, MA: Harvard University Press.

Armstrong, Tim 1998. *Modernism, Technology and the Body: A Cultural Study.* Cambridge: Cambridge University Press.

Armstrong, Tim 2000. 'Two Types of Shock in Modernity', *Critical Quarterly*, 42: 60–73.

Baker, Houston 1987. *Modernism and the Harlem Renaissance.* Chicago: Chicago University Press.

Banfield, Ann 2000. *The Phantom Table: Woolf, Fry, Russell and the Epistemology of Modernism.* Cambridge: Cambridge University Press.

Banta, Martha 1993. *Taylored Lives: Narrative Productions in the Age of Taylor, Veblen, and Ford.* Chicago: University of Chicago Press.

Beer, Gillian 1993. 'Wave Theory and the Rise of Literary Modernism', in *Realism and Representation: Essays on the Problem of Realism in Relation to Science, Literature, and Culture*, ed. George Levine. Madison: University of Wisconsin Press, 193–213.

Beer, Gillian 1996. *Open Fields: Science in Cultural Encounter.* Oxford: Clarendon Press.

Bell, Ian F. A. 1981. *Critic as Scientist: The Modernist Poetics of Ezra Pound.* New York: Methuen.

Benstock, Shari 1987. *Women of the Left Bank: Paris 1900–1940.* London: Virago.

Berger, John 1980. *The Success and Failure of Picasso.* New York: Pantheon.

Berman, Jessica 2001. *Modernist Fiction, Cosmopolitanism and the Politics of Community.* Cambridge: Cambridge University Press.

Berman, Marshall 1988. *All that is Solid Melts into Air: The Experience of Modernity.* Harmondsworth: Penguin.

Bernstein, Richard J., ed. 1985. *Habermas and Modernity.* Cambridge: Polity.

Birkin, Lawrence 1988. *Consuming Desire: Sexual Science and the Emergence of a Culture of Abundance 1871–1914.* Ithaca: Johns Hopkins University Press.

Bradbury, Malcolm, and James McFarlane, eds. 1976. *Modernism: 1830–1930.* Harmondsworth: Penguin.

Braddick, Mike 2000. *State Formation in Early Modern England, c. 1500–1700.* Cambridge: Cambridge University Press.

Bradshaw, David 1992. 'The Eugenics Movement in the 1930s and the Emergence of *On the Boiler*', *Yeats Annual*, 9:189–215.

Bradshaw, David, ed. 2003. *A Concise Companion to Modernism.* Oxford: Blackwell.

Braun, Marta 1992. *Picturing Time: The Work of Étienne-Jules Marey.* Chicago: University of Chicago Press.

Brown, Gillian 1990. *Domestic Individualism: Imagining Self in Nineteenth-Century America.* Berkeley: University of California Press.

Bürger, Peter 1984. *Theory of the Avant-Garde*, trans. Michael Shaw. Manchester: Manchester University Press.

Burke, Carolyn 1996. *Becoming Modern: The Life of Mina Loy.* New York: Farrar, Straus, & Giroux.

Burwick, Frederick, and Paul Douglass, eds. 1992. *The Crisis of Modernism: Bergson and the Vitalist Controversy*. Cambridge: Cambridge University Press.

Bush, Ronald 1976. *The Genesis of Ezra Pound's Cantos*. Princeton: Princeton University Press.

Butler, Christopher 1994. *Early Modernism: Literature, Music and Painting in Europe 1900–1914*. Oxford: Clarendon Press.

Calinescu, Matei 1987. *Faces of Modernity: Modernism, Avante-Garde, Decadence, Kitsch, Post-Modernism*, rev. edn. Durham, NC: Duke University Press.

Childs, Donald J. 2001. *Modernism and Eugenics: Woolf, Eliot, Yeats and the Culture of Degeneration*. Cambridge: Cambridge University Press.

Clark, Suzanne 1991. *Sentimental Modernism: Women Writers and the Revolution of the Word*. Bloomington: Indiana University Press.

Clark, T. J. 1999. *Farewell to an Idea: Episodes from a History of Modernism*. New Haven: Yale University Press.

Clarke, Bruce 1996. *Dora Marsden and Early Modernism: Gender, Individualism, Science*. Ann Arbor: University of Michigan Press.

Clarke, Bruce, and Linda Dalrymple Henderson, eds. 2002. *From Energy to Information: Representation in Science and Technology, Art, and Literature*. Stanford: Stanford University Press.

Conrad, Peter 1998. *Modern Times, Modern Places*. London: Thames & Hudson.

Cooper, Helen M., et al, eds. 1989. *Arms and the Woman: War, Gender and Literary Representation*. Chapel Hill: University of North Carolina Press.

Crary, Jonathan 1993. *Techniques of the Observer: On Vision and Modernity in the Nineteenth Century*. Cambridge, MA: MIT Press.

Crary, Jonathan 1999. *Suspensions of Perception: Attention, Spectacle and Modern Culture*. Cambridge, MA: MIT Press.

Crawford, Robert 1992. *Devolving English Literature*. Oxford: Oxford University Press.

Daly, Nicholas 1999. *Modernism, Romance and the Fin de Siècle: Popular Fiction and British Culture*. Cambridge: Cambridge University Press.

Danius, Sara 2002. *The Senses of Modernism: Technology, Perception and Aesthetics*. Ithaca: Cornell University Press.

Davis, Alex, and Lee M. Jenkins, eds. 2000. *Locations of Literary Modernism: Region and Nation in British and American Modernist Poetry*. Cambridge: Cambridge University Press.

Deane, Patrick, ed. 1998. *History in Our Hands: A Critical Anthology of Writings on Literature, Culture and Politics from the 1930s*. London: Leicester University Press.

DeKoven, Marianne 1991. *Rich and Strange: Gender, History, Modernism*. Princeton: Princeton University Press.

Deloria, Philip 1998. *Playing Indian*. New Haven: Yale University Press.

De Man, Paul 1970. 'Literary History and Literary Modernity', *Daedalus: Journal of the American Academy*, 99: 384–404.

Dettmar, Kevin and Stephen Watts, eds. 1996. *Marketing Modernisms: Self-Promotion, Canonization, Rereading*. Ann Arbor: University of Michigan Press.

Doane, Mary Ann 1996. 'Temporality, Storage, Legibility: Freud, Marey and the Cinema', *Critical Inquiry*, 22: 313–43.

Douglas, Ann 1996. *Terrible Honesty: Mongerel Manhattan in the 1920s*. London: Picador.

Doyle, Laura 1994. *Bordering on the Body: The Racial Matrix of Modern Fiction & Culture*. New York: Oxford University Press.

DuPlessis, Rachel Blau 2001. *Genders, Races and Religious Cultures in Modern American Poetry 1908–1934*. Cambridge: Cambridge University Press.

Dyer, Geoff 1994. *The Missing of the Somme*. London: Hamish Hamilton.

Dyer, Geoff 1998. *But Beautiful*. London: Abacus.

Eksteins, Modris 1990. *Rites of Spring: The Great War and the Birth of the Modern Age*. London: Black Swan.

Ellmann, Maud 1987. *The Poetics of Impersonality: T. S. Eliot and Ezra Pound*. Brighton: Harvester.

Eysteinsson, Astradur 1990. *The Concept of Modernism*. Ithaca: Cornell University Press.

Feudtner, Chris 1993. 'Minds the Dead have Ravished: Shell-Shock, History and the Ecology of Disease Systems', *History of Science*, 31: 387.

Fer, Briony, et al. 1993. *Realism, Rationalism, Surrealism: Art Between the Wars*. New Haven: Yale University Press/Open University Press.

Ferrall, Charles 2001. *Modernist Writing and Reactionary Politics*. Cambridge: Cambridge University Press.

Foucault, Michel 1970. *The Order of Things: An Archaeology of the Human Sciences*. London: Tavistock.

Foucault, Michel 1979. *The History of Sexuality*. Vol. I: *An Introduction*, trans. Robert Hurley. Harmondsworth: Penguin.

Fraser, Robert, ed. 1990. *Sir James Frazer and the Literary Imagination: Essays in Affinity and Influence*. Basingstoke: Macmillan.

Fuss, Diana 1995. *Identification Papers*. New York: Routledge.

Fussell, Paul 1977. *The Great War and Modern Memory*. Oxford: Oxford University Press.

Fussell, Paul 1980. *Abroad. British Literary Traveling Between the Wars*. New York: Oxford University Press.

Gammel, Irene 2002. *Baroness Elsa: Gender, Dada, and Everyday Modernity*. Cambridge, MA: MIT Press.

Gardiner, Muriel, ed. 1989. *The Wolf Man and Sigmund Freud*. London: Karnac Books.

Gikandi, Simon 2003. 'Picasso, Africa, and the Schemata of Difference', *Modernism/modernity*, 10/3: 455–80.

Gilroy, Paul 1993. *The Black Atlantic: Modernity and Double Consciousness*. London: Verso.

Gilbert, Geoff 2004. *Before Modernism Was: Modern History and the Constituencies of Writing 1900–30*. Basingstoke: Palgrave.

Gilbert, Sandra M., and Susan Gubar 1988–94. *No Man's Land: The Place of the Woman Writer in the Twentieth Century*. 3 vols. New Haven: Yale University Press.

Gillies, Mary Ann 1996. *Henri Bergson and British Modernism*. Montreal: McGill-Queen's University Press.

Gitelman, Lisa 1992. 'Negotiating a Vocabulary for Urban Infrastructure, or, The WPA Meets the Teenage Mutant Ninja Turtles', *Journal of American Studies*, 26: 147–58.

Godden, Richard 1997. *Fictions of Labour: William Faulkner and the South's Long Revolution*. Cambridge: Cambridge University Press.

Goldman, Arnold 1975. 'Yeats, Spritualism, and Psychic Research', *Yeats and the Occult*, ed. G. M. Harper. New York: Macmillan. 108–29.

Goldman, Jane 1998. *The Feminist Aesthetics of Virginia Woolf: Modernism, Post-Impressionism and the Politics of the Visual*. Cambridge: Cambridge University Press.

Goldman, Jane 2004. *Modernism 1910–1945*. Basingstoke: Palgrave.

Goodrum, Charles and Helen Dalrymple 1990. *Advertising in America: The First Two Hundred Years*. New York: Harry N. Abrams.

Greenslade, William 1994. *Degeneration, Culture and the Novel 1880–1940*. Cambridge: Cambridge University Press.

Hanscombe, Gillian, and Virginia L. Smyers 1987. *Writing for their Lives: The Modernist Women 1910–1940*. London: Women's Press.

Head, Dominic 1992. *The Modernist Short Story*. Cambridge: Cambridge University Press.

Hewitt, Andrew 1993. *Fascist Modernism: Aesthetics, Politics and the Avant-Garde*. Stanford: Stanford University Press.

Hoffman, Frederick J., and Charles Allen 1946. *The Little Magazine*. Princeton: Princeton University Press.

Horne, Philip 1996. 'Henry James and the Economy of the Short Story', in *Modernist Writers and the Marketplace*, ed. Ian Willison, Warwick Gould and Warren Chernaik. Basingstoke: Macmillan. 1–36.

Hutchinson, George 1995. *The Harlem Renaissance in Black and White*. Cambridge, MA: Belknap Press.

Huyssen, Andreas 1986. *After the Great Divide: Modernism, Mass Culture, Postmodernism*. Bloomington: Indiana University Press.

Hynes, Samuel 1991. *War Imagined: The First World War and English Culture*. London: Bodley Head.

Isaak, Jo Anna 1986. *The Ruin of Representation in Modernist Art and Texts*. Ann Arbor, UMI Research Press.

Jameson, Fredric 2002. *A Singular Modernity: Essay on the Ontology of the Present*. London: Verso.

Jochum, K. P. S. 1993. 'Yeats's Vision Papers and the Problem of Automatic Writing', *English Literature in Transition*, 36: 323–36.

Kadlec, David 2000. *Mosaic Modernism: Anarchism, Pragmatism, Culture*. Baltimore: Johns Hopkins University Press.

Kahn, Douglas 1999. *Noise, Water, Meat: A History of Sound in the Arts*. Cambridge, MA: MIT Press.

Keating, Peter 1989. *The Haunted Study: A Social History of the English Novel 1875–1914*. London: Secker & Warburg.

Kenner, Hugh 1971. *The Pound Era*. Berkeley: University of California Press.

Kenner, Hugh 1975. *A Homemade World: The American Modernist Writers*. New York: Knopf.

Kermode, Frank 1979. *The Genesis of Secrecy*. Cambridge, MA: Harvard University Press.

Kern, Stephen 1983. *The Culture of Time and Space 1880–1918*. Cambridge, MA: Harvard University Press.

Kibble, Matthew 2002. '"The Betrayers of Language": Modernism and the *Daily Mail*', *Literature & History*, 11: 62–80.

Kittler, Friedrich A. *Discourse Networks 1800/1900*, trans. Michael Metteer. Stanford: Stanford University Press.

Knapp, James 1988. *Literary Modernism and the Transformation of Work*. Evanston, Northwestern University Press.

Koestlenbaum, Wayne 1989. *Double Talk: The Erotics of Male Literary Collaboration*. New York: Routledge.

Kouidnis, Virginia 1980. *Mina Loy, American Modernist Poet*. Baton Rouge: Louisiana State University Press.

Krebs, Paula 1999. *Gender, Race, and the Writing of Empire: Public Discourse and the Boer War*. Cambridge: Cambridge University Press.

Kuna, David P. 1976. 'The Concept of Suggestion in the Early History of Advertising Psychology', *Journal of the History of the Behavioral Sciences*, 12: 347–53.

Laplanche, J. and J. B. Pontalis 1988. *The Language of Psychoanalysis*, trans. Donald Nicholson-Smith. London: Karnac Books.

Larrissy, Edward 1990. *Reading Twentieth-Century Poetry: The Language of Gender and Objects*. Oxford: Blackwell.

Leach, William 1994. *Land of Desire: Merchants, Power, and the Rise of a New American Culture*. New York: Vintage.

Lears, T. Jackson 1981. *No Place of Grace: Antimodernism and the Transformation of American Culture 1880–1920*. New York: Pantheon.

Leed, Eric J. 1979. *No Man's Land: Combat and Identity in World War I*. Cambridge: Cambridge University Press.

Levenson, Michael 1984. *A Genealogy of Modernism*. Cambridge: Cambridge University Press.

Levenson, Michael, ed. 1998. *The Cambridge Companion to Modernism*. Cambridge: Cambridge University Press.

Lewis, Pericles 2000. *Modernism, Nationalism, and the Novel*. Cambridge: Cambridge University Press.

Light, Alison 1991. *Forever England: Femininity, Literature and Conservativism Between the Wars*. London: Routledge.

Lipking, Lawrence 1981. *The Life of the Poet*. Chicago: University of Chicago Press.

Longenbach, James 1988. *Stone Cottage: Pound, Yeats and Modernism*. New York: Oxford University Press.

Luckhurst, Roger 2002. *The Invention of Telepathy 1870–1901*. Oxford: Oxford University Press.

Lukács, Georg 1965. *Essays on Thomas Mann*, trans. Stanley Mitchell. New York: Grosset & Dunlap.

Luhmann, Niklas 1994. 'How Can the Mind Participate in Communication?', in *Materialities of Communication*, ed. Hans Ulrich Gumbrecht and Ludwig K. Pfeiffer. Stanford: Stanford University Press. 371–88.

Lutz, Tom 1991. *American Nervousness 1903*. Ithaca: Cornell University Press.

Lyon, Janet 1992. 'Militant Discourse, Strange Bedfellows: Suffragettes and Vorticists before the War', *Differences*, 4/2: 100–33.

Lyotard, Jean-François 1989. *The Lyotard Reader*, ed. Andrew Benjamin. Oxford: Basil Blackwell.

McGann, Jerome 1993. *Black Riders: The Visible Language of Modernism*. Princeton: Princeton University Press.

Mao, Douglas 1998. *Solid Objects: Modernism and the Test of Production*. Princeton: Princeton University Press.

Marchand, Roland 1985. *Advertising the American Dream: Making Way for Modernity 1920–1940*. Berkeley: University of California Press.

Marcus, Laura 1997. *Virginia Woolf*. Plymouth: Northcote House.

Marek, Jayne E. 1995. *Women Editing Modernism: 'Little' Magazines and Literary History*. Lexington: University Press of Kentucky.

Melman, Billie 1988. *Women and the Popular Imagination in the Twenties: Flappers and Nymphs*. London: Macmillan.

Michaels, Walter Benn 1995. *Our America: Nativism, Modernism, and Pluralism*. Durham: Duke University Press.

Miller, Tyrus 1996. 'Poetic Contagion: Surrealism and Williams's *A Novelette*', *William Carlos Williams Review*, 22/1: 17–27.

Miller, Tyrus 1999. *Late Modernism: Politics, Fiction and the Arts Between the World Wars*. Berkeley: University of California Press.

Montefiore, Janet 1996. *Men and Women Writers of the 1930s: The Dangerous Flood of History*. London: Routledge.

Morrisson, Mark S. 2001. *The Public Face of Modernism: Little Magazines, Audiences, and Reception 1905–1920*. Madison: University of Wisconsin Press.

Murray, Stuart 1998. *Never a Soul at Home: New Zealand Literary Nationalism and the 1930s*. Wellington: Victoria University Press.

Murphet, Julian, and Lydia Rainford, eds. 2003. *Literature and Visual Technologies: Writing After Cinema*. Basingstoke: Palgrave-Macmillan.

Nelson, Cary 1989. *Repression and Recovery: Modern American Poetry and the Politics of Cultural Memory 1910–1945*. Madison: University of Wisconsin Press.

Nicholls, Peter 1995. *Modernisms: A Literary Guide*. Basingstoke: Macmillan.

North, Michael 1994. *The Dialect of Modernism: Race, Language and Twentieth-Century Literature*. Oxford: Oxford University Press.

North, Michael 1999. *Reading 1922: A Return to the Scene of the Modern*. New York: Oxford University Press.

North, Michael 2002. 'Words in Motion: The Movies, the Readies, and "the Revolution of the Word"', *Modernism/modernity*, 9: 205–23.

Norris, Margot 1996. 'The Trace of the Trenches: Recovering Modernism's World War I', in *America's Modernisms: Revaluing the Canon*, ed. Kathryn V. Lindberg and Joseph G. Kronick. Baton Rouge: Louisiana State University Press. 135–51.

Ohmann, Richard 1996. *Selling Culture: Magazines, Markets and Class at the Turn of the Century*. London: Verso.

Parsons, Deborah L. 2000. *Streetwalking the Metropolis: Women, the City and Modernity*. Oxford: Oxford University Press.

Passerin d'Entrèves, Maurizio, and Seyla Benhabib, eds. 1997. *Habermas and the Unfinished Project of Modernity: Critical Essays on The Philosophical Discourse of Modernity*. Cambridge, MA: MIT Press.

Pease, Alison 2000. *Modernism, Mass Culture, and the Aesthetics of Obscenity*. Cambridge: Cambridge University Press.

Peppis, Paul 2000. *Literature, Politics, and the English Avant-Garde: Nation and Empire 1901–1918*. Cambridge: Cambridge University Press.

Perloff, Marjorie 1985. *The Dance of the Intellect: Studies in the Poetry of the Pound Tradition*. Cambridge: Cambridge University Press.

Perloff, Marjorie 1986. *The Futurist Moment: Avant-Garde, Avant-Guerre, and the Language of Rupture*. Chicago: University of Chicago Press.

Poole, Roger 1990. 'The Real Plot Line of Ford Madox Ford's *The Good Soldier*: An Essay in Applied Deconstruction', *Textual Practice*, 4: 390–427.

Prendergast, Christopher 2003. 'Codeword Modernity', *NLR*, 24: 95–111.

Rainey, Lawrence 1998. *Institutions of Modernism: Literary Elites and Public Culture*. New Haven: Yale University Press.

Raitt, Suzanne 2000. *May Sinclair: A Modern Victorian*. Oxford: Oxford University Press.

Remy, Michel 1999. *Surrealism in Britain*. Aldershot: Ashgate.

Roberts, Neil 2004. *D. H. Lawrence, Travel and Cultural Difference*. Basingstoke: Palgrave.

Rose, Jonathan 2001. *The Intellectual Life of the British Working Classes*. New Haven: Yale University Press.

Ross, Dorothy, ed. 1994. *Modernist Impulses in the Human Sciences 1870–1930*. Baltimore: Johns Hopkins University Press.

Ross, Cathy 2003. *Twenties London: A City in the Jazz Age*. London: Philip Wilson.

Ruthven, K. K. 2001. *Faking Literature*. Cambridge: Cambridge University Press.

Sartre, Jean-Paul 1995. 'John Dos Passos and *1919*', in *Literary and Philosophical Essays*, trans. Annette Michelson. London: Rider. 88–96.

Schnapp, Jeffrey T. 1999. 'Crash (Speed as Engine of Individuation)', *Modernism/modernity*, 6: 1–50.

Schleifer, Ronald 2001. *Modernism and Time: The Logic of Abundance in Literature, Science, and Culture, 1880–1930*. Cambridge: Cambridge University Press.

Schneidau, H. N. 1991. *Waking Giants: The Presence of the Past in Modernism*. Oxford: Oxford University Press.

Schwartz, Hillel 1986. *Never Satisfied: A Cultural History of Diets, Fantasies and Fat*. New York: Free Press.

Scott, Bonnie Kime 1995. *Refiguring Modernism: The Women of 1928*. Bloomington: Indiana University Press.

Smith, William Kay 1961. *The Spectra Hoax*. Middletown: Wesleyan University Press.

Smith, Stan 1994. *The Origins of Modernism: Eliot, Pound, Yeats and the Rhetorics of Renewal*. New York: Harvester Wheatsheaf.

Stein, Sally 1989. 'The Graphic Ordering of Desire: Modernization of a Middle-Class Women's Magazine 1914–39', in *The Contest of Meaning: Critical Histories of Photography*, ed. Richard Bolton. Cambridge, MA: MIT Press. 145–62.

Stonebridge, Lyndsey 1998. *The Destructive Element: British Psychoanalysis and Modernism*. Basingstoke: Macmillan.

Strychacz, Thomas 1993. *Modernism, Mass Culture, and Professionalism*. Cambridge: Cambridge University Press.

Surette, Leon 1993. *The Birth of Modernism: Ezra Pound, T. S. Eliot, W. B. Yeats and the Occult*. Montreal: McGill–Queens University Press.

Surette, Leon 1999. *Pound in Purgatory: From Economic Radicalism to Anti-Semitism*. Urbana: University of Illinois Press.

Sword, Helen 2002. *Ghostwriting Modernism*. Ithaca: Cornell University Press.

Szalay, Michael 2000. *New Deal Modernism: American Literature and the Invention of the Welfare State*. Durham: Duke University Press.

Tallack, Douglas 1993. *The Nineteenth-Century American Short Story: Language, Form and Ideology*. London: Routledge.

Tate, Trudi 1998. *Modernism, History and the First World War*. Manchester: Manchester University Press.

Taylor, Charles 1975. *Hegel*. Cambridge: Cambridge University Press.

Taylor, Charles 1989. *Sources of the Self: The Making of Modern Identity*. Cambridge: Cambridge University Press.

Thomas de le Peña, Carolyn 2003. *The Body Electric: How Strange Machines Built The Modern America*. New York: New York University Press.

Thompson, Emily 2002. *The Soundscape of Modernity: Architectural Acoustics and the Culture of Listening*. Cambridge, MA: MIT Press.

Thurschwell, Pamela 2001. *Literature, Technology and Magical Thinking 1880–1920*. Cambridge: Cambridge University Press.

Tichi, Cecelia 1987. *Shifting Gears: Technology, Literature & Culture in Modernist America*. Chapel Hill: University of North Carolina Press.

Tiffany, Daniel 1995. *Radio Corpse: Imagism & the Cryptaesthetic of Ezra Pound*. Cambridge, MA: Harvard University Press.

Tiffany, Daniel 2000. *Toy Medium: Materialism and Modern Lyric*. Berkeley: University of California Press.

Torgovnik, Marianna 1990. *Gone Primitive: Savage Intellects: Modern Lives*. Chicago: University of Chicago Press.

Tratner, Michael 1993. 'Sex and Credit: Consumer Capitalism in *Ulysses*', *James Joyce Quarterly*, 30–1: 695–716.

Tratner, Michael 1995. *Modernism and Mass Politics: Joyce, Woolf, Eliot, Yeats*. Stanford: Stanford University Press.

Tratner, Michael 2001. *Deficits and Desires: Economics and Sexuality in Twentieth-Century Literature*. Stanford, CA: Stanford University Press.

Trotter, David 1986. 'Modernism and Empire: Reading *The Waste Land*', *Critical Quarterly*, 28: 143–53.

Trotter, David 1993. *The English Novel in History 1895–1920*. London: Routledge.

Trotter, David 2001. *Paranoid Modernism*. Oxford: Oxford University Press.

Warner, William 1998. *Licensing Entertainment: The Elevation of Novel Reading in Britain 1684–1750*. Berkeley: University of California Press.

Watson, Steven 1991. *Strange Bedfellows: The First American Avant-Garde*. New York: Abbeville Press.

Weir, David 1997. *Anarchy and Culture: The Aesthetic Politics of Modernism*. Amherst: University of Massachusetts Press.

Wertheim, Arthur Frank 1976. *The New York Little Renaissance: Iconoclasm, Modernism and Nationalism in American Culture 1908–1917*. New York: New York University Press.

Weston, Richard 1996. *Modernism*. London: Phaidon.

Wexler, Joyce 1997. *Who Paid for Modernism?* Fayetteville: University of Arkansas Press.

Whalan, Mark 2003. '"Taking Myself in Hand": Jean Toomer and Physical Culture', *Modernism/modernity*, 10: 597–616.

Will, Barbara 2000. *Gertrude Stein and the Problem of 'Genius'*. Edinburgh: Edinburgh University Press.

Williams, Raymond 1989. *The Politics of Modernism: Against the New Conformists*, ed. Tony Pinkney. London: Verso.

Willison, Ian, Warwick Gould and Warren Chernaik, eds. 1996. *Modernist Writers and the Marketplace*. Basingstoke: Macmillan.

Winter, Alison 1998. *Mesmerized: Powers of Mind in Victorian Britain*. Chicago: University of Chicago Press.

Winter, Jay 1995. *Sites of Memory, Sites of Mourning: The Great War in European Cultural History*. Cambridge: Cambridge University Press.

Yaguello, Maria 1991. *Lunatic Lovers of Language: Imaginary Languages and their Inventors*, trans. Catherine Slater. London: Athlone.

Index